Global Education Series—6

WOMEN AND EDUCATION

Global Education Series—6

WOMEN AND EDUCATION

Edited by

B. M. Sharma

Commonwealth

Women and Education

Edition : 2025

ISBN 81-7169-308-3

Published by :
COMMONWEALTH PUBLISHERS (P) LTD.
4831/24, Govind Lane,
Ansari Road, Darya Ganj,
New Delhi - 110002
Ph. : 23272541, 23242541
e-mail : commonwealthpublishers2016@gmail.com

Distributed by :
ARJUN PUBLISHING HOUSE
4831/24, Govind Lane,
Ansari Road, Darya Ganj,
New Delhi - 110002
Ph. : 23272541, 23242541
e-mail : arjunbooks2001@gmail.com

Laser Typesetting by :
Dimple Computers
Delhi

Printed at :
Milan Enterprises
Delhi

Preface

In 1965, the United Nations embarked upon a long-term programme to improve the status of women in all fields. A decade later 1975 was designated as International Women's Year and UNESCO declared its belief that 'in the long run, education will prove to be the most effective channel for achieving equality between men and women and ensuring the full participation of women in development'.

In the attention that was focused in 1975 on the status of women, and as the United Kingdom introduced its own legislation to promote equality between the sexes (the *Sex Discrimination Act, 1975*), the role of education has emerged as of increasing importance. As this book goes to press, indeed, we in the United Kingdom are reviewing two years of anti-discrimination legislation. In the public debate that this has provoked, the role of education and training has emerged as even more central than hitherto. This book is an attempt, at least partly, to fill the gap that exists in the general knowledge and consciousness of the actual, and of the desired, character of the education of girls and women and the situation of girls and women in education today.

It is not only an attempt to provoke new thought and to strengthen existing knowledge; it is an impassioned call to all educated women (and men) to accept their own responsibility and direct duty, to walk back down the ladder which they have climbed, and to build in all the missing rungs to help less fortunate girls and women (both here and abroad) to the freedom of status, career, and personal fulfilment to which only the fullest educational opportunity is the key.

India as a member of UNESCO and as a leading Third World Country has also embarked upon a massive programme of women's education through its Five Year Plans and its special efforts for the advancement of women's education. Education has been rightly considered as a means to remove under-development and gender bias. This book gives an idea of Women and Education at a holistic level.

EDITOR

Contents

1

Gandhi on Women

No leader in history has commanded such a large following during his lifetime either in his own country or the world as Gandhiji. And certainly no man has evoked such whole-hearted devotion from women. The reason is not far to seek. Gandhiji has the enviable capacity of being able to put himself into the shoes of another person, more especially when that person is the under-dog.

In spite of the unrivalled culture and high ideals of society that ancient India placed before us, we have to bear witness to the tragic fact that we have fallen ever so far from that happy estate, and perhaps in no sphere of life has that fall been so great as in that of woman. From being man's co-equal and co-sharer and helpmeet she has become his subordinate—a mere chattel to be used at will for satisfying his wants with no rights or will of her own. Custom and usage have dealt harshly with her. As a matter of fact this subordination has been a world factor, for it is only in very recent times that the women of the "advanced" Western hemisphere have come into their own after a struggle, and even there they have not gained all they want for in some countries many disabilities still attach to them.

A passionate lover of humanity, an implacable foe of injustice in whatsoever form or sphere, it is small wonder that Gandhiji early espoused the woman's cause. And, as in every thing that he has preached, he began the reform in his own home. Being as harsh as truth and a merciless critic of himself, the moment he realised he was a 'slaveholder' as he has called himself, his attitude to his wife changed, and with that change began his work for the emancipation of womankind as a whole. With his masterly pen and from every platform he has, throughout his long life of service, preached against the wrongs done to women in the name of law, tradition and even religion. He has spoken out fearlessly against enforced widowhood, pardah, the dedication of girls to temples, prostitution, early marriage, the dowry system, the economic bondage and marital slavery of women. "Man and woman are equal in status." "I am uncompromising in the matter of woman's rights. In my opinion she should labour under no legal disability not suffered by man. I should treat daughters and sons on a footing of perfect equality." "It is sad to think that the Smritis contain texts which can command no respect from men who cherish the liberty of woman as their own and who regard her as the mother of the race." "The saying attributed to Manu that for woman there can be no freedom' is not to me sacrosanct."—are but a few lines from the many he has written on behalf of suppressed woman and are enough witness, if witness, were needed, of his burning desire to see woman restored to her natural and rightful place in society.

In his own institutions and programme of work he has paid equal attention and given equal place to girls and women. There is an air of freedom and self-confidence in the girls and women that have lived with him or been under his care whether in Sabarmati or Sevagram or elsewhere, which is a joy to behold and rarely visible in Indian society elsewhere. Nothing delights him more than the success of women in any sphere of life. The Spinners' Association, the child of his creation which is perhaps nearest his heart, is in essence a woman's association. It is not for nothing that he named it thus. Those of us who have been privileged to come close to him and serve him have found in him not only "Bapu"—a wise father, but what is far more precious a mother, before whose all-embracing and understanding love all fear and restraint vanish.

He has paid the best tribute our sex could wish when he says, "Woman is the embodiment of sacrifice and suffering." But with all his championship of our cause and his appreciation of our difficulties he has not withheld just criticism of our many defects. In the matter of birth control Gandhiji's writings have found a good deal of opposition from many of the leaders of the women's movement. But he has put the question on a high moral plane and appealed to woman not to sell her birthright for a mess of pottage. It is not for lack of sympathy with the sufferings of women because of frequent giving birth to children that he has voted unequivocally against the use of contraceptives but because in every sphere of life he wants to protect women from losing that moral force which is at once her crowning glory and her fortress against all attack and temptations. For while he has praised us much he expects much of us too—especially of those who are educated. He is of opinion that subservience to man or any power on earth need not be if we realise our inner strength. We have consented to be called the weaker sex. we have considered ourselves unable to strand without man's protection, we have tacitly acknowledged that we cannot compete with him intellectually, we have been flattered by man's tributes to woman's physical beauty and powers of attraction and have thereby lowered our own status and standard. In fact we have willingly subscribed to the doctorine that 'might is right'. Inasmuch as the spring of all Gandhiji's thought and action is non-violence, he has naturally pointed the way of *ahimsa* as the way of freedom for women not only from their own shackles but for the permanent removal of the world's ills. "If only women will forget that they belong to the weaker sex, I have no doubt that they can do infinitely more than men against war," he said to women in Paris in 1932; and again in Switzerland, "I do not know if I have the courage to give a message for the women of Europe that you have asked for. If I am to do so without incurring their wrath. I would direct their steps to the women of India who rose in one mass last year, and I really believe that if Europe will drink in the lesson of non-violence it will do so through its women." Alas! that this advice fell on stony ground with the result that Europe today is bathed in blood and being consumed in the hideous fire of hatred and revenge. There is no doubt that of all the factors contributing to the awakening of women in India none has been so potent as the field of non-violent action which Gandhiji offered to women in his 'war' against British domination of India. It brought them out in their hundreds from sheltered homes to stand the furnace of a fiery trial without flinching. It proved to the hilt that woman was as much able as man to resist evil or aggression. To the thinking mind it has also proved that resistance without arms was not only equally efficacious but more ennobling for the resisters as also for those who were being resisted. In any event it gave woman a definite place so far as the salvation of India was concerned.

Today the question of violence versus non-violence is a vital one. Gandhiji's message is a clarion call for those who believe in non-violence as the strait and narrow road that leads to heaven to muster strong on his side. Only the other day when talking to some friends about the constructive programme which he has put before the nation as a concrete plan for the attainment of Swaraj, he said in regard to women's part in it: "But my greatest hope is in the women. They want a helping hand to lift them out of the well in which they have been kept. The slightest thing will work wonders. They made a record contribution during the satyagraha of 1931-32, and even now they are playing their part nobly but not to the utmost advantage. So little work has been done among them. They are waiting to be organsied. They have the capacity for suffering evoked by non-violent effort and they will suffer silently." Are we going to fulfil that hope is the question before those of us who are in a position to lend that helping hand for our own souls' sake no less than for the country and the world.

While Gandhiji's utterances and writings on behalf of the woman's cause should evoke a responsive chord in every well-wisher of humanity and even in the most hardened conservative, they are meant primarily for women, for they touch on every department of her life and can serve as an unerring guide to her in times of stress and strain. Above all they call to her for service—utter and devoted—for her own kind, for the country and for humanity at large. It is in this spirit that every woman should read this book. We stand to make an epoch-making decision. May we be given the wisdom and strength to choose the better part so that there may, as Gandhiji once said, rise up from among us "women pure, firm and self-controlled as Sita, Damayanti and Draupadi" who will command the homage of society as have done through the ages these immortal heroines of yore.

2

On Education and Training

DONALD K. STEWART

Introduction

The term "system" has many applications and is often used to refer to such things as a telephone system, payroll system, transportation system, school system, etc. During and after World War II, researchers developed a special meaning for the term "system" which concerned man-machine relationships such that as a particular machine was designed, developed, and completed, the necessary training of personnel to operate and work with the particular machine was designed, developed, and completed simultaneously. A critical part in this "system" was the specification of the operational objectives or purposes of the machine, of the man or men working with the machine, and their interrelationships. It was not until after the advent of programmed instruction that this system concept could applied to education with a meaning similar to that just described. Programmed instruction introduced the need for specifying educational objectives and the techniques for making general and ambiguous objectives more specific. Although education has been concerned with stating educational objectives for decades, these objectives were not specific and measurable. As a result, educators stated objectives, described educational activities, and then designed tests almost as three separate functions with little if any correlation between them.

In adapting the system concept to education, several differences must be noted. In industry, the end product or goal is a machine of some kind with trained people to operate and work with the machine; consequently, this system is often referred to as a man-machine system. In education, the end product, or goal, is learning; consequently, this system is referred to as a learning system. Machines are the major emphasis throughout the man-machine system, whereas in a learning-systems concept, the importance of machines is dependent upon their contribution to the learning process. Although the man-machine system and the learning system differ in several respects, there are also similarities. In industry, quality control is built into the man-machine system to increase the effectiveness and efficiency of the developmental processes. Likewise, in education, quality control can be built into the learning system to increase its effectiveness and efficiency. In both the man-machine system and the learning system, all activites should be based on verifiable or measurable specific objectives, not on guesses, opinions, or other nebulous or ambiguous statements.

Why should educators consider the use of a learning-systems concept? What is wrong with the present educational system which has been used as an example for the whole world to follow? In order to answer such questions, let us look at our present educational system.

The Existing Educational System

Society expects educational institutions to carry out at least the following three functions:

1. prepare students in such a way that they will have an even happier and more successful life than their parents;

2. be sure that the experiences necessary for each student to achieve the first function happens by choice—not by chance;
3. develop each child to the maximum of his capabilities.

These three functions are stated in various ways in most educational institution charters or constitutions. They sound good, but the implied goals are often not achieved because those goals implied by the first function have never been specified precisely enough to allow absolute measurement. In fact, very few teachers have ever specified, in measurable terms, the terminal objectives which are the desired student behaviours at the end of a course. Various state departments of public instruction have tried to define the content of each course at each grade level in the form of guidelines for the teachers. Most of these guidelines describe activities for the teacher or for the students. Objectives that are listed are so general that the interpretation of any one objective is actually up to the individual teacher.

If teachers do not know specifically what the termin objectives of their courses are, then how can students be teste for achievement that has not been defined? Consider th following questions:

1. Can you make a test that would *fall all of the students* in your class? (yes or no)
2. Can you make a test that would *pass all of the students* in your class? (yes or no)

If you answered "yes" to both questions, then consider this question: If you can make up a test that could pass all of your students and you can also make up one that could fail all of your students, where do you find that magic something to help you select test items that will pass those who should pass and fail those who should fail? This magic something does not exist, so most teachers grade according to some kind of curve (normal or skewed) which indicates more about how a student learned in comparison to his classmates than in comparison to the objectives of the course. When grading "by the curve." a failing student in a class of smart students could be an "A" student in a class of not-so-smart students without any difference in the amount learned by the student.

If a teacher knows precisely what the student is supposed to learn, and test are designed to measure to achievement of the specific content, then a student's grade should reflect his progress towards the course goals.

In a situation where the teacher is a "presenter of content," and the schools concentrate on moving students through the system *regardless* of learning, the system fosters "cumulative ignorance" (the cumulative effect of non-learaing that inhibits subsequent learning). Cumulative ignorance is responsible for a majority of dropouts and discipline problems. Consider the following anomalies:

(a) Almost every tenth-grade teacher will agree that any given class of tenth-grade students will contain students with reading levels from fourth or fifth grade up to college level. Knowing this fact, teachers will give these students tenth-grade reading level materials in literature, history, geometry, biology, etc., and when some of the students are unable to comprehend what they are reading, they are failed.

(b) Students who go through the "fail one year, pass the next" cycle several times usually find themselves in a situation where they couldn't learn if they wanted to because they don't have the prerequisite knowledge and/or skills.

(c) If a "C" grade in addition and subtraction means that a student didn't learn everything he was supposed to know about addition and subtraction, then chances are that this student will get a "C" or a "D" in multiplication and division, a "D" or an "F" in decimals and fractions, and an "F" in algebra, if the student elects to take it. Most educators would say that some students just are not capable of doing mathematics. Could the "F" in algebra be a result of "cumulative ignorance" rather than lack of innate ability?

The Learning-Systems Concept

To many professional educators, the notion of a systems approach, which has been borrowed from engineering and industry, may seem harsh and ominous in its implications for the management of instructional processes. But instructional planning in modern educational institutions cannot be conducted on a piecemeal basis without some effort toward a rational and efficient deployment of human and technical resources. Consequently, the use of the systems concept is intellectually and practically inescapable.

For the purposes of this chapter, a "Learning-Systems Concept" will be defined as follows:

(a) The requirements or objectives of the system will control the design of the system.

(b) The system will maximize learning effectiveness through procedures such that all, or almost all, of the stated objectives of the system are achieved; i.e., 90 per cent of the students will learn 90 per cent of the material.

(c) The system will maximize learning efficiency by adapting the system to the learner rather than making the learner fit the system.

(d) The design and procedures of the system will reflect the educational philosophy consistant with the requirements of the system and society.

Learning can occur under almost any set of circumstances; in fact, a great deal of learning takes place without the assistance of formal instruction. Experience itself is learning. The contribution of formal instruction is to assure that the student's learning experiences will occur by choice and not by chance.

A learning-systems concept, when applied to educational or training courses, offers an opportunity to develop or redesign courses that will be significantly more effective and efficient in relation to the learning tasks and goals of students.

It is necessary to begin with two objectives that exist irrespective of course content. They are:

1. to utilize more fully available educational resources and enriched teaching techniques;
2. to develop course patterns so that students can pursue their education or training as much as possible at their own pace, on their own schedule, and at a convenient site.

The first objective is particularly important in a society where both knowledge and the population are expanding at an ever-increasing rate. Educators must investigate ways of making our educational process more efficient and effective. Changes must be made in existing educational patterns.

The first objective is based on the following assumptions:

— Education's primary purpose is to facilitate learning by establishing an appropriate environment conducive to learning.

— In any programme, it is necessary to find out where the student is on the ladder of learning and to proceed from that point without gaps or unnecessary overlap.

— Programmes must be revised if it is found that learning has not taken place. Revisions should be made after an examination of the learner, method, media, and environment.

— If the learning objectives of a particular course could be definitely stated, and if all of the learners could achieve these objectives, they would all receive an "A" or some equivalent symbol indicating 90-100 per cent achievement.

— Some learning objectives cannot be defined specifically, but can be described as a result of other specific observable and measurable behaviours.

— Grades based on undefinable objectives and temperament of the grader do not contribute to an effective and efficient educational system and should not be included as a course requirement for grading procedures.

The second objective of the learning-systems concept, as stated previously, is to develop course patterns so that stadents can pursue their education or training as much as possible at their own pace, on their own schedule, and at a convenient site. This objective is important because students taking educational or training courses are "individuals" with different abilities, interests, past experiences, and environmental limitations. Most educators subscribe to this concept of individuality, yet in our schools they continue to insist on uniformity in performance within scheduled slots of time and at specific locations only.

The second objective is based on these assumptions:

— As educators, we want *to help* as may students through high school and college as possible.

— Many capable ex-students would like to continue their education or training if they could proceed at their own pace. A higher percentage of students could graduate from high school, and from college, if education could be geared to individual needs.

— "Cumulative knowledge," which is best defined as a situation where a student learns 90 per cent of each unit before he can proceed to the next unit, can be self-motivating and rewarding.

— Teachers can utilize the time released from presenting information, to "individualize" and make meaningful the learning experiences of the student.

The learning-systems concept should be considered from two points of view: the development, testing, and revising of the software system which actually helps the student learn; and the design and development of the hardware system which will store, transmit, and present the software.

Learning-Systems Approach to the Development of Software

What is the student's greatest problem in a learning situation? All too often, students have to play a guessing game with teachers concerning the content of the course to be learned. If the students guess wrong, it is reflected in their grades. Most teachers probably believe that they have pointed out the learning objectives of their courses, but if the students do not understand, then there is a problem in communication and in perception as well. Of course, communication, in a sense, is teaching; and perception, learning.

In the process of communication, there are four levels of communication which can occur.

1. *Independent*

This is a level of communication carried on by everyone in the form of self-communication thinking to oneself).

2. *Physical Interdependence.*

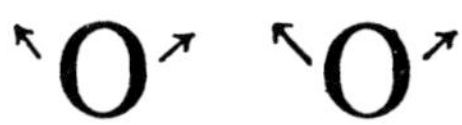

This is a type of communication in which the communicator just needs a "warm body" to talk to. Illustrations of this level of communication were typified in recent television commercials in which a man talks to his wife about his business and the wife talks about a new soap. Although both talk, neither one listens to the other.

3. *One-way*

This is a type of communication which predominates the present educational system and is typified by the one-way lecture presentations or by most other instructional materials including books. Over the years, this one-way form of communication in education has been portrayed in cartoons by a teacher pouring knowledge from a pitcher into a student's head. With one-way communication, there is no way to know to what degree the student is attending to the message and learning, or even whether or not the student is capable of attending to the message and learning from it

4. *Two-way* O——————→O

This is a type of communication that is typified by the tutorial approach to teaching and recent instructional approaches such as programmed learning and computer-assisted instruction.

Although all four of these levels of communication exist in education, learning which is a result of the association or interaction between teachers, of the association or interaction between teachers and students, or between instructional materials and students (fourth level), is the most effective and efficient. The major problem consists in the development of materials to be used at the third level which, through appropriate developmental techniques, takes on characteristics of the fourth level.

A brief review of David Berlo's communication model will be of value in laying the foundation for a learning-systems approach to the development of instructional materials. Berlo's S-M-C-R model breaks the communication process into the characteristics of four parts: the Source, the Message, the Channel, and the Receiver.

Three points should be kept in mind.

1. The most important feature of Berlo's model is that the characteristics of the Receiver are identical.
2. One of the most important assumptions of the learning-systems concept is that educators "*want* to help students

Source	*Message*	*Channel*	*Receiver*
Communication	Code	Seeing	Communication
Skills			Skills
Knowledge	Content	Hearing	Knowledge
Attitudes	Structure	Touching	Attitudes
Social	Elements	Tasting	Social
Cultural	Treatment	Smelling	Cultural

Fig. 2.1. S-M-C-R Communication Model.

progress through our educational institutions." This does not mean just to give the students good grades, it means to *help* the student learn what is appropriate and necessary.

3. In the communication process, the Receiver or learner can mentally "turn off or tune out" the Source at any time much easier and faster than closing a book, hanging up the telephone, or changing a television channel.

In order to help the student learn, we must design massages that will motivate the learner to keep his communication channels open to teachers' messages. For example, if the *Source* uses one language but the *Receiver* uses a diffrent language, communication is impeded. In many schools, teacher using a sophisticated from of classroom English are teaching culturally disadvantaged students who speak and understand an entirely different form of English. The teacher must change the message to fit the students' needs. In other words, *instructional messages need to be learner-oriented.*

In presenting information, we often make the assumption that the students perceive the information in the same manner and with the same meaning that we do. This is especially true in regard to verbal information. For some reason, many of us are under the impression that words have meanings. Words *do not* have meanings. People give meanings to the symbols we refer to as words, and because each of us has had a unique combination of experiences, these meanings may be highly personal or they may be almost coincident with the meanings held by other people.

Visual perception has a great deal to do with learning. It is of value, therefore, to consider the validity of what we see. In Figure 2.2 does the line *AB* appear to be equal to the line *BC*? Measure them and you will see that they are equal.

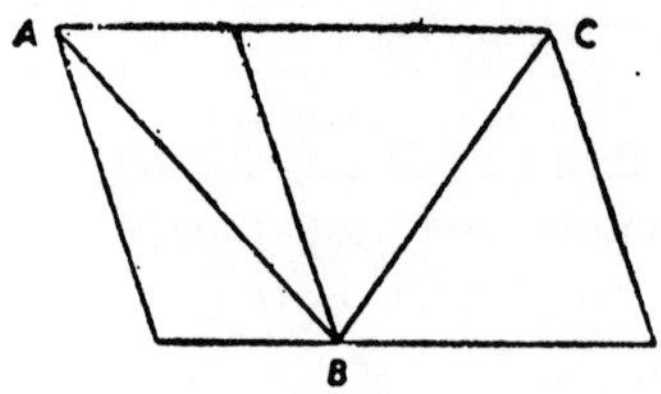

Fig. 2.2

Figure 2.3 is disturbing to many people. The amount of disturbance appears to be in relation to prior exposure to art, mechanical drawing, etc. Young children are not as bothered as are adults. In fact, some young children see nothing wrong with the picture. If you cover up one side or the other, the figure looks all right. It is the middle section that is distracting because prior experiences preclude a rationali-

Fig. 2.3

zation of the two extensions becoming three. The interpretation of information sent to the brain from the different senses are mediated by past experiences; consequently, perceptions of this information may vary from person. Therefore, if we are truly concerned that students perceive a specific message and have a meaning for that is coincident or at least similar to our own meaning, we must be willing to vary the mode of presentation until this condition occurs.

Few people can see it right away. Some see the face only after hours of study and some never see it at all. In education, the learner is often expected to "see" a visual concept, or a situation with the same perspicacity as the teacher. If he fails to see this "something," he may not learn material that is important to his future progress. In the learning-systems concept, if the learner does not see what he should see, the stimulus is changed.

Even more detail has been added to make it easier for the viewer to "see" the face. Even so, it may be necessary to study the illustration for a moment. Once you see the face look again. Perhaps now the face will be visible in the first illustration.

Usually, by increasing the visual clues. learning can take place, whereas initially, many would fail to achieve the objective (in this case a recognition objective).

Because of the restrictions of the printed medium, it is difficult to present actual examples concerning the problems of perception through our other four senses, but without too much trouble, examples of mis-perception in hearing, tasting, touching, and smelling can be demonstrated. An understanding of the communication process and how perception affects the fidelity of communication is vital to a succrssful use of a learning-systems approach to the development of instructional materials.

Development of a Course

The development of a course utilizing a learning-systems concept includes the same steps that are followed when preparing materials for programmed instruction. A programme consists of a sequence of carefully constructed items leading the student to mastery of a subject through self-study

The change from programmed instruction to the learning-systems concept is a matter of a greater degree of sophistication. The name change is necessary because "learning system" is more descriptive of the process involved and because the stereotype already established by those familiar with the term "programmed instruction" limits the mode of presentation to some kind of verbal format presented in a textbook form or by a teaching mrchine· People who are unfamiliar with the term often confuse it with computer technology. Extra steps are necessary, however, in order to apply a systems concept to the process.

Course development involves two major stages:

1. the behavioural analysis of the course content which is the preconstruction stage; and
2. the synthesis of learner behaviour which is the construction stage.

Lerner behaviours are anything that a student does purposely in response to an appropriate stimulus and which results in observable and measurable activities; *e.g.*, writing, speaking, performing, etc.

In the first stage, the task is to specify learner behaviours and learning objectives so that the nature of the behaviour can be discovered, past learning can be measured, behaviours to be modified can be identified, and objectives can be communicated.

The development of a typical course during this first stage follows a sequence designed to analyze and delimit the course content.

1. The first step in the analysis is the specification of the terminal behaviours (*i.e*,, those behaviours which the course instructor wishes the learner to exhibit upon

completion of a course). After each terminal behaviour (objective) is stated, the following three questions should be asked:

(a) Why should the student learn this behaviour?
(b) What is the student supposed to do with the behaviour once he has attained it?
(c) How long should the student retain the behaviour after once attaining it?

Answers to the first two questions could affect the inclusion of the objective in the course content and answers to the third question could affect the design of the instruction materials.

2. The construction of a post-test is the next step and will enable the observer to determine whether or not the terminal behaviours caa be exhibited by the learner. Usually, a slight change in the wording of the specified behaviour will result in the test item for this behaviour.

3. The third step is the specification of the assumed entry behaviours of representative learners *i.e.*, those behaviours pertinent to the course content that are exhibited by prospective learners of the course—(see Figure 2.4) and the relevant characteristics of these learners (*e.g.*, I.Q. level, educational background, etc.—see S.M.C.R Model).

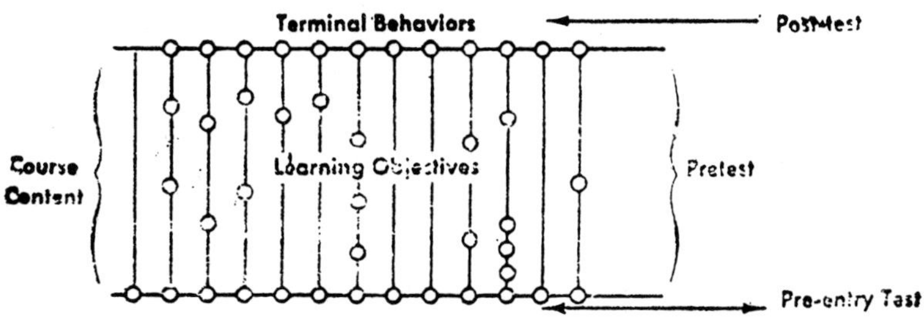

Fig. 2.4. Behavioural Analysis Outline

4. The fourth step is the construction of a pre-entry test will enable the observer to determine whether or not the assumed entry behaviours can actually be exhibited by representative learners who would take the course.
5. The fifth step is the specification of learning objectives of the course content which will be achieved through learning experiences and convert the learner's entry behaviours into terminal behaviours.
6. The sixth step is the construction of a pretest that will enable the observer to determine which of the learning objectives of the course content, if any, have been learned previously by representative learners.
7. The last step of the analysis is a preliminary tryout of the pre-entry test, pretest, and post-test on a sample of students that are representative of the intended learners for the course.

The tryout of three tests is to verify the existence of assumed entry behaviours the lack of terminal behaviours, and the lack of knowledge concerning the learning objectives which constitute the course content. Ideally, the learners would score 100 per cent on the pre-entry test and zero on the pretest and post-test. This would indicate that the entry assumptions made by the course instructor were correct (see Figure 2.5).

The tryout test scores will usually vary from the ideal. If the pre-entry test scores are less than 100 per cent, it is an indication that the course instructor's assumption regarding student entry behaviours were overstated (see Figure 2.7).

If one were to write programmed materials without testing for the existing entry behaviours of the intended audience, one would probably find many errors during the tryout of the complete programme. Most writers would tend to expand the programme by making the steps smaller and by overcueing the required responses to make up for the missing entry behaviours. Very seldom will a programme developed under these circumstances be successful; a high percentage of the dropouts will

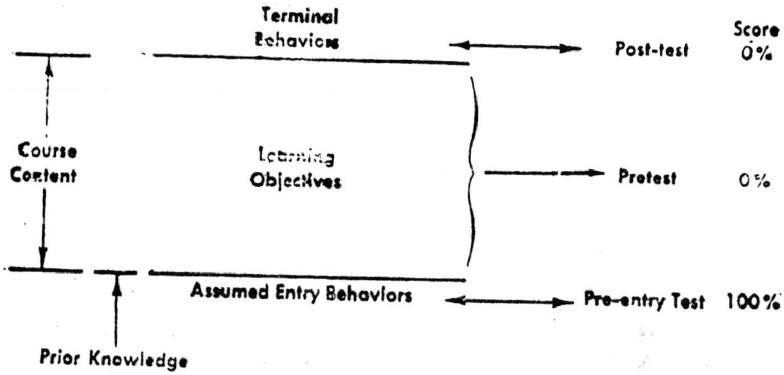

Fig. 2.5. Ideal Assumed Entry Behaviours

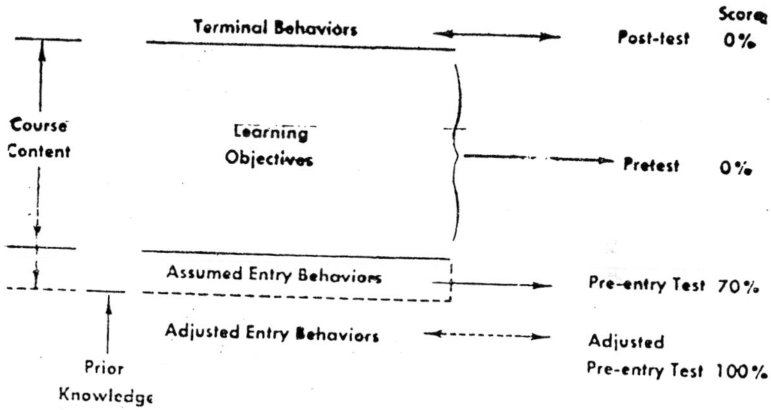

Fig. 2.6. Assumed Entry Behaviours—Too High

result because the steps will be too small and students working through the programme will consider it very dull and an insult to their intelligence.

If the pre-entry test scores were 100 per cent, the pretest scores greater than zero, it is an indication that the course instructor's assumptions regarding student entry behaviours were understated (see Figure 2.7).

Programmed materials developed without testing for existing entry behaviours might enable learners to reach the terminal

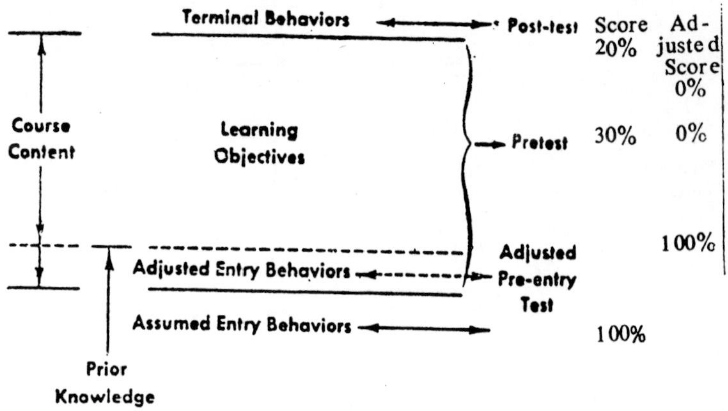

Fig. 2.7. Assumed Entry Behaviours—Too Low

behaviours, but there is a built-in boredom factor which will inhibit positive growth of motivation as learning takes place during the programme.

Programmes of this type are exemplified by situations where learners are able to score high on the post-test without going through the programme. A review of the literature on research concerning programmed instruction reveals that many programmes fall into this category. Almost every research article, where the pretest data are given, indicates that students knew from 30 per cent to 75 per cent of the content of the programme before even going through the programme. Generally, the programme is written before the students are tested, the excess frames stay in. It is not surprising that many students make the statement about programmed instructional being boring and repetitious.

Often, when the intended audience is heterogenous, students will be found in all three levels; above, below, and right at the assumed entry behaviours. Such data indicate the need for branching, and the same data can be used to locate and construct the appropriate branches.

This discussion has some rather obvious implication for the

use of pre-entry tests and pretests in the classroom. If tests of this kind are not used, and subjective intuitive measures or traditional course lights are relied upon, the studedts' fund of cumulative ignorance may grow because the material presented may be too far above or below them. Such a situation fosters low grades and/or potential dropouts.

In either of these two situations, overstated or understated entry assumptions, it is important to go back over the first six steps of the pre-construction stage and make appropriate adjustments in the behaviour analysis statements and the accompanying tests before going into the synthesis stage of the development of instructional materials.

The most successful programmes start the learner from where he is. This gives support to a very important learning principle: *Paths of learning proceed most effectively and efficiently when going from the known to the unknown.*

The analysis stage concerns the use of this principle in locating the begining point for a course, but not necessarily the sequence during the course. The need for a specific sequence varies from subject to subject and from unit to unit within a given subject. The achievement of some learning objectives is more dependent upon prior learning than the achievement of other objectives. In determining sequence, the developers should remember that the best sequence is ultimately the one that results in the greatest progress for the learner. As a starting point, the sequence could follow tradition or an experienced instructor's best guess. To develop a sequence that will proceed from the know to the unknown, a matrix method can be used. This method becomes cumbersome with a large number of objectives (over 50). Therefore, it may be useful to perform the matrix method using units or groups of objectives when a great uumber of objectives are involved.

The Matrix Method for Sequencing

List the learning objectives (represented by numbers) across the top of a matrix and duplicate the list of numbers down the left hand side of the matrix (see Figure 2.8).

Identify any and all telationship between the learning objectives by placing an (X) in the sequare representing the intersection between the objectives represented by columns and the objectives represented by rows. (See Figure 2.9). The diagonal from the upper left-hand corner represents the intersection of the column and row designated by the same object number.)

Rearrange the vertical columns aud the corresponding horizontal rows (some objective number; *i.e.*, column 5 and row 6) in such a manner that the (X)'s on the matrix, indicating

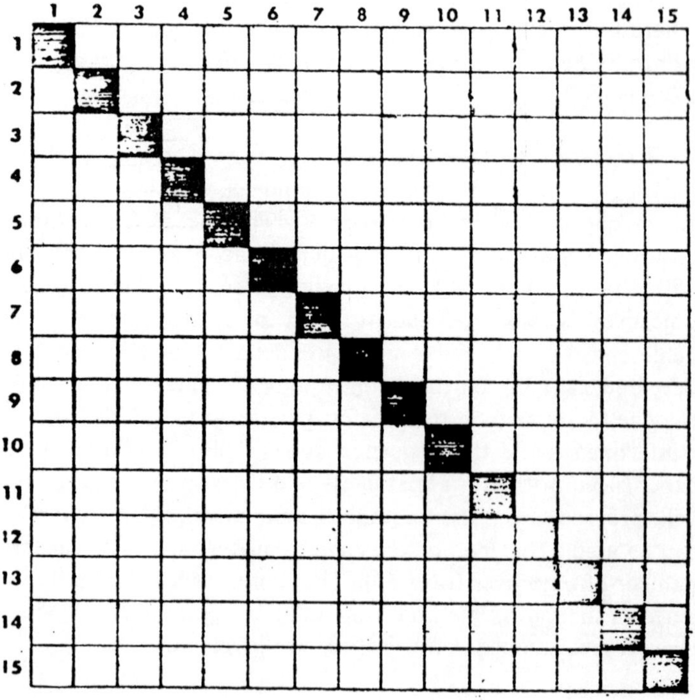

Fig. 2.8. Matrix Method for Sequence

relationships between learning objectives, are brought closer and closer into an elliptical pattern with the matrix diagonal as the major axis (see Figure 2.10). The ultimate goal of this step is to fill all the spaces adjacent to the diagonal with (X)'s. This would result in a particular sequence of objectives in which each objective would have some relatienship with the previous objective and also with the subsequent objective or "the path of learning could proceed from the known objective to the unknown objective." The extra (X)'s not along the diagonal indicate relationship which can be used in testing, review, or for presenting content from a different point of view.

The second stage, the synthesis of learner behaviours, can start after all of the objectives havs been defined, tests constructed and tried out on representative students, and objectives sequenced. The synthesis of the course content should not be started until all necessary adjustments indicated by the results of

Specific Learning Objectives

	1	12	2	3	5	14	7	11	13	4	8	15	9	6	10
1		X													
12	X		X	X	X										
2		X		X	X										
3		X	X		X	X									
5		X	X	X		X		X							
14				X	X				X		X				
7						X		X	X						
11					X		X			X	X	X			
13							X			X	X		X		
4								X	X		X	X	X		
8								X		X		X			
15								X		X	X		X	X	
9									X	X		X			
6												X			X
10														X	

Fig. 2.9. Matrix Method for Sequence

Specific Learning Objectives

	1	2	3	4	5	6	7	8	9	10	11	12	13	14	15
1												X			
2			X		X							X			
3		X			X							X		X	
4								X	X		X		X		X
5		X	X								X	X		X	
6										X					X
7											X		X	X	
8				X							X		X		X
9				X									X		X
10						X									
11				X	X		X	X							X
12	X	X	X		X										
13				X			X	X	X						
14			X		X		X						X		
15				X		X		X	X		X				

Fig. 2:10. Matrix Method for Sequence

the tryout of the tests have been made in the terminal and entry-behaviour lists and in the learning-objective list.

The first step in the synthesis or course-construction stage is the examination of the adjusted learning objectives to determine the most efficient and effective media and methods to be used in presenting the material associated with each objective (see Figure 2.11), keeping in mind what that particular objective or terminal behaviour is desired, what the learner is expected to do with this behaviour, what budget is available, what the feasibility is of the media and method‘ how portable the course materials have to be, etc.

The second step of the construction or synthesis stage is the construction and preparation of the materials necessary to help the learner attain the learning objectives and terminal behaviours of course, keeping in mind these four principles:

1. The content of the course is presented to the learner in small, single-concept steps or units that are appropriate to the learner's abilities; *e.g.*, reading level, educational level, age, etc.

TERMINAL LEVEL

Group

Demonstration

Trip

ETV

Face-to-Face

Film

P.I.

Audio

Models

ENTRY LEVEL

Fig. 2.11

2. For each step or unit, the learner is covertly or overtly involved, depending upon the behavioural requirement of that step.

3. In steps or units where the system requests specific responses, immediate confirmation of the correct reponses is *usually* available.

4. The course materials are self-paced to meet individual differences. This may necessitate a certain amount of branching from the main system to accommodate differences in the needs for the terminal behaviours of the course, the differences in learner abilities or differences is entry behaviours (see Figures 2.12 and 2.13).

The form in Figures 2.12 allows check points from time to

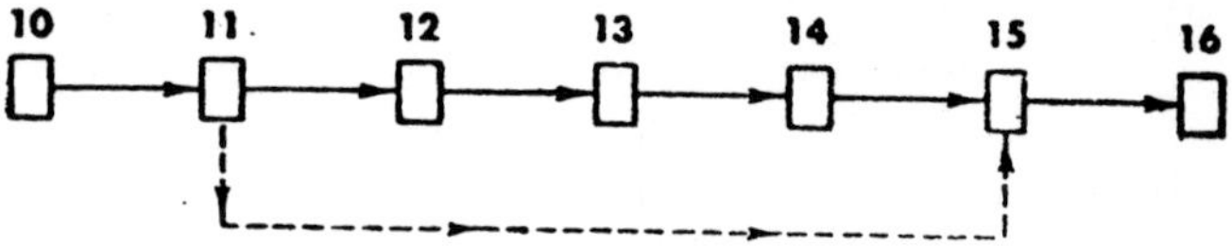

Fig. 2.12. Modified Linear

time, such that if a student answers frame 11 correctly he may be able to skip further redundency by being advanced to frame 15. Another version of this form will send the student back to frame 11 for further review if he answers wrong on frame 15. In one case, redundency is avoided, while in the second version, redundency is increased.

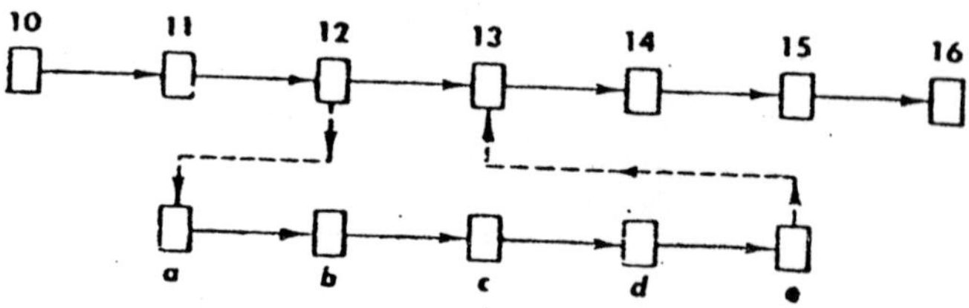

Fig. 2.13. Linear with Subroutines

Figure 2.13 illustrates another from that can be used in two ways. For the advanced and interested student, this form may allow him to pick up additional information relevent to the topic but not necessary for the terminal behaviours—an embellishment. For the slow student who was unable to answer frame 12 correctly, a variation of the previous frames may be used to present the particular topic or point from another viewpoint; *i.e.*, frames *a* through *e* will be essentially the same as frames 8 through 11.

For the student without some specific entry behaviours necessary to continue on with frame 13, the branch (*a* to *e*) could be used to teach the student the necessary material. In instance, frame 12 acts as a testing frame or "gate keeper" to be sure the learner is capable of continuing the course successfully.

The third step is the assembly of course materials and examination of them for clarity, continuity, and subject-matter validity.

The fourth step, and one of the more important steps of the course development, consists of trying out the course materials on representative learners and revision of the materials based on learner comments and errors. This "tryout-and-revision" process is repeated enough times so that 90 per cent of the learners are able to exhibit 90 per cent of the terminal behaviours.

This last step is very important in the development of a course where materials are "learner-oriented" rather than "instructor-oriented," and will enable students to master the materials to the appropriate level.

In testing out the units or total courses, the *developer* has to be especially aware of individual differences. The following learning variables should be kept in mind as being contributing factors to individual differences:

(a) rate of learning;

(b) amount to be learned;

(c) mode of learning;

(d) interpersonal relationships in learning;

(e) motivation to learn.

The fact that students *learn at different rates* is probably accepted by most teachers. The problem is, that while most teachers agree that students learn at different rates, their teaching behaviours in the classrooms are based on techniques that require all students to learn at the same rate. If the students in a learning situation do not learn at the same rate, both techniques and materials must be changed.

The *amount to be learned* varies from student to student.

The amount to be learned can be identified through the use of pre-entry tests, pretests, and post-tests (see Figure 2.14).

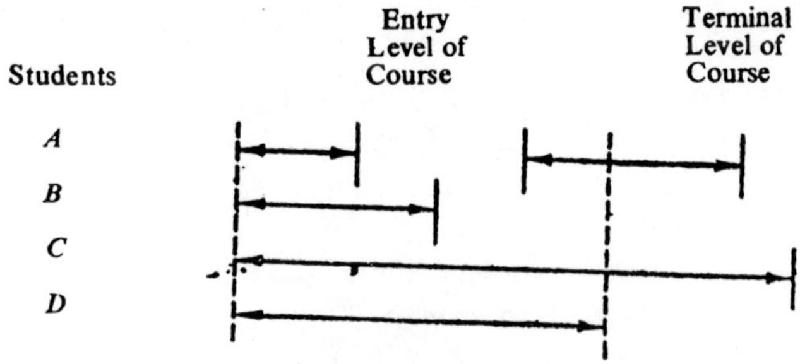

Fig. 2.14. Amount to be Learned

For example, student *A* has the right entry behaviours for the course and doesn't know any part of the course. Student *B* needs some remedial work before he can start the course. Whether or not student *B* takes his remedial work prior to the course or concurrently with the course depends upon the subject matter, the student, and the dependency of the course on the student's knowledge of prerequisite material. Student *C* knows most of the course and in most instances would be wasting his time if he were to go back through material he already knows. Student *D* is more typical of most of the students today. Even though he knows a considerable part of the material he also needs a certain amount of remedial study. Some kind of branching is indicated in dealing with students like *C* and *D*.

Mode of learning is also an important learning variable. One's assumptions about how students learn will usually determine the teaching methods used. For the purpose of this chapter, a presentation will be considered a "simulation" of the real-life situation when the same set of related objectives can be learned from various methods of presentation in a synthetic situation or learned by chance in a real-life situation.

A better understanding of the concept of simulation will be assured by beginning with a statement of the assumptions upon which this concept is based.

(a) There is such a thing as a "life environment."

(b) There is such a think as an "academic environment."

(c) The purpose of the academic environment is to preparc the learner for the life environment.

(d) The value of exposure to the academic environment is measured by the learner's performance in the life environment as a consequence of behaviours that have been transferred and adapted from the academic environment.

In real life, the learner's performance usually consists of perceiving certain stimuli and responding to them appropriately. The learner's response generally is not made to one stimulus, but to patterns of stimuli. An objective of the academic environment is to present certain stimulus patterns that represent the appropriate specific experiences from which it is hoped the learner will be able to generalize when meeting real-life experiences. Transfer of learned responses from the academic environment to the stimulus patterns met in life is referred to as "stimulus generalization."

Because the evaluation of the academic environment is measured by the learner's performance in life as a result of "stimulus generalization," it is important that the stimulus patterns in the synthetic situations of the academic environment be such that;

(a) they establish in the learner certain responses;

(b) the responses transfer positively to the real-life or operational situation; and

(c) the responses constitute the desired and appropriate reaction to the real-life stimulus patterns.

When there is a demand for transfer of learning to superficially different situations, some modes of learning which emphasize response to *pattern of cues* will be more effective than others emphasizing responses to *specific cues.* Learning which directs response to the total configuration of the life environment will therefore enable the student to cope with wider varieties of real-life situations, including transfer from synthetic to life environments.

The process of setting up a synthetic situation which enables the learner to learn responses, which through "stimulus generalization" are desired and appropriate in a real-life situation, is called *simulation.*

As a process, simulation can be positive or negative. In the concrete-abstract continuum (Fig. 6.15), positive simulation refers to the condition wherein the synthetic situation (S_2) is *more concrete* than the real life situation (S_1). Examples of positive simulation are the three-dimensional models used in

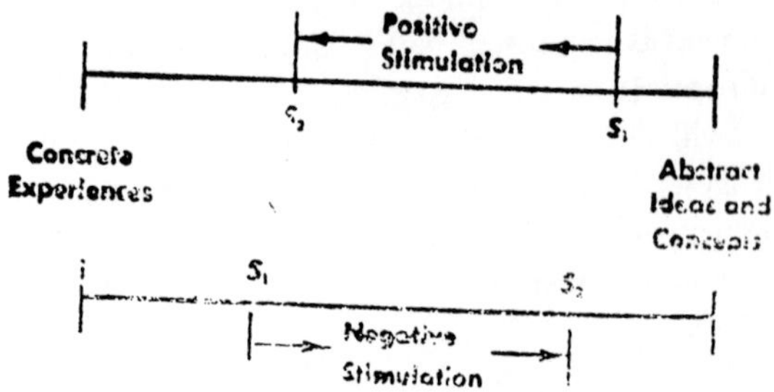

Fig. 2.15. Concrete-Abstract Continuum

chemistry and mathematics as concrete demonstrations of abstract ideas or concepts. Negative simulation refers to the condition wherein the synthetic situation (S_2) is less concrete than the real-life situation (S_1). Examples of negative simulation are the simulated cars used in driver training, the simulated planes used in air-crew training, and the scenery in theatrical plays.

Simulation is made up of two components: physical simulation—the copying of that part of the real-life situation which is physically involved in the desired responses or behaviours of the learner; and psychological simulation—the copying of that part of the real-life situation which is psychologically necessary to obtain the desired responses or behaviours of the learner. Psychological simulation can be divided into three distinct types:

(a) the copying of that part of the physical environment of the real-life situation that is *not* physically involved in the desired responses of the learner but nevertheless does affect the learning of the desired responses. Examples of this are the use of films with the driver-training simulators and the airplane cabins in the air-crew training simulators;

(b) the substitution of symbolic stimuli for physical realism based on stimulus generalization. Examples of this are the use of stubby wings on the flight simulators and the use of a small hood on the driver-training simulator to symbolize the real thing;

(c) the use of symbolic stimuli (words and/or visuals) to retrieve from the learner's memory information concerning past experiences that will help in the setting up of a synthetic situation. An example of this is the use of directions given prior to role-playing (a form of simulation); *i.e.*, "You are the owner of a toy manufacturing business doing three million dollars worth of business a year. You have 100 employees, etc."

Given the task of simulating a real-life situation, one may be tempted to produce a physical replica of the real-life situation, limited only by available budget and the state of the engineering art. There are kinds of behaviours and degrees of learning which may profit from a high degree of physical fidelity in the simulated environment, but other behaviours may be learned and may transfer quite adequately from synthetic situations having relatively little physical or functional realism.

Once it is recognized that there are degrees of both physical simulation and psychological simulation, practical decisions about the specifications for a synthetic environment will rest on economic and learning-objective compromises. From the standpoint of economy, the development of synthetic situations should rest on psychological simulation because as the degree of physical simulation increases, the physical environment (models, films, equipment, etc.) becomes more expensive to build and maintain. However, with low degrees of physical simulation, the student will be making verbal responses and will be transferring to the real-life situation little more than identifiation of specifies, and perhaps, certain ways and means of dealing with these specifics. This is adequate only if learning such specifics is the objective.

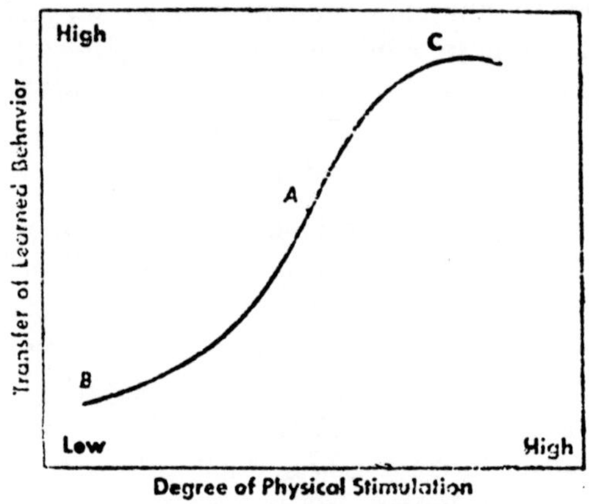

Fig. 2.16. Relationship between Degree of Physical Simulation and Transfer of Learned Behaviour.

Up to a point, increased increments of transfer of learned behaviours result from increased degrees of physical simulation (*A* section of transfer curve, Fig. 2.16). Human receptor channels, like other receivers, have limitations in sensitivity. For any stimulus imput, there will be ranges of physical differences in the synthetic situation which will not be matched with behavioural differences (*B* and *C* sections of transfer curve, Fig. 2.16).

In setting up a synthetic situation, various instructional media and varied methods and degrees of utilizations can be integrated providing flexibility in the desired simulation. It is important to remember that a particular synthetic situation (simulation) which involves a variety of instructional media should be designed in accordance with the predetermined learning objectives and not according to the characteristics of the instructional media. In other words, *fit the media to the objectives, not the objectives to the media.*

Fig. 2.17 is, in a sense, a continuum ranging from abstract to concrete, The placement of a specific medium in a specific tier is based on the general use of the medium; the number of senses involved; whether a synthetic situation is perceived directly (or indirectly through media); whether the synthetic situation is observed, heard, or both; and whether the perception involved is a synthetic situation or a verbal description of a synthetic situation. It is relatively easy to affect the placement of a specific medium by incorporating some new features or characteristics that would relate to the criteria used for deciding placement on the diagram; *e.g.*, adding sound to filmstrips would move the combined media to the next tier below.

Simulation in a specific synthetic situation can be evaluated for its effectiveness. *Perfect simulation* results in the performance of specified terminal behaviours in the real-life operational situation as a consequence of the transfer of learned behaviours from the synthetic situation. If some behaviours are not being performed adequately, it is an indication of a need for a greater degree of simulation.

For example, if, in the testing of learners who have taken a course or unit utilizing a specific media group or tier, it is found that only 50 per cent of the terminal behaviours are transferred to the operational situation (thus sindicating 50 per cent successful simulation), then the course materials should be restructured utilizing the media represented in the next lower tier or group—increasing the degree of simulation. The testing of learners who have taken the restructured course should indicate an increased transfer of learned behaviours as a result of a greater degree of

ABSTRACT

↑

S_8 Verbal description of the S.S.* *heard* (audio-tapes, lectures, radio recordings, etc.).

S_7 Verbal description of the S.S.* observed (book, pamphlets, periodicals, and other printed matter).

S_6 S.S.* is *heard* through a medium which presents the appropriate sound effects of the real-life situation (audio-tapes, radio, recordings, etc.).

S_5 S.S.* is *observed* through a medium which presents the visual stimuli of the real-life situation (silent motion pictures, slides, filmstrips, photographs, etc.).

S_4 Synthetic situation is perceived indirectly through a medium which presents the visual and audio stimuli of the real-iife situatlon (television, video tape, sound motion pictures, sound slides, etc.).

S_3 Synthetic situation is perceived directly without any intervening media allowing use of visual, audio, and alfactory stimuli of the real-life situation (exhibits, field trips, demonstrations, models, mock-ups, etc.).

S_2 The learners are *physically involved* in the synthetic situation through contrived or dramatized experiences allowing the use of all five senses (driver training or pilot training simulators, role playing, sociodrama, puppetry, mock-ups, models, etc.).

S_1 REAL-LIFE OPERATIONAL SITUATION

↓

CONCRETE

Fig. 2.17. Simulation through Use of Instructional Media (°Synthetic Situation).

simulation which has been set up in the synthetic situation. In a similar way, if, in the testing for retention of learned behaviours over a period of time, a decrease or loss is noted, increased simulation should be built into the course materials to increase retention.

One of the reasons programmed instruction has been so successful is that it combines active involvement along with the verbal content. When programmed materials utilize records, films, or kits of materials, the resultant is even greater because the experiences are more concrete.

Throughout the research literature, the reader is confronted with conflicting comments, *i.e.*, students were bored—students were captivated; students learned faster through programmed instruction—students learned faster through television; students learned more—students learned less; students learned better by branching programmed instruction—students learned better by linear programmed instruction; etc. Because of their varied abilities, interests, and prior experiences, some students will learn better and faster in certain subject areas through one mode or combination of modes while other students will learn better and faster in the same subject areas through a different mode or combination of modes. The teacher should manipulate the learning environment for each student in order to facilitate learning rather than spend his time presenting the course content which limits the students to one mode of learning. This method necessitates the efficient utilization of a variety of media and materials for presenting course content: programmed instructional materials, films, slides, demonstrations, face-to-face lectures, etc. It is not an efficient use of learning time to have a student go through an hour of the stereotyped, textbook form of programmed material when the same learning objectives could be accomplished by haviag him read a regular textbook for ten minutes or view a five-minute demonstration; or have teachers and students in a lecture situation for an hour when the same learning objectives could be accomplished in fifteen minutes through independent study of a programmed text.

The fourth learniing variable, the *interpersonal relationships in learning*, has received increasing attention of late. Many people have been aware of this variable for years, but little, if any efiort has been made to classify it as a learning variable and to take it into account in the learning situation. For instance, in a programmed instruction project, it was found that not all students like a particular programmed text: when given a choice of three programmed texts covering approximately the same content, each student was able to choose a text that he liked and from he could learn.

Why do we expect the learners to all like the same programmed text, textbook, or even the same teacher? *If our ultimate goal is learning, then whatever will facilitate learning should be a part of the system.* If a student is not learning and a change in the textbook or a change in the teacher does result in learning, then why not do it?

The fifth learning variable, *motivation*, has been the topic of many conferences during the past two decades. For the purposes of this chapter, it is enough to say that, in general, educational institutions and educators are not paying enough attention to the need for motivation to stimulate learning. The concept of motivation is like the concept of individval differences; almost all educators will agree that what will motivate one child will not necessarily motivate another. Yet, in the classrooms, it is continually assumed that all children are motivated in the same manner with no individual differences.

These five learning variables are not taken into account largely because the teachers are too busy presenting the content of their courses. When a teacher is presenting the content of a course:

1. the student's rate of learning is determined by the teacher's rate of presenting;
2. the amount the student learns is limeted by the amount the teacher presents;
3. the mode by which the student learns is determined by

the mode the teacher decides to use to present the course;

4. the interpersonal relationship between the teacher and student is restricted to the teacher that is presenting: or

5. if the teacher is presenting, the teacher does not have time to worry about individual motivation.

In the typical classroom situation, the teacher is the presenter of information, and is generally the focus of attention Courses developed in accordance with a learning-systems approach replace the teacher as the presenter of information. Learning now becomes the focus of attention, and the teacher, who has been relieved of the time-consuming task of repeatedly presenting the same information, can concentrate on the task of *teaching*. The teacher becomes an educational diagnostician, a director, or a guide to meaningful learning experiences, adapting available materials and environment to the needs of the learner.

Testing and Evaluation

Testing and evaluation are very important in the development of materials utilized in the learning-systems concept as well as for any significant improvement in learning.

In order to conserve time, energy, and money, one unit that resents a good sample of the skills and knowledge to be learned from the entire course should be selected and developed first. Once the media and instructional methods which will bring about the desired transfer of learning for the specific unit have been determined and tested, the development of the balance of the course may be carried out with a minimum of restructuring.

The most dificult job in testing and evaluation is to define what is to be tested and evaluated; consequently, meaningful testing and evaluation should be based upon specific objectives measuring achievement of course content. Tests developed from non-specific or non-definable learning objectives tend to show a very low correlation between the course content and the tests. Learning objectives may be classified as shown in Fig 2.18.

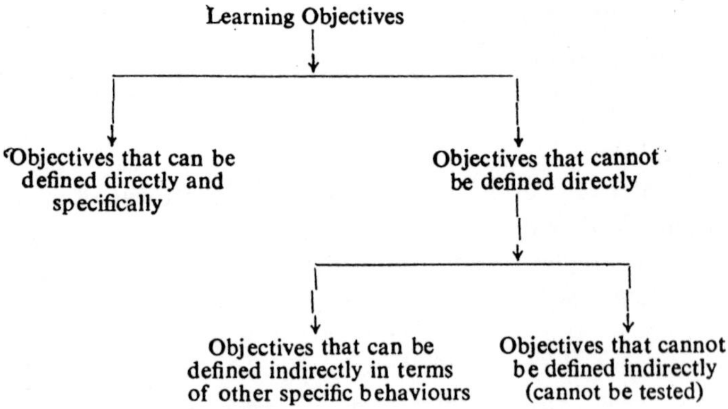

Fig. 2.18. Classification of Learning Objectives

A test made from definable objectives (directly or indirectly) may serve three purposes, depending on the point of view, without changing the test from. It may serve as:

1. a *teaching test*, to help the learner become aware of what he has already learned and what he may have to review;

2. a *measurement test*, to determine what the learner knows at a given time. The learner can then be placed in a learning situation which will enable him to proceed without either an unnecessary review, or a gap in his knowledge in going from the known to the unknown (pre-entry tests, pretests, and placement tests):

3. a *mastery test*, to determine if the learner has achieved mastery of the specified objectives of the course content (post-test).

It is useful to remember that the synthetic situation which has been validated by the transfer of appropriate learned

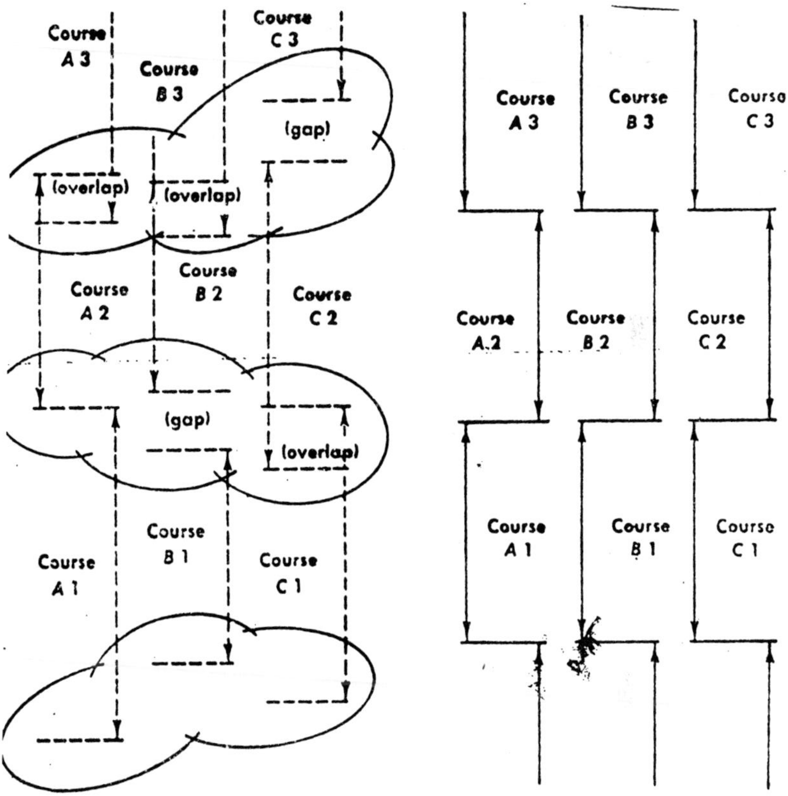

Sequence *A* Sequence *B* Sequence *C*

Traditional Patterns

Typified by obscure entry and terminal course behaviours permitting gaps and overlaps in a sequence of course

Sequence *A* Sequence *B* Sequence *C*

Learning System Patterns

Typified by defined entry and terminal course behaviours such that the terminal behaviours of one course are the same as the next course.

Fig. 2.19. Patterns of Course Sequences.

behaviours to the real-life operational situation can be very effectively and efficiently used to evaluate student achievement. In almost all courses, some simulation other than at the verbal level is integrated into the course materials; *e.g.*, films, models, artifacts, chalkboard, flannelboard, graphs. pictures, tapes, discs, and so on. If these materials are used in the teaching-learning process, why not use them in the testing of learning? Verbal tests of behaviours which were learned in response to more concrete forms of simulation may not only be testing the learned behaviours of the learner, but may also be testing the learner's ability to correctly interpret the instructor's verbalization of the desired behaviours. The same general considerations which go into the decisions of what to include in a course also go into the decisions of what to include in a valuation of the course.

Suggested Areas for Course Development

Several areas of education would benefit from courses that have been developed in accordance with the learning-systems concept: sequential courses having long-range goals such as those in elementary, secondary, and higher education: and non-sequential courses such as those found in continuing and adult education and in vocational- and industrial-education programmes having short-range goals: *e.g.*, learning of a psychomotor skill, gaining a fine unit of knowledge. etc.

In the area of sequential courses, it is important to point out one of the major differences between elementary, secondary, and higher education in regard to their developmental patterns. In elementary education, almost all students take the same content and follow the same pattern. In secondary education, almost all students follow one of four or five patterns. At the present time, the pattern which a student might follow in secondary education is determined to a large extent by the amount of "cumulative ignorance" acquired by a student in elementary school. One can only estimate the effects of the approach to elementary education which would enable 90 per cent or more of the students to learn 90 per cent or more of the content.

1. The elementary curriculum would be completed by a high majority of students in a much shorter time.
2. Because of the decrease in learning time necessary to

achieve the elementary curriculum, certain portions of the traditional secondary education curriculum would be transferred into the elementary curriculum.

3. Almost every student would enter and complete secondary education (only 71 per cent complete secondary education now).

Two approaches can be utilized in the development of instructional materials for sequential courses. One approach is the development of a subject from its introduction to some finite level; *e.g.*, mathematics from kindergarten to twelfth grade. This is essentially a *vertical systems analysis and development.* The second approach is the simultaneous development of all the basic subjects from their introduction to some finite level; *e.g.*, grades one through four, or kindergarten through eighth grade. This is basically a *horizontal systems analysis and development.*

It would be most efficient to apply the systems design at the elementary level before and of the other educational levels, because almost all students follow the some curriculum patterns and there is a need for interrelationships between basic subject areas. The horizontal systems analysis and development would be the best approach for a systems design at this level. It would allow the development of a continuous-progress type scale in each subject upon which a student's overall achievement profile could be recorded. The student, then, would experience a minimum of gaps and overlaps when transfering from school to school—or even from teacher to teacher. By varying the amount of time spent in each subject area in accordance with the student's needs, and by concentrating time and effort on the weak areas of the student's achievement profile, students should be able to complete eighth grade with a solid background and foundation in all subject areas.

Although the required courses in secondary education provide a core of course content which lends itself to a continuation of the horizontal systems analysis and development, several curriculum patterns in secondary education would benefit more from a vertical systems analysis and development. The are of mathematics provides one good example.

Staff Requirements to Develop a Course

Course development is a complex process. As a general estimate, 25-150 man-hours of labour are required to produce one hour of instructional materials for the average learner. This estimate can vary considerably depending on such factors as the degree of competence of those involved in regard to their particular specialty and the complexity of the subject matter.

In order to develop quality courses in accordance with the learning-systems concept the services of a number of specialists may be needed.

1. Subject-matter experts or analysis are specialists who have taught the course content and are interested in learning-system orientation and behavioural analysis. Their job is to specify the entry and terminal behaviours and the mediating learning objectives necessary. They also act as subject-matter editors for accuracy of content of the final course materials.

2. Media specialists or examiners must be acquainted with the advantages and disadvantages of various instructional media. Their task is to determine collectively the media to be utilized in the presentation of each step or unit for maximum effectiveness and efficiency, and to initiate the preparation of the necessary materials.

3. Subject-matter synthesists develop and synthesize the steps or units of the course on the basis of the behavioural analysis in the preconstruction stage. They are involved in the revision of those materials that have been tested with representative students.

4. Learning-system coordinators (behavioural technologists) must have a knowledge of a variety of media. In order to obtain the maximum benefits from utilizing the learn-

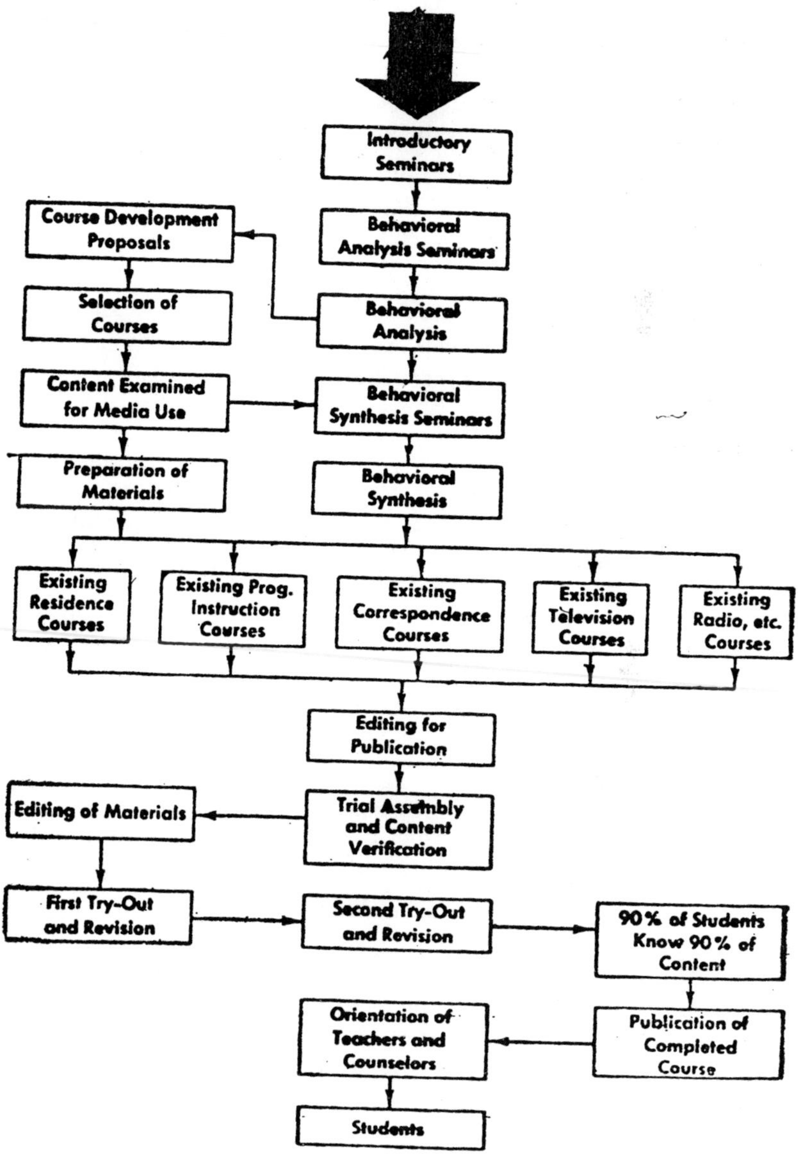
Introductory Seminars
Course Development Proposals
Behavioral Analysis Seminars
Selection of Courses
Behavioral Analysis
Content Examined for Media Use
Behavioral Synthesis Seminars
Preparation of Materials
Behavioral Synthesis
Existing Residence Courses
Existing Prog. Instruction Courses
Existing Correspondence Courses
Existing Television Courses
Existing Radio, etc. Courses
Editing for Publication
Editing of Materials
Trial Assembly and Content Verification
First Try-Out and Revision
Second Try-Out and Revision
90% of Students Know 90% of Content
Orientation of Teachers and Counselors
Publication of Completed Course
Students

Fig. 2.20.

ing-systems approach in course development, their tasks are to conduct seminars; hold follow-up individual conferences; help define and analyze course content and accompanying tests as outlined in the preconstruction stage of the course development, and help in the validation of tests; make recommendations regarding the appropriate media for specified learning objectives; supervise the trial assembly of course materials; and help in the testing and revision of the completed courses.

5. Production specialists from television, radio, graphics, films, computers. etc., produce materials designed to maximize learning most effectively and efficiently from the student's point of view.
6. Publication editors edit the course materials prior to testing, after each revision, and prior to final publication for correct English, structure, continuity of format, etc.

Fig. 2.20 indicates the sequence of events which might be followed in the implementation of a systems approach in education.

Closing Comments

The use of the *total* learning-systems concept involves a lot of time, effort, and money. In order to facilitate educational innovation, several aspects of such an approach could easily be adapted into on-going courses as listed below.

1. Specify precisely the course objectives without using such vague and non-measurable terms as "understanding," "appreciation for," "familiarity with," "a knowledge of," etc. Robert Mager's book, on *instructional objectives*, has been helpful in the formulation of specific objectives. Just as it is possible to make test items out of specific objectives by a slight change of wording, it is also possible to make specific objectives

out of test items. At the very least, specify the "critical objectives" of the course. "Critical objectives" are learning objectives which, if not achieved by the student, will inhibit or prevent learning in subsequent courses. Students should not be permitted to pass on to the next course without them.

2. Develop pretests which will clarify the student's standing in his class work, and indicate whether specific remedial work or advance placement is needed. A ready-made source of a pretest is a combination of a final examination from a prerequisite course or courses (just using the test items that are pertinent to the course for which you want the pretest) plus the first major test in the course itself (six- or nine-week examination). In this way, it is possible to measure whether the student has the necessary knowledge and skills to take the course and whether he already knows part of the course.

3. Look upon student errors as indications of possible learning problems. Most students try to answer test questions to the best of their ability. If a student's answers are incorrect, check into the learning situation. May be the objective was not taught right!

4. Make sure that tests are valid and actually measure the behaviours that represent the learning objectives of the course; test only behaviours which the student has had an opportunity to learn (no hidden objectives). For example, if a teacher wants a student to learn specific facts or to deal with facts in certain ways, a multiple-choice test may not identify whether or not the student has actually achieved these objectives. Multiple-choice tests usually measure ability to discriminate between answers (process of elimination) rather than demonstrate knowledge of a specific item or skill.

5. Keep in mind the five learning variables discussed earlier in this chapter concerning individual differences.

In education, students come to teachers in order to learn. Generally, if the student does not learn by whatever method the teacher uses, he fails. The cumulative effect of failure cannot be measured in dollars and cents. Teachers have a moral responsibility to society to do everything in their power to help students learn to live.

3

Women and Human Resource Development

Education has been regarded both as an end in itself and as a means of realizing other desirable ends. It develops the personality and rationality of individuals, qualifies them to fulfil certain economic, political, and cultural functions and thereby improves their socio-economic status. It has been recognized as a major instrument which societies can use to direct the process of change and development towards desired goals. It provides for vertical mobility and can thereby help to equalize status between individuals coming from different social strata. The Universal Declaration of Human Rights regards it as one of the basic rights of every human being.

The movement for improving women's status all over the world has always emphasized education as the most significant instrument for changing women's subjugated position in society. The Indian social reformers of the nineteenth century also accepted this view. Their aim, however, was to use education to make women more capable of fulfilling their traditional roles as wives and mother and not to make them more efficient and active units in the process of socio-economic or political development. The colonial authorities generally supported this limited view of women's education. The expansion of education and heath services in the twentieth century, however, precipitated a need for women 'teachers' and doctors and resulted in the incorporation of these two non-familial vocations in the programmes for women's education.

The attainment of independence and the constitutional guarantee of equallty introduced new dimensions with the call on women to play multiple roles in the polity, the economy, and the society. In the years after the second world war, international agencies also emphasized the role of education as an instrument thant can equip women to build the new social order. In spite of this new emphasis, however, attitudes to women's education in India have displayed an ambivalence between the traditional, limited view on the one hand and this broad new concept on the other and it is this ambivalence which has influenced academic planning, allocation of resources and development of value in society, both for men and women.

Progress of Women's Education : Quantitative Aspects

We have examined women's educational development:

(1) by quantitative indicators like enrolment, outturn, educational facilities, literacy rates, and total stock of educated women, and

(2) in the light of the stated national objective of integration of women as equals of men in all aspects of national development.

(1) *Enrolments*: The constitutional directive to provide free and compulsory education for all children up to the age of 14 years has remained unfulfilled till now. Educational experts admit that this failure is mainly due to the slow progress of education among girls. Scheduled Castes, and Scheduled Tribes. In the group 6-11, only 66% of the girls were in schools at the end of the Fourth Plan period. In the age group 11-14, this figure was only 22%. The comparative figure boys were 100% and 48% respectively.

When compared to the progress of women's education in the pre-independence period, however, the development of women's education of the post-independence period has been phenomenal. The expansion of women s education, which began at the primary stage, was also mostly confined to that stage only in the earlier period. In 1947, the number of girls enrolled in primary schools (3,475,165) represented 83% of all the girls in the educational system. The middle schools had an enrolment of only 321,000 and represented 9% of the total enrolment. The secondary schools with their enrolment of 281,000 represented only 7% of the total enrolment ; and even though the Indian universities had proved to be more liberal than their western counter parts in admitting women, their enrolment in higher education (23,000) was only less than one-half of 1% of the total enrolment. The number of girls per 100 boys at different levels in 1947 was 36 at the primary level, 22 at the middle level, 14 at the secondary level, and 19 at the university level. By 1973-74, the number of girls enrolled at different stages as well as their proportion to boys had increased tremendously. At the primary level, girls enrolled numbered over 24.4 million (ratio 62 per 100 boys), at the middle level, over 4.5 million (ratio 43), at the secondary level, over 2.3 million (ratio 36) and in colleges and universities, about 0.9 million (ratio 31). The destribution of all girls enrolled between different stages of the educational system also changed during the period. By 1970-71, 73% were in primary schools, 14% in middle schools, 7.3% in secondary schools, 2.4% in universities and colleges, and 3.3% in professional sechools.

In spite of this unprecedented advance, the overall situation left a good deal to be desired. Some of the major weaknesses of the position were the following:

1. In classes I to V, one girl out of three is out of school. The drop-out rate is also high—of every 100 girls enrolled in class I, only about 30 reach class V.
2. In classes V to VIII, only one girl out of five is at school. The step fall from an enrolment of 66% of the

population in the age group 6-11 to 22% in the age group 11-14 indicates the tremendous drop-out rate between the primary and the middle stage

3. At the secondary stage the population of girls enrolled group to only 12% of the population in the age group 14—17 which implies that only one girl out of eight is in school. Secondary education even now is largely confined to the upper and the middle classes it means if the rural area is namely utilized by well-to-families, particularly from the middle classes.

4. As a result of special efforts, girls' enrolment was stepped up from 1960. We regret to observe, however, that these efforts were slackened after 1966. The quinquennial growth rate in enrolment of girls declined at the primary stage from 56.1% in 1961-66 to 30.7% in 1966-71. At the secondary stage, the decline was from 70.6% to 30.5%. At the university stage, however, the decline was relatively less, from 109.4% to 78.4%. In professional and special schools the decline was from 74.6% to 34.6%. This is a matter of deep concern.

5. While enrolment is generally regarded as the main indicator for measuring educational progress, the problems of wastage and stagnation impose certain limitations. The all-India average of drop-outs at different stages of the school system has alway been higher for girls than for boys. The Education Commission had found this to be 62% at the lower primary stage as against 56% for boys. At the higher primary stage, it was 34% as against 24% for boys. A latter study* found the rate of wastage and stagnation to be 62.3% for boys and 71.3% for girls in primary and middle schools, the maximnium difference being in grades I and II.

(2) *Outturn.* In the outturn of students from schools and the unlversity system the most significant features are the slower rate of increrse in number of girls per thousand boys

who pass the matriculation and higher secondary examinations and the much faster rate of increase at the university stage, particularly at the first degree level. The gap between qualified mean and women is declining more rapidly in higher education than at the school level. Since higher education in India is still confined to a small minority, the impact of this trend on the educational development of women as a whole is marginal. During 1947-48 to 1965-66 the number of girls per thousand. boys passing the matriculation examination increased from 12 to 31. Admission to engineering and technology became possible only after 1948 Considering this late start, women's success in these courses has been significant, though their representation in other professional fields still remains very low. Similarly, women's entry into research was mainly a post-independence development and their progress at this level is satisfactory. The earlier widespread beliefs that girls have less aptitude and intelligence than boys higher studies, particularly in subjects like mathematics of science, has been disproved by their success, success which often outstrips that of boys, in various examinations.

(3) *Growth of Institutions*; The National Committee on Women's Education had advocated provision of separate institutions for girls to break down the prejudice against their education. In the period after 1960-61, exclusive institutions for girls multiplied rapidly. In 1947-48, these represented only 10.3 per cent of the total number of educational institutions. By 1967-68, they formed 29 per cent of the total, the number increasing from 16,951 to 230,032.

While welcoming the growth of institutional facilities for spread of education among women, we have to point out some adverse features of this rapid growth. The large number of single-teacher primary schools suffer from frequent closures because of absence of teachers, which has discouraged many parents from sending girls to school. Many girls to sehools at the middle and secondary level suffer from inadequate teaching facilities and low standards, particularly for subject such as science and mathematics. limiting the students' choice of subjects. The extremly rapid expansion of women's colleges (from 81 in 1953-54 to 435 in 1971-72) has introduced a number of institutions with very low enrolment (256 have more than 500; 55 less than 100), which are financially non-viable and provide very low standards of teaching. This has been possible because of the policy to encourage women. In our view the spread of sub-standard or limited education will not help the achievement of equality of opportunities and may even damage the cause of women s education. Vigilance regarding standards is imperative and must from a part of the policy of encouragement and assistance.

(4) *Women Teachers*: It has always been recognized that increasing the number of women teachers is an essential condition for development of women education. In 1947, only 14.4 per cent of school teachers were women. In 1973-74, their population had increased to 26 per cent in primary schools. 37 per cent in middle schools, and 30 per cent in secondary schools. In the universities and colleges their population increased from 8.5 per cent in 1950-51 to 15 per cent in 1970-71 the highest representation being in education (23.9 per cent), arts (19.7 percent), and medicine (19.2 per cent). They constituted 13.6 per cent of the university teaching staff in sciences and 10.8 per cent in law, their position in other faculties being negligible. The low proportion of women among primary school teachers is mainly due to difficulties that women have to face in serving in rural areas, caused by resistance from their families, the fear of insecurity in villages, and the lack of physical amenities such as accommodation, schooling, transport, and medical facilities. In our view these need to be solved on a priority basis to reduce the present imbalance in the development of women's education between urban and rural areas and to prevent increasing unemployment among trained and qualified women teachers. We were also informed that the inadequacy of women inspectors creates certain difficulties for women teachers particularly in single teacher school. In some States which do not have a women's cadre

of inspectors, women teachers complained of misbehaviour. blackmail, or exploitation by male inspectors.

Literacy

In spite of all the expansion that has taken place in the formal educational system, the vast majority of India women have remained outside the reach of all education and are illiterate. While the female leteracy rate has increased from 0.69 per cent in 1901 to 18.4 per cent in 1971, and the number of literate females per thousand males from 68 to 435, the number of illiterates women has also increased from 161.9 million in 1950-51 to 215.3 million in 1970-71. The comparable figures for illiterate males are 139.9 million and 172 miliion. In the 15-24 age group, 29.8 million or 41.5 per cent of the women are illiterate. In the 25 and above age group, this number inereases to 94.5 million of 88.6 per cent. Of the small proportion of literate women in these two age groups, the large majority have only primary and middle level education.

The challenge of this widening illiteracy gap will have to be borne in mind in determining priorities in educational development in the years to come. The claims of the formal educational system which can cater to the needs of only a minority, and mainly the younger generation, will have to be balanced against the educational needs of this group of adult women who constitute the workers and the mothers of the society.

Attitudes to Women's Education

Social attitudes to girls' education vary from acceptance to absolute indifference. According to our survey, only 16.8 per cent of the respondents felt that girls should not be given any education, but 64.5 per cent observed that girls should not go in for higher education even if they are very intelligent. About 77.5 per cent, both male and female, supported compulsory education for girls up to the 8th class. Educationists and administrators were generally in favour of compulsion for this purpose. We found the acceptance of girls' education to be far wider in urban areas, being the highest among the middle classes. A small group of affluent families still oppose it for traditional reasons, but others regard it as an accomplishment and a symbol of modernization. Among the lower middle class, an increasingly large section is now ready to make substantial sacrifices for girls' education because of economic need, but a very large section still finds itself unable to do so for economic and social difficulties. For the majority of the people below subsistence level, powerty is the predominant factor that governs their attitude to girls' education.

A large majority of girls have to undertake domestic chores, including looking looking after the siblings, by the time they reach the age of 8 years. A very large number are also engaged in earning for the family. We found girls from the age of five working with their parents in bidi factories and other industries in the unorganized sector for 12 hours a day and also as helpers of their mothers in domestic service. Some teenagers were supporting entire families of sick and unemployed parents and young siblings on their sole earnings. It should be noted that girls constitutes a higher proportion of the unpaid family workers throughout the country and that is a major reason for their exclusion from schools. Other social reasons for this adverse attitude to girls' education are early marriages or betrothal, though these are on the decline, except in the admittedly educationally backward States of Bihar, Orissa, Madhya Pradesh, Rajasthan, and Uttar Pradesh. The social restriction on girls pursuing their studies after marriage is, however, considerably less now. The other reasons mentioned to us, which stand in the way of girls' education, are inadequacy of facilities, particularly distance of schools; irrelevance of the content of education; and fear of the alienation of girls from their environment as a result of education.

The strongest social support for girls' education comes from its increasing demand in the marriage market. About 64.5 per cent of our respondents stated that education helped to improve the girls' marriage prospects. This relationship between marriage prospects and education, however, operates in different ways. Since it is considered necessary to find bridegrooms with still higher education, education of girls contributes to an increase of dowry, and the double expenditure acts as a deterrent to girls' education. We were told by many parents that this was the reason for their withdrawing their girls from schools after the primary stage.

Other Imbalances in Educational Development

Education is a double-edged instrument which can eliminate the effects of socio-economic inequalities, but can also introduce a new kind of inequality between those who have it and those who do not. Apart from the sharp increase in the number of illiterate women and the disparity in educational development between rural and urban areas, there are severe imbalances in educational development between advanced and backward classes and between regions. Imbalances in women's education and literacy are the consequences of these regional disparities, which reflect, to a great extent, variations in regional attitudes to women. A detailed analysis of State-wise progress in women's education at different levels revealed that while all of them have made rapid progress, the rate of progress has been uneven between different States. While Bihar and Rajasthan show uniformly lowest performance at all levels. States such as Andhra Pradesh, Assam, Maharashtra, Karnataka, Uttar Pradesh, Himachal Pradesh, Manipur, and Tripura have achieved a higher rate of progress at the pr imary level. The only States where progress of enrolment at both primary and middle leves have been equally high are Jammu and Kashmir, Kerala, Nagaland, Delhi, and Tamil Nadu. The case of West Bengal is rather unique, as it has merely maintained its position at the primary level and lost ground at the middle level during this period. At the secondary !evel only Kerala, Tamil Nadu, and Delhi registered definite progress. At the university level, the majority of the States registered a distinct improvement, but progress in vocational and technical courses at the school level has been slow and even static in many States, with the exception of Assam, Maharashtra, and Delhi. Progress in professional and technical education at the university level is marginal in all States. This is not conductive to the diversification of women's education or to the employment of educated women

While we found a significant correlation between the growth of girls' education and the female literacy rate, no 'such significant relationship could be established between girls' education and

1. Per capita income of the State;
2. Density of population; and
3. Sex ratio.

Female literacy rate, in turn, is influenced greatly by population composition. Cities and regions with a high proportion of Muslim or Scheduled Castes and Tribes are marked by low literacy rates, while those with a relatively high percentages of Christians have a high literacy rate. While there is a big gap in urban and rural literacy rates, broadly speaking, the southern States have always maintained a higher rate of female literacy.

Apart from the lower literacy rate among Muslim women, our survey of minority communities definitely revealed that the number of Muslim women with no formal education continues to be very high even in those States which have otherwise progressed considerably in the development of women's education (e.g. Kerala). Similarly, women in Scheduled Castes and Scheduled Tribes continue to any demand other women and the men in their own communities very greatly in both literacy and education. According to the census of 1961. (the comparable figures for males being 865 and 696). The large majority of the small literate group are literates without educational level.

The influence of these sociological factors on women's education reduces the value of national or State averages in assessing educational progress. Female literacy rates in different districts of the same State vary sometimes from 6.4 to 29.5 per cent (Andhra Pradesh); 4.8 to 33.8 per cent (Uttar Pradesh); 4 per cent to 31.4 per cent (Madhya Pradesh). In our opinion, plans for educational development which do not take these soeial and regional imbalances into account, will intensify inequalities between different, section of the population. It is necessary to identify factors responsible for them and seek their removal with the aid of special programmes.

Co-education

Co-education represents a controversy of longstanding in Indian education. While arguments in its defence from the point of view of fuller utilization of resources and economy are gradually gaining ground, it has been generally objected to by the defenders of women's education out of an apprehension that social prejudices against women's education can be removed more easily if girls are taught in separate institutions. We found continued evidence of this divergence of view during our investigation. Communities which observe *purdah* naturally demand separate schools. (There was, however, no such demand in Kashmir.) In some areas this resistance to co-education is higher among Hindus than Muslims. We also found this resistance to be more of an urban middle class phenomenon, explained by the increasing indiscipline and rowdyism in institutions for secondary and higher education. The under-privileged classes, whether in urban or rural areas, do not have such objections to co-education. A new argument in favour of co-education coming even from an educationally socially backward State like Bihar is that co-educational institutions provide better teaching standards and show better performance of students. An opinion poll among officials, from Directors of Public Instruction to field staff working in rural areas, elicited a strong support for co-education at the primary and middle levels

In our opinion, the considerations of efficiency, economy and equal opportunities require the acceptance of co-education as a long-term policy. However, in view of the divergent social attitudes, we recommend:

1. its adoption as the general policy at the primary level;
2. provision of separate schools at middle and secondary levels in areas where there is a great demand, along with an effort to persuade public opinion in favour of co-education;
3. its adoption as a general policy at the university level, discouraging opening of new colleges exclusively for girls;
4. removal of ban on admission of girls to all-boys' institutions;
5. vigilance regarding required standards in all exclusive institutions for girls;
6. acceptance of the principle of mixed staff as the condition of recognition for all mixed schools—to be reviewed a few years after implementation; and
7. provision of separate toilets and retiring rooms for girls in all mixed institutions.

Curricula

The traditional view regarding women's education had resulted in an emphasis on different curricula for girls, with accent on subjects which were considered specially suitable for them such as domestic science, need-work, or fine arts. This also resulted in failure to provide subjects such as sciences and mathematics in most girls' institutions. This practice was challenged by the Committee on Differentiation of Curricula for boys and girls (1964) which recommended a common course at all levels to counteract the influence of traditional attitudes which regard certain tasks as 'manly' and others as 'womanly'. The Education Commission (1966) endorsed these recommendations We found wide acceptance of this new trend of thought, but some States continue to prescribe different curricula for boys and girls.

We recommend a common course of general education till the end of class X with all optional courses open to boys and girls. Simple needle craft, music and dancing should be taught to all children at the primary stage. From the middle stage, variations may be permitted under work experience with no compulsion or exclusion for students of either sex. Vocational and technical courses in class XI and XII should be open to girls.

Pre-Primary Schools

Good pre-school education helps children to overcome their environmental disadvantages and to develop egalitarian values as they are unaware of differences of caste, class, creed, or sex at this age. We were greatly impressed by the achievement of the rural Balwadis in this respect. These pre-primary schools also help to relieve mothers of small children and increase the chances of schooling for older girls. We recommended the provision of three-year's pre-school education for all children and special efforts to increase the number of Balwadis in rural areas and in urban slums. They should be located as near as possible to the primary and middle schools of the locality.

Primary and Middle Level Education

We recommend:

1. provision of primary schools within walking distance from the home of every child within the next five years;
2. establishment of Ashram or residential schools to serve clusters of villages scattered in difficut terrains;
3. mobile schools for children of nomadic tribes, migrant labour, and construction workers;

4. sustained propaganda by officials and non-officials to bring every girl into school; and
5. provision of incentives (including mid-day meals, free uniforms, scholarships and stipends, free supply of books and special awards or recognition to the community, teachers, students) in order to prevent dropouts;
6. provision of at least two teachers in every school and raising the proportion of women primary teachers to 50 or more;
7. adoption of the multiple-entry system and a system of part-time education for girls who cannot attend school continuously on a full-time basis;
8. provision of some space in every school for the care of younger siblings who are the charges of schools-going girls; and
9. provision of sex education from the middle stage in schools. (An expert group should be appointed to prepare graded teaching material for this purpose.)

Seconday Education

We recommend:

1. free education for all girls upto the end of the secondary stage;
2. improving teaching facilities in science, mathematics, and commerce;
3. introduction of job-oriented work-experience relating it to the needs, resources, and employment potential of the region;
4. adequate arrangements for co-curricular activities; and
5. greater provision of need-cum-merit scholarships and hostel facilities for girls.

Higher Education

While progress of women in this sector has not been as unsatisfactory as at the school stage, we disagree with the view which considers higher education of girls as a waste because many of them do not use their knowledge for any social purpose. It is for the socicty to provide greater opportunities for such educated women to be of social use by utilizing their talents for social and national development. We therefore recommend:

1. development of more employment opportunities, particularly of a part-time nature; and
2. improvement in employment information and guidance services for women entering higher education.

Non-formal Education

The greatest problem in women's education in India today is the provision of some basic education to the overwhelming majority who have remained outside the reach of the formal system because of their age, social disabilities on the literacy gap. In order to integrate women in the process of national development, it is imperative to provide some education to the vast mass of illiterate and semi-literate women in the 15-25 age group. The government's efforts in the field of adult literacy and education have been rather ineffective so far; and even the non-formal training programmes such as functional literacy for women and non-student youth, show surprising biases by drawing distinction in educational content for men and women and emphasizing family life, health. nutrition, and child care for the latter. In our view, these distinctions have now become meaningless, since a proper management of family life requires joint efforts of men and women. At the same time, women's needs for vocational and occupational skills have become even greater than those of men. The greatest handicap of these programmes, however, is their *ad hoc* approach and the lack of co-ordination between different agencies that take up such programmes. There is considerable wastage of resources on duplication of administrative machinery. What is necessary, now, is to design a non-formal system of education using all available educational resources in the community (*e.g.* teachers, health service personnel, agricultural extension, workers, successful farmers, mechanics, welfare workers, and other educated persons). The system should be continuous and emphasize learning useful things in spare time, the object being to provide women with easy access to information and use of information for better participation in social life. Functional literacy would certainly have to form the core of the package.

In our view, the organization and management of this programme for women could be entrusted to the women's panchayats that we have recommended. Government's role should be limited to providing technical guidance and advice, permitting government functionaries at the local level to participate in the programme and supportive assistance in the form of literature and reading material, and development of basic libraries in villages and slum areas. We recommend concentration of government efforts on providing this infrastructure.

Equality of Sexes as a Major Value to be Inculcated Through the Educational Process

The educational system is the only institution which can counteract the deep foundations of the inequality of the sexes that are built in the minds of men and women through socialization process. It must make a deliberate, planned, and sustained effort to replace the traditional value system, based on inequality, by the new value system which accepts equality of the sexes. Unfortunately, the educational system, instead of accepting this responsibility, has helped to perpetuate traditional prejudices through its curricula, classification of subjects on the basis of act and the unwritten code of conduct enforced on the pupils. This is one area where a major change is needed in the content and organization of education.

4

Political Status of Women in India

The political status of women can be defined as the degree of equality and freedom enjoyed by women in the shaping and shaping of power and in the value given by society to this role of women. The recognition of women's political equality in the Indian Constitution was a radical departure, not only from the inherited norms of traditional Indian society, but also from the political norms of most advanced countries at that time.* The two major forces which acted as catalysts in the achievements of political equality of women were the national movement and the leadership of Mahatma Gandhi.

The nineteenth century reform movements had limited their efforts to improving the position of women within the traditional family structure. The turn of the century, however, saw a minority of women paticipating valuntarily in social welfare activities outside their homes, particularly in the cause of women's education, welfare of the weaker sections in society and relief to distressed persons. A still smaller group participated in the revolutionary movement. The early twentieth

*With the exception of socialist countries, no other state in the world had accepted women's equality as a matter of course.

century saw the birth of women's organizations and the beginnings of the demand for political rights. In 1917, a deputation of Indian women led by Shrimati Sarojini Naidu presented to the British Parliament a demand for the enfranchisement of women on the basis of equality with men. The Reforms Act of 1921 extended the franchise only to wives who had property and education. The foreign rulers could not believe that Indian society would ever regard women as equal partners of men. Nor did they regard women in a saperate partner.

In sharp contract to such attitudes was that of Mahatma Gandhi. He had declared himself to be 'uncompromising in the form matter of women's rights'. He believed that women had a positive role to play in the reconstruction of socity, and that the recognition of their equality was an essential step to bring about social justice. He had also extended his continued and unqualified support to the enfranchisement of women. This, added to the massive participation by the women in Freedom Movement, had a direct impact on the political and social elite, including women of these classes. In 1930, a meeting of represantative women's organizations demanded immediate acceptance of adult franchise without sex discrimination. Though rejected by government, the Karachi Session of the Indian National Congress in 1931 accepted the demand and committed itself to women's political equality, regardless of their status and qualifications. This promise was redeemed after independence, when the Constitution pledged the nation to the principles of equality and dignity of the individual, and proclaimed the fundamental right of women to political and legal equality and guaranteed non-discrimination in employment and office under the state.

In examining the impact of these rights in the years since independence, our basic position is the same as that of Mahatma Gandhi who looked upon them as instruments for achieving general equality of status and opportunities and social, economic and political justice. We also propose to use three main indicators to assess the political status of women, *viz.*,

1. Participation in the political process as voters and candidates in elections;
2. Political attitudes such as awareness, committment and involvement in politics and autonomy in political action and behaviour; and
3. Their impact on the political process.

Participation as Voters and Candidates in Elections

The percentage increase from 45.4 per cent in 1962 to 55.4 per cent in 1967 and 49.1 per cent in 1971, when there was a general decline in participation of all voters. The difference between percentage turnout of men and women voters declines from 15.4 per cent to 11.8 per cent during this nineyear period. The States of Orissa, Bihar, Madhya Pradesh, Rajasthan, Uttar Pradesh and Himachal Pradesh which are generally known for the educational and social backwardness of their women have had persistently low mobilization of women voters during elections. While States with a high literacy rate show a higher mobilization of women, it is not possible to establish a similar correlation between education or economic development and evercise of franchise by women. Patterns of political behaviour from different regions indicate influences of various inter-related factors such as the social status of women, their economic position, the cultural norms, and the overall regional outlook towards women's participation in the wider society.

In the case of candidates, the difference between men and women is much sharper. For the Lok Sabha, only 17 per cent of the total seats were contested by women in 1971, the highest so far. As compared to the total number of candidates, women have never exceeded 4 per cent. Interestingly enough, the maximum number of candidates are found in Uttar Pradesh, Bihar, and Madhya Pradesh, where the general mobilization of women voters has been consistently low. This indicates that there is no correlation between the level of women's participation and the selection of women candidates. Punjab, were women voters have outstripped the men in the urban areas, had an extremely poor number of candidates. Kerala and Maharashtra, with high level participation, show a slow increase in the number of candidates over the years, and West Bengal a sudden one in 1971. But the most visible trend is of stagnation or even decline in their number in most States. Karnataka, which is not a backward State, did not put up a single woman candidate in three of the general elections, and only one in the other two. Women in Manipur, Andhra Pradesh, Tamil Nadu, Karnataka, and Orissa were extremely vocal in criticizing the political parties for not sponsoring women candidates. In their view, the small number of candidates represented not the aspirations of women, but the indifference of political parties.

Apart from election data, our discussion with different groups of women lead to certain general conclusions:

1. The study increase of women voters at each election shows that the response of women to the political rights conferred on them by the Constitution is improving. Keeping other things equal, development of literacy, and mass communication may help to draw an even larger number of women into the political mainstream.
2. While there has been a substantial number of new entrants among women candidates, a large number of the older ones have also dropped out from active participation in politics. Where these come from families with long polltical traditions, such dropout indicates a degree of disillusionment with the political process.
3. Muslims and tribal women show a lower level of participation, both as voters and as candidates, although there are exceptions to this rule. Our survey of Muslim women indicates that a large number of the respondents had also voted in the previous election. We also met tribal women in Tripura, Meghalaya, and Bastar (M.P.) who, though not formally educated, took a keen interest in politics and participated regularly.

4. Women of the intermediate and scheduled castes have a higher participation rate. We met many women from these communities in villages in different States and found them determined to participate in elections.

5. Rural-urban difference in voting participation of women is narrowing down, though the belief in the lower participation of rural women still remains widespread. Our investigations indicate that urbanization does not have much influence on women's participation in politics. On the other hand, urban women, particularly those from the middle classes, plead that domestic duties prevent their participation.

6. Awareness of the power that the right of franchise gives to them is far more widespread among women than is generally believed. We found evidence of this even among Muslim, tribal and Scheduled Caste women in villages of Madhya Pradesh, U.P. and Tripura. Most of these women were also aware of the reasons for the secrecy of the ballot and observed that this permitted them to exercise their independent judgement in voting.

7. There is a general feeling that political parties have neglected their task of politically educating and mobilizing women adequately.

8. The majority of women candidates come from relatively well-to-do families, with a sprinkling of members of old princely houses. Most of them are educated through the levels of their education vary. A smaller group comes from families with fairly long traditions of political activity. Consequently they are more articulate and have continued in the struggle for power for a longer period. The larger group are new entrants, with no previous political experience; and their entry into the political arena has been through elections only.

9. Factors which deter women from active participation in politics are; the increasing expense of elections (this

constitutes the biggest handicap, as the majority of women do not command any independent means); threats of violence; and character assassination. The two latter factors have increased recently and have also prevented many women from contesting elections.

Political Attitudes

Levels of political awareness of women vary from region to region, class to class, and community to community. They are conditioned greatly by the political culture of the area, the approach of political parties to women, and the quality of the local leadership. We found that the influence of education, urbanization, and exposure to mass media is not always uniform. While literacy seems to have a direct influence on both awareness and participation, the relationship between education and awareness does not always evtend to pnrticipation. Political awareness of women also does not differ significantly between urban and rural areas.

On the whole, working women, including professionals, have greater awareness but this is not always reflected in participation. Nor is there any positive relationship between higher socioeconomic status and political awareness. Some of the studies initiated by us revealed that political awareness is less among women in the higher income groups, who have a negligible interest in politics, though many of the women legislators come from well-to-do families.

The influence of husbands on women exercising their right of franchise seems to be on the decline. In rural areas, the influence of village elders is still strong, but there are significant exceptions to this rule. In spite of such changes, the differences in the level of political information and understanding between men and women still continue, mainly due to the indifference of political parties to women. Women's organizations and pressure groups have also failed to provide political education to women.

There is some evidence of disillusionment among women with the political process, partly because of the prevalence of corruption and inefficiency in political circles, and also because women feel that politics has not solved the problems which affect their daily lives. About 42 per cent of women interviewed in a study supported revolution for social progress as opposed to the 'ritual' of election. The majority felt that the greatest problems before the country were unemployment and poverty. rising prices, corruption, and breakdown of law and order.

Our investigation in different States indicates one common trend, that women are more concerned with problems that affect their day-to-day lives. They have shown themselves ready to protest against rising prices, adulteration of food. unemployment, and poverty. The unity between political, economic, and social issues that characterized the freedom movement was one of the causes for the high degree of women's participation. The absence of a similar movement in the period after independence and the divorce between social problems that affect women directly and the political process has been one of the major Causcs for lower participation of women in politics in recent years.

Impact of Women on the Political Process

Women's participation in politics has not been reflected in their record of success at elections. The number and pereentage of successful women candidates for the Lok Sabha has been declining steadily from 33 (50.6 per cent) in 1962 to 21 (25.9 per cent) in 1971. The sharp decline in 1971 is due to the increase in the number of independent women candidates most of whom were defeated. The increase in independent candidates was mainly due to the failure of the parties to sponsor an adequate number of women. It has generally been found that the success of women eandidates depends upon party backing, the compaign strategy adopted and the personality including the family background of candidates. Since 1952, 212 women have served in the Indian Parliament.

Women leaders in the period immediately after independence were mostly veterans from the freedom struggle. They had also worked in the movement for women's welfare and development, were spokesmen of the women's cause in the representative bodies, and played an important role in mobilizing public opinion in support of the social legislation that changed the legal status of women within the first few years after independence. Some of them also helped to shape the policies and the programmes for women's development that were taken up by Government at that time. Most of these leaders, who had attained a national stature during the freedom struggle, became members of the Central Government or Parliament. In States, a new generation entered politics. Our investigations suggest that while experience of social work among women is still considered a qualification for candidates to local bodies, it has ceased to be so for entry to the legislature. We were informed by political workers that politics at the State level seldom reflects social differences at present. The women involved in State politics mostly come from the economic and political elite of States and enter the representative process, more because of support within a party, rather than through work among the people.

Women from the minority among the party workers. When elected to the legislature, they see their role as representatives of the people with no special responsibility to women. In earlier years, their championship of women's causes was concerted, cutting across party lines. In recent years, however, women legislators have not shown such concern or interest in problems that affect women specifically. This criticism was voiced by many women outside the circle of active politicians. Debates and discussions in the legislative bodies have given very meagre attention to women's problems.)

We are of the view that the political elite of the country, of both serve, has prepare some to other that this problem of tae women had practically been saved with the easy and administrative measure adopted in the first few years after indapendence. The very articulate debates of earlier years on women's problems, in which women members played a major role, have not been repeated since. The absence of an active women's movement and the failure of political organizations to mobilize women for the solution of their problems have prevented women from exerting adequte pressure on political institutions. The small number of women in the legislatures and their lack of position in the decision-making bodies within the parties have limited their capacity to voice women's problems in these institutions.

Political Parties and Women

The election manifestoes of the political parties agree that women constitute a backward section of the society to whom special privileges have to be granted to bring them at par with men.

1. The *Indian National Congress* whose recent manifestoes have emphasized development of education and employment opportunities for women has been sponsoring the largest number of women cadidates at all elections, but has still failed to reach its repeatedly stipulated target of 15 per cent. In spite of a woman being the undisputed leader of this party, women's position in the party hierachy is not particularly impressive. Though the Working Committee contains three women out of a total of twenty-one and two out of four General Secretaries are women, it is evident that, without pressure from the Working Committee, party committees in many States would exclude women. Women workers in the party complain of denial of opportunities to develop or demonstrate their organizing ability and of neglect of women's demands by the leadership.

2. The *Communist Party of India* believes that women can be fully liberated only in a socialist system. The must play a role in bringing about the social revolution. It has, therefore, been demanding equal pay for equal work and removal of all restrictions and discriminations against women in employment, inheritance of property, education and socal laws. The party

claims that 5 per cent of its members are women. The National. Council of the Party with a membership of 110 has four women members. Their representation on State bodies of the party is, however, uneven. The party's representatives en emphasized the removal of economic dependence and poverty to enable women to enjoy their legal rights, and argued that, without fuller participation in the process of social production, reservation of jobs in selected industries, free legal aid and greater educational opportunities, it will be difficult for women to achieve the equality to which they are entitled by law.

(3) The *Communist Party of India* (*M*) holds similar views regarding women and is critical of the poor progress in the field of women's welfare since independence. The nation cannot progress if its women remain in their present condition as victims of women's welfare since independence. The nation cannot progress if its women remain in their present condition as victims of obscurantist customs and prejudices and with limited opportunities for development. Women constitute about 1 per cent of the party's membership with one woman out of a total of thirty-one members in the Central Committee. Their representation on State Committees varies according to regions. The representatives of the party emphasized the need for economic independence without which women were as good as private property of men. The growing problem of rural unemployment with increasing landlessness and decay of village industries threatened the security and status of women in these areas. and made them unable to enjoy their constitutional and legal rights, even more than urban women. The party suggests mass employment and mass education (including the education of women about their emancipation), inclusion of the principle of equal pay for equal work in the Fundamental Rights, and equal shares of land and job facilities for peasant women, as necessary steps to achieve genuine equality for women.

4. The *Bharatiya Jana Sangh* supports advancement of women and special steps to remove their social and educational disabilities, without any change in the traditionally established principles of social organization. The Central Executive of the

party has five women and the All India Council eighty-three. The constitution of the various committees of the party provides for inclusion of one or more women though it has been found difficult to meet this target at the level of local committees. The party's representatives emphasized the need to increase plitieal participation and consciousness of women since the conservation of a women presents an obstacle to their development. They criticized the use of female figures in advertising and the image of women projected by other mass media as derogatory to women's status.

5. The *Indian National Congress* (*O*) promises to implement the constitutional guarantees and Directive Principles of State Policy regarding women. Out of a total membership of twenty-eight in the Working Committee, two are women (one of them is the General Secretaıy). The 20 per cent quota reserved by the party for women candidates has not been filled due to decline in political interest among women and in members seeking nomination. In the opinion of the party's representative, economic backwardness and competition in obtaining nominations at different levels deter women candidates.

6. The *Socialist Party* believes that women still suffer from social inequalities. The party's representative emphasized the ignorance and indifference of women regarding their legal and constitutional rights. A determined effort has to be made by social workers to remove this difficulty. Government and other institutions should educate men and women against outmoded traditions and superstitions. The women's front of the party has adopted a charter of Women's Rights, demanding free education, vocational and technical training, part-time employment, uniform Civil Code, social mobilization against dowry and greater scope for women in elections and party organizations.

Positions in Government

Though only a few women reached the highest level of power and authority, those who did so have been recognized for their administrative skills and capacity to manage their own affairs.

Since 1952, thirteen women have served the Union Government as Ministers and several have served as Chairmen of both Houses of Parliament. Many have been members of Standing and *ad hoc* Committees. In States, two women have been Governors, two Chief Ministers, one Speaker, and one Deputy Speaker. Though few have held Cabinet rank, women have held office in most of the States. Compared to their overall number in the legislature, the number of women holding offices was not low.

Effectiveness of Campaigns to Activite Women

Though women constitute nearly 50 per cent of the electorate, the experience of all the general elections proves that they are not aware of their strength nor has thir source been adequately tapped by any political party. There has not been any bargaining on the part of organized women with political parties for their support, except in Jammu. The parties generally tend to seek the support of the male active heads of families expecting that their wishes would prevail with the women, particularly in rural areas. In larger cities, some attempt has been made to activize women voters, making specific promises to them and using a house-to-house approach.

Among the non-political organizations, the most important are the Ail India Women's Conference, the National Council of Women in India, the Bharatiya Grameen Mahila Sangh, and the National Federation of Indian women. The first two are mainly deliberative bodies and have concentrated more on welfare and relief activities. The Bharatiya Grameen Mahila Sangh works among rural women and has been active in rural development. The National Federation aims to raise the political and social awareness of women and has been mobilizing women's protest against such issues as rising prices, hoarding, and adulteration. All these organizations admit that they have not been fully successful in carrying the message of their new rights to all women in the country.

While women leaders in the trade union movement have played a major role in bringing about changes in labour laws to provide protection to women, most trade unions admit that they have not made many efforts to mobilize women to assert their legal and constitutional rights. Whenever these organizations have worked together to defend the rights of women, however, their influence as pressure groups has been fairly effective. They played an important role in the enactment of social laws after independence.

We find that, in spite of increase in participation, women's ability to produce an impact on the political process has been negligible. Parties have tended to see women as appendages of the males. Among women, the leadership has become diffused and diverse, with sharp contradictions in their regard and concern for the inequalities that affect the status of women in every sphere—social, economic, and political, The revolution in status of women for which constitutional equality was to be only the instrument, still remains a very distant objective. While the position of some groups has changed for the better, the large masses of women continue to lack spokesmen in the representative bodies of the State. Though women do not constitute a minority numerically, they are acquiring the features of one by the inequality of class, status, and political power. The chasm between the values of the new social order proclaimed by the Constitution and the realities of contemporary Indian society as far as women's rights are concerned remains as great as at the time of Independence.

This right to political equality has not enabled women to play their role as partners and constituents in the polltical process, because Gandhiji's message to treat political rights, not as an end, but only as a means. has been forgotten. Instead, these rights have helped to build an illusion of equality and power which is frequently used as an argument to resist special protective and ameliorative measures to enable women to achieve a just and equal position in society. In spite of special powers provided by Article 15(3) of the Constitution, almost no efforts have been made to redress the unequal status of women in different spheres. The fact that the country has been ruled by a woman for the past nine years is not an indicator of the real status of women in this country. Though men recognize and advocate the desirability of giving equal opportunities to women in economic and political spheres, the norms and attitudes regarding a woman's role in society remain traditional. In this sense, the new rights provided to them seem to be only concessional.

Women in Local Bodies

In order to provide greater opportunities to women to actively participate in the decision-making process, it is imperative to recognize the true nature of the social inequalities and disabilities that hamper them. This can best be achieved by providing them with special opportunities for participation in the representative structure of local government. The present form of associating women in these bodies, through co-option or nomination, has become a kind of tokenism. The time has come to move out of this token provision to a more meaningful association of women in local administration, and to counteract the general apathy and indifferenee of the local bodies to women's development and change of status. We therefor recommend the establishment of statutory women's Panchayats at the village level with autonomy and resources of their own for the management and administration of welfare and development programmes for women and children, as a transitional measure, to break through the attitudes that inhibit most women from articulating their problems and participating actively in the existing local bodies. They should be directly elected by the women of the village and have the right to send representatives to the Panchayat Samitis and/or Zila Parishads. A viable relationship with the Gram Panchayats should be maintained by making the Chairman and Secretary of both bodies *ex-officio* members of the other.

At the level of municipalities, the principle of reservation of seats for women is already prevalent in certain States. This should be adopted by all States as a transitional measure* In addition, permanent committees should be constituted in

*This was a majority decision, two members dissenting

municipalities to initiate and supervise programmes for womens' welfare and development.

Reservation of Seats in Legislatures

Political parties should adopt a definite policy regarding the percentage of women candidates to be sponsored by them for elections to Parliament and State Assemblies. While they may initially start with 15 per cent, this should be gradually increased so that, over time, the representation of women in legislative bodies has some relationship to their position in the total population of the country or the State. We also received a demand for reservation of seats for women in State Assemblies and Parliament, but rejected the suggestion after examination, with two members dissenting.

Association in Important Bodies

Women should be included in all important committees, commissions, or delegations that are appointed to examine socio-economic problems.

5

Policies and Programmes for Women's Development

Development in its wider perspective covers all aspects of community life. The accepted goals of national development such as maximum production, full employment, and attainment of economic equality and social justice apply equally to men and women. Their realization in an inegalitarian society is not, however, possible, unless special efforts are made to assist the underprivileged groups. Our Constitution therefooe stresses the urgent need for promoting the educational and economic interests of the weaker sections of the people; and as women are handicapped by social customs and traditions, they need special attention to help them to play their full and proper role in national life.

Plans and Women's Development

The Planning Commission has defined three major areas for women's development: education, health, and welfare. Among the programmes specially designed in these areas, the priorities have been the same till the end of the Fourth Plan. There has been a continued emphasis on women's education in all the plans . The other programmes for women mainly concentrated on maternal and child welfare services, health, nutrition, and family planning. As regards social welfare, the voluntarys ector operated the bulk of the programmes, the efforts of the Government being confined to provide institutional services. The Second Plan emphasized the need for special attention to the problems of women workers who suffered from certain handicaps, *e.g.*, unequal pay, lack of adequate training facilities to enable them to compete for higher jobs, and lack of opportunities for part-time employment; and the Draft Fifth Plan gives priority to the training of needy women from low-issues families, a programmes of 4 functional literacy for the age-group 15—45 (which includes child care, nutrition, health care, and home economics), placement and follow-up of successful candidates under the present scheme of condensed courses of education, and socio-economic programmes. In addition to production-cum-training units, managerial and sales training will also be introduced to promote marketing of goods. Under health programmes the primary objective is to provide minimum public health facilities and integrated family planning and maternal and child care programmes.

In spite of this policy of emphasis on welfare or development of human resources, the proportional allocation for these programmes has been steadily declining in successive plans and the total allocation for education, health, and welfare has come down from 24.1 per cent in the First Plan to only 11.17 per cent in the Fifth Plan.

Programmes for women's welfare and development may be broadly classified as follows:

1. Programmes under statutory obligations such as the Suppression of Immoral Traffic Act, 1956, or the Maternity Benefit Act, 1961.
2. Development programmes which provide essential services and opportunities such as education, health, maternity and child welfare, family planning, nutrition, and training.
3. Programmes for special groups of women such as assis-

tance to widows, aged and destitute women, hostels for working women in urban areas, scholarships for girls of Scheduled Castes and Tribes, and free residential schooling in Ashram Schools.

Since the administrative system under the colonial regime was not geared for these tasks, and most welfare services were in the hands, of voluntary agencies, a central official agency was created in 1953 to promote welfare and development services for women, children, and other under-privileged groups. The Central Social Welfare Board (CSWB) provides assistance to voluntary agencies, improves and develops welfare programmes and sponsors them in areas where they do not exist.

There is three-tier structure for planning and administering women's welfare and development programmes with agencies at the Central, State, and local level. However, the major responsibility for implementing these programmes lies on various departments and other agencies of Government. At the Centre, the main agencies for planning and implementation are the Planning Commission, Ministry of Education and Social Welfare with with its two specialized agencies—Central Social Welfare Board and National Council of Women's Education, Ministry of Health and Family Planning, Ministry of Home Affairs, and Ministry of Labour and Employment. At the State level, there is no uniform pattern and the programmes for women are administered by a large number of departments.

We tried to collect information from all the Central and Ltate Departments regarding their special programmes for women. The replies were not comprehensive; but from the information supplied by 12 Ministries of Central Government, 19 States and one Union Territory, two points seem to emerge:

1. Despite their cemmon objectives, these programmes are implemented by a large number of departments without any effective machinery to co-ordinate their functions; and

2. Government departments do not always seem to be clear in their understanding of what constitutes welfare or development.

A few adopt a rather limited approach to welfare and equate it with giving assistance to distressed women.

With the exception of the Second Five Year Plan, no Plan has shown concern for generating and improving employment opportunities for women. However, it is interesting to note that all the agencies engaged in implementing women's programmes attach the highest priority to increasing women's earning power. Even the Fifth Plan which accepts the 'utilization of idle manpower as a tremendous force to spced up the process of development,' visualizes no change in the present low representation of women in the labour foree.*

Health and Family Planning

The health status of women, which includes their physical mental, and social condition, is affected, in addition to their biological and physiological problems, by the prevailing norms and attitudes influence the provision and utilization of preventive and curative health care facilities, including maternal care services. Several studies have shown a definite correlation between the low status of women and deficiencies in the knowledge and utilization of prevention health services.

The cultural norms the particularly affect women's health are attitudes to marriage. age of marriage, fertility rate and sex of the child, the pattern of family organization, the place of the woman in the family, and the expected role of the woman as defined by social convention. All these factors have important demographic implications. Cultural insistence on early marriage, high fertility, idealization of the roles of mother and house-wife affect her physical and mental health. According to

*Its labour force projections up to 1986 indicate a constant sex ratio with women constituting only 16 per cent of the total. This is even lower than the 17.35 per cent recorded by the census of 1971.

our Survey, 48.53 per cent respondents stated that women serve the family first and eat last. In poor families, this results in still greater malnutrition of women. This process of subservience starting at a young age, taboos and restrictions which start with menstruation, and reluctance to consult a doctor, particularly a male doctor, result in a general neglect of women's health.

Various studies, particularly from developing countries, indicate that the main health problems of women are: higher maternal and infant mortality, maternal morbidity; lower expectation of life at birth; malnutrition; mental disorders; high suicide rate; and certain sex-selective diseases. As child-bearing and rearing is still the dominant role assigned to women, maternity becomes a special problem in the population with inadequate housing, sanitation, and poor medical facilities.

The indications of women's health in India are drawn from two sources: demographic trends and access to health service.

1. *Demographic trends*: The census studies drew attention to the declining sex ratio and higher female mortality (specially in the age-groups 15—44), Neglect, rather than under enumeration, is the explanation of the adverse sex ratio. The census of 1931 drew pointed attention to the higher female mortality in the age-group 5—10 and 'at the reproductive age'. According to Vital Statistics of India, the incidence of female mortality in the age-group 15—29 is high, both in rural areas and in the whole country. Female mortality in the age-group 1—4 has increased during 1960-68. Some scholars observe that vital statistics regarding infant deaths and births are under-estimates, particularly in the case of females, the difference between estimated and reported deaths being as high as 75.69 per cent for rural and 59.07 per cent for urban areas. The recent SRS data for 1968-69 also indicate that female mortality continues to be higher in the age-groups 0—4 and 15—34. It is also observed that the reason for the low sex ratio is the high maternal mortality which is reported to be 252 per 1,00,000 live births in 1964 for the whole country and as high as 573 for 1,00,000 live births in rural areas in 1968.

Recent medical research, while trying to identify the contributory factors for higher female mortality, has concentrated more on meternal mortality and has identified different factors such as pregnancy wastage (abortions and still births) which have remained constant over the period 1957-68 and mostly prevail in low-income groups. One study reported that pregnancy wastage of malnourished mothers was as high as 30 per cent in 1972.* Still births constituted 11 per 1,000 live births. Perinatal mortality was the result of maternal malnutrition, iron deficieney; and anaemia. Another cause of infant and maternal mortality was related to higher birth orders and frequent pregnancy, causing protein malnutrition. 10—20 per cent deaths are known to be due to nutritional anaemias and 16.44 per cent to pregnancy complications and morbidity. Besides, a WHO report indicates that psychiatric morbidity is more prevalent among women than mens.**

2. *Access to health services*: The broad objectives of the health programmes have been ;to provides both curative and preventive health services in rural areas through the Primary Health Centres, and to train medical and para-medical personnel. The Fifth Plan, while realizing the shortfalls and inadequacy of staff, medical supplies and equipment, and trained personnel, envisages an integrated programme of family planning and maternity and Child Health Services. The lowest unit of the Health Services structure is the P.H.C. The Bhore Committee (1946) had recommended that each centre should cater to a population of 40,000, with a 30-bed hospital, two medical officers, four mid-wives, and four trained 'dais' as the 'irreducible minimum'. The Mudaliar Committee (1964), while reiterating these recommendations, suggested the additional provision of three specialists in medicine, surgery, obstetrics, and gynaecology and 75 maternity and 50 paediatric beds for each district hospital. When PHCs were established they had to serve a population of 60,000—70,002. Their number has increased from 67 in the First Plan to 5,195 in 1972;and the sub-centre have increased from 17,522 in 1967 to 32,218 in 1972. From

*Gopalan, C. and Naidu, A.N., "Nutrition, and Fertility", *The Leucet*, No. 18, 1972.

**WHO, *Vital Statistics of South East Asia Region, 1966*.

1963, family planning services were initiated with one medical officer, one extension doctor, one ANM and two family workers to supervise four sub-centres. Each sub-centre was expected to cater to a population of approximately ten thousand.

An expert committee appointed by the Ministry of 'Health and Family Planning in 1973 to examine the full utilization of the existing beds in PHCs observed that, apart from West Bengal and Kerala where utilization was 50 per cent, in States such as Bihar. Rajasthan, U.P., Orissa, M.P., and Jammu and Kashmir it was hardly between 5 and 15 per cent. The reasons were the apathy of the staff, the status barriers between the doctor and the people of a low socio-economic group and the absence of a lady doctor in many centres. Emphasizing the need to improve maternity and child welfare services, this Committee recommended the provision of domiciliary maternity services.

The present pattern of health services puts more emphasis on curative services on which the expenditure is three times more than on preventive services, and most of it is urban-centred. Only 10 per cent of the hospital beds are meant for four-fifths of the population living in rural areas.

Maternity services show wide regional variations. The report of the Study Group on Hospitals (1968) estimated that maternity beds (45,000) constituted less than 17 per cent of total hospital facilities.

The health statistics for the States reveal that Kerala, which stands out for provision of maternity services also, has the highest expectancy of life for women which is 60.7 as compared to Uttar Pradesh where it is 53.7, nearly the lowest in India. Kerala also has the lowest infant mortality rate. Other States such as Tamil Nadu, Andhra Pradesh, Punjab, Assam, Karnataka, and West Bengal which have paid some attention to these services have helped to improve the expectations of life for women.

The impact of these services have not been uniform because factors such as education employment, and cultural norms are important variables influencing the utilization of these services. Apart from regional variations in both attitudes and norms, the accessibility of health services is also affected by rural-urban and socio-economic differentials, including a broad pattern of sex differentials. Sex differentials are deep-rooted in attitudes regarding the needs of women for care and assistance during ailments. The studies in nutritional deficiencies of women indicate that though the incidence of diseases caused by malnutrition is higher not only among adult women but also among female infants, the hospital records reveal that more male children are treated for such diseases.

Two-thirds of the total number of doctors and nurses and most hospitals are concentrated in urban areas (which have only one-fifth of the total population) and the rural population get a much smaller share. The National Sample Survey (19th Round) found that 46 per cent of all births in urban India are attended by trained medical personnel as compared to 9 per cent in rural areas and that the average per capita private monthly expenditure on medicine and medical services is Rs. 1.01 in urban areas and about half of that in rural areas. A recent study on rural health services pointed to the inadequacy of medical personnel, especially ANMs in the villages. Consequent upon the small number of ANMs the area covered by one ANM is too large, with consequent difficulties of transport and accommodation, and night halts and problems of security which effect their functioning. Second, for an outsider like the average ANM, a degree of acceptance and security by influential members of the village community is essential. But as they very often monopolize her services, the gap between the ANM and the masses of women who need her services is widened.

Family Planning: Relationship with Women's Status

In our opinion, the neglect of maternity and child health services and over-concentration of efforts on family planning have contributed to the trends discussed above and have defeated the ultimate objective of the family planning programme itself.

Propagators of the family planning movement in India have been keen to emphasize improvement in the status of women as one of the direct consequences of family planning. Recent researches in this field, however, seem to agree more on the obverse of the relationship, *viz.*, improved status of women, with a rise in the age of marriage, better education, employment, better living conditions, and greater general awareness, has a direct impact on the acceptance of family planning methods. There is no doubt that knowledge of family planning releases women from the bondage of repeated and frequent child birth, gives them a greater control over their life and future, and prevents excessive drain on their physical resources. A third consequence which is sometimes emphasized is the possible change in husband-wife relationship and improved position in decision-making within the family. Each of these developments is integrally connected with a complex set of variables—social, economic, demographic, and political, among which the woman's ability to control the size of her family could be a contributory factor for improving her status.

An enormous volume of research has developed out of the need to evaluate the progress of family planning in India. The results of a national survey* indicatr that the percentage of couples using family planning methods increases with the age of wife, number of living children, education of wife, family income, size of city or village. Some studies reported a reluctance for family planning among Muslims, but others, and our own evidence, do not indicate any disapproval on religious grounds as such. Most studies found a direct relationship between education and employment status of women and their readiness to accept family planning. Other associational factors include:

(i) rise in the age of marriage;

(ii) standard of living and socio-economic status of the couple;

*Conducted by the Operations Research Group, Ministry of Health and Family Planning during 1970-71.

(iii) mobility; and

(iv) exposure to mass-media and knowledge of diverse methods of contraception.

The IUCD* which was introduced in 1965 was initially successful, but showed a reverse trend. During our tours we were informed that careless handling of IUCD insertions by the para-medical staff and Inadequate follow-up treatment had caused this loss of popularity.

Tubectomies accounted for two-thirds of all sterilizations during 1956—58, and up to 1959, they exceeded the number of vasectomies. After 1960, the number of vasectomies increased more rapidly and in 1965 and 1972 and, accounted for more than 80 per cent of all sterilizations. Since this is a terminal method, women are reluctant to adopt tubectomy because of the uncertainty regarding the survival of their children. We were told by women doctors of two specific arguments against tubectomy:

1. cases of 'post-ligation syndrome' where women developed psychological disturbances; and
2. cases where the operation is dangerous because of extremely anaemic conditions of a large number of women.

Another measure adopted by Government, *viz.*, the Medical Termination of Pregancy Act, 1971, aims to reduce the incidence of criminal abortions. The Act allows termination of pregnancy on therapeutic grounds, eugenic grounds, humanitarian grounds, and social grounds. Hospital records indicate that 15 per cent to 20 per cent of maternal deaths arise from abortions. The vital statistics, 1966-67, indicate that abortions form a high percentage of causes of all deaths due to child birth. Two studies of the National Institute of Nutrition, Hyderabad, show that pregnancy wastage from miscarriage and abortions ranges from 16—19 per cent to 28—32 per among low-income groups.

*Intra-uterine co ntraceptive device.

While the Medical Termination of Pregnancy Act emphasizes its importance as a health measure, the permission given under section 3(2)(b) for termination of pregnancies for married women in cases of contraceptive failure. emphasizes its importance as an instrument of population control. The available evidence shows that it is used more for birth control than as a health measure

All the studies indicate that most of these women who go in for induced abortions are in favour of small families, if not planned parenthood, and can be persuaded through counselling, to adopt safer methods of birth control. Medical practitions are convinced of the serious psychological hazards of both unwanted pregnancies and sterilization. Systematic research in this field is imperative, Several medical practitioners are reluctant to perform this operation because of ethical considerations, long recording procedures and paper work, and lack of proper medical facilities especially in rural areas. We were informed that some hospitals insist on sterilization or the husband's consent before performing abortion. We feel that while the doctors should have the authority to discourage an abortion when it posses a definite risk to the health, the imposition of such conditions will only drive women to unqualified persons and defeat the main purpose of Act.

Changes in Government Policy

During the First and the Second Five Year plans, Government regarded the problem of population control as a long-term objective which depended as much on 'improvement in living standards and more widespread education, especially among women' as on making the people adopt methods for family planning. In the Third Plan, the programme received greater emphasis and priority, with time-bound targets for reduction of the birth rate, a large administrative network, and adoption of such methods as mass camps or monetary incentives for sterilization. Legalization of abortion was another step in that direction. Some State Governments even restricted the right to maternity benefits of women government servants to three children only.

This change in emphasis indicates excessive reliance on the clinical rather than on the welfare approach to family planning. While the Plan allocation for all other health programmes went up from Rs. 98 crores in the First Plan to Rs. 226 crores in the Fourth Plan, that on family planning went up from Rs. 6.50 crores in the First Plan to Rs. 315 crores in the Fourth Plan. Thus other health services did not develop adequately because of the excessive emphasis on population control. It has been now realized that a purely clinical and target-oriented approach cannot overcome the socio-psychological resistance caused by poverty, ignorance, and low survival rate of children among the poorer sections. The Fifth Plan visualizes integration of family planning into the general health services such as maternity, child care, and nutrition programmes. The proposed integrated health services will provide a far greater incentive to the adoption of family planning measures than the earlier reliance on 'motivation' and 'incentives' which have come in for severe criticism. In our opinion the inadequacy of qualified medical personnel, specially in rural area, and absence of mature counselling are the greatest drawbacks to the success of family planning.

Welfare Programmes

The programmes to promote women's welfare and development have been evolved separately for rural and urban areas. Apart from certain general programmes there are others meant for specific groups of women.

(1) *Programmes in Rural Areas* aim to train and mobilize women in villages for their development and are modelled on Gandhian ideas for women's progress to which the Kasturba Memorial Trust gave a concrete shape. Education. health services, and socio-economic programmes (in the form of khadi and village industries) to relieve economic distress formed the three prongs of this composite programme. In 1954, when the Central Social Welfare Board decided to launch the Welfare Extension Projects (WEP), this three-fold approach was adopted as the basic framework and their activities included Balwadis,

maternity services and general medical aid, social education, and craft training for women. Since the objectives and methodology of this programme was similar to the community development programmes, initiated in 1952, similar projects were started in CD Blocks on a co-ordinated basis and the budget was shared by the CSWB, the State Government, and the CD Block in the ratio of 12:6:5 for the first five years and in the ratio of 24:12:5 thereafter.

In 1966, 1,629 centres of WEP were handed over to Mahila Mandals run by voluntary agencies. On the recommendation of the CSWB and an Evaluation Committee of the WEP, it was decided to develop a countrywide programme of integrated welfare services for children and thus the scheme of Family and Child Welfare Projects (F & CWP) was initiated in 1967 and funded by the Central and the State Governments in a 75:25 ratio and aided by UNICEF. This services provided by F & CWP are: integrated services to the pre-school child, training to young mothers including home management, health education, nutrition education and child care, assistance to women through Mahila Mandals and existing welfare agencies, and cultural education and recreational activities.

In the First Plan, Maternity and Child Welfare Services were taken up by the Ministry of Health as part of the overall development programme in health. At the same time, the Community Projects Administration also undertook these services in the CD and NES Blocks. Other Ministries such as Railways, Defence, and Labour also promoted maternity and child welfare programmes. Since it was realized from the beginning that the objectives of these programmes could not be achieved without the active participation of the members and leaders of the local community, it was decided to constitute committees of local women to guide or run these programmes. Mahila Mandals were organized in villages and blocks for promoting women's programmes. Various villages functionaries needed for these development schemes were trained by Government agencies and non-government organizations such as the

Kasturba Memorial Trust, Visva Bharati, and Jamia Milia with assistance from the CSWB.

(2) *Programme in Urban Areas*: Apart from some WEPS, most programmes in urban areas have been left to voluntary organizations receiving grants from the CSWD. The best known is the scheme for Working Women's Hostels.

(3) *Other Programmes*: These include condensed courses of education for adult women and socio-economic programmes (*e.g.*, training-cum-production centres in simple crafts), which were initially started for the rehabilitation of refugee women and were later on taken up by the CSWB to provide an extra source of income to needy women. The CSWB also provides financial assistance to voluntary welfare institutions and cooperative societies for small production units. A number of Ministries such as Railways, Labour, Agriculture, and Community Development have schemes for providing craft training for women.

While most welfare programmes attempt to improve earning power, they do not have the desired impact. Difficulties in getting raw material, credit marketing finished products make many of them commercially non-viable. The training imparted is only in production skills, not in organization and marketing. Handicapped by their lack of command over modern markets, sales promotion methods, and regular organized production, these programmes often fail to achieve their objective. Strangely enough, the government agencies responsible for promoting industrial development completely ignored them.

The nutrition programmes which were emphasized in the plans as a major need of lower income groups, are being operated by the Department of Social Welfare and CSWB, the Ministry of Health and Family Planning, the Department of Community Development of the Ministry of Agriculture and the Ministry of Education. The Fourth Plan Special Nutrition Programme for pre-school children and expectant and nursing mothers has been redesignated as the Integrated Child Development Programme (ICDP) in the Fifth Plan and is proposed to be implemented by co-ordination between the ministry of Health, State Health departments, Community Development Department, and the Department of Social Welfare. The entire expenditure for the ICDP during the Fifth Plan will be met by the Centre.

Social Defence Programmes for the correction and rehabilitation of women, (*i.e.*, suppression of immoral traffic, after-care services, and welfare services in prisons), are provided by the Department of Social Welfare and the Rehabilitation Directorate at the Central level. State Governments are assisted to set up protective homes. At present, there are 33 protective homes and 68 reception centres and district shelters in the country. The inmates of these homes are given training in sewing and embroidery to help them become self-employed when they are discharged. There are no formal arrangements for marketing these products nor are the inmates given any training to organize production and marketing. Various reports by social workers indicate that these women find it difficult to earn a living from effort is wasted as many of them are compelled to return to their old prefessions. The homes which are provided for the aged and destitute women are highly inadequate in terms of the population to be covered.

Role of Voluntary Organizations

The grants given to registered voluntary institutions during the four Plans indicate that Government's dependence on these bodies has registered a decline during the Third and Fourth Plans. Voluntary welfare programmes co-exist with governmental programmes and provide a supportive base to them since it is not possible for Government to look after all the welfare needs of the people. Voluntary organizations, whose basic assets are flexibility, and greater capacity for experimentation, nearness to the people, and sensitivity to new problems could be of great assistance. We met representatives of women's voluntary organizations in every State. Most of these are confined to the urban areas and their membership is drawn mainly from the educated middle class women. Few organizations have worked among rural women. In some cases, the grant was given for administration and maintenance while, in other cases, for programmes only. Apart from the CSWB's grants-in-aid programme, there is no machinery to co-ordinate the efforts of these agencies and ensure even distribution. The resources of majority of these organizations are inadequate to maintain trained staff. The relative importance of the role of the state and the role of voluntary agencies has bcen engaging attention of the planners, policy-makers, administrators and social workers, but this is hardly an either-or issue. What is needed is a well-coordinated effort on both fronts.

Governmental Administration of Welfare Programmes

Welfare, which is a non-productive item, gets a low priority in financial allocations in comparison to other sectors. A major part of the allocations made for these programmes is spent on maintenance and establishment charges, leaving little for actual services. The administration and handling of welfare programmes has becomes increasingly technical.

The administrative tradition in India, which emphasized maintenance of law and order and economic development, has been slow in accepting the need for technical competence and difference in orientation necessary for social welfare administration. Limited resources and lack of emphasis on technical competence have had an adverse impact on the quality of the programmes.

There are other factors which impede the adoption of a rational organization and flexible approach in operation:

1. In the federal structure of our polity, the responsibility for implementing social policies and programmes rests with States and local authorities while the resources and the planning agencies are at the Centre.
2. The State Governments give still lower priortiy* to

*All programmes for women in the Same of Uttar Pradesh once described as a model for co-ordination, efficiency and achievement were closed down by Shri Charan Singh as Chief Minister, presumably on growth of economy.

social welfare programmes. The policy for women's welfare and development is limited to education or welfare of special groups such as handicapped or destitute women. The interests of the weaker sections who are less vocal and powerful than the dominant sections, generally suffer in State and local administrations.

3. Most State Governments do not have any machinery for collection of data or planning welfare services. The State Boards which might have undertaken this role, serve mainly as link organizations to supervise, implement, and report on the working of voluntary agencies getting aid and as agents of the CSWB.

4. The relationship between the CSWB and the State Boards is not clearly defined and the status of the State Boards differs from State to State.

5. Local administrations show even more apathy to women's welfare programmes. We were informed that the rural elite are not favourably disposed towards changing the position of women and that the co-opted women members of Panchayats have not been very effective. Women's programmes have generally been starved of funds.

All these have led to an increasing burden on the Centre. The Centre provides assistance for the development programmes during the Plan period and at the end, the full responsibility for their maintenance devolves on the States which are not always willing to assume it. In some cases, the programmes have been redesignated so as to get continued Central assistance.

This centralization has overshadowed the concept of local need-based approach to social welfare. The programmes and policies initiated at the Centre also widen the gap between the levels of policy-making and the levels of implementation and defeat the very objective of social welfare. It has further prevented the State Governments from assuming their due responsibility in the field of welfare. The authority and initiative of the field staff is greatly impaired since they are not consulted in framing programmes. The State Boards have little authority to either initiate or review the programmes of the CSWB. Bureaucratization also hampers the progress of the programmes through delays in sanction and release of grants, standardization of programmes without reference to local needs, and multiplicity of programmes, agencies and functionaries leading to a waste of resources. There is very little co-ordination at the State level also. The CSWB's efforts to co-ordination its activities with the local bodies have evoked little response.

The Central Social Welfare Boards

As the most important central agency for the implementation of welfare activities, the CSWB enjoyed, in its initial years, some autonomy, although it had no legal, independent existence.* In fact the only justification for its creation lay in the nature of welfare work which cannot be easily administered within the procedural framework of a Government department. But this autonomy has been considerably eroded since then. When the CSWB was created as a specialized agency, there was no Central department of Social Welfare. With the establishment of the Department of Social Welfare in 1966 and its increasing role in planning and execution of welfare programmes the position of the Board has become anomalous, with an adverse effect on its functioning. At the Conference of State Ministers of Social Welfare in 1972 and 1974, recommendations were made for the reorganization of the Central Social Welfare Board, giving representation on it to all the State Governments and Union Territory Administrations. No action has, so far, been taken to give effect to these recommendations.

For a satisfactory implementation of welfare programmes, it is essential that the relationship of the voluntary and the government sector should be complementary. The voluntary sector should provide services and the financial contribution

* I was crented in 1953 by a Resolution of the Ministry of Education to promote welfare and development services for women, children, and other underprivileged groups.

should come from Government. At present, however, voluntary organizations are totally excluded from the decision-making process and are reduced to a status of grant-receiving agencies. They also lack technical and organizational competence and trained staff and are unable to utilize the available resources in a fruitful manner. The Conference of State Ministers and Secretaries of Social Welfare held in 1974 agreed that procedures and rules for making grants should be liberalized and that due provision should be made for training voluntary workers. The need for greater co-ordination between governmental and non-governmental sectors at all levels, and particularly at district level, has also been emphasized.

The staff of the CSWB and State Boards is also not on par with government employees. The field staff is temporary, depending on allocatious and the continuity of the Project.

Progress in the development of welfare programmes for women and children has been hampered by several factors such as the *ad hoc* nature of the programmes, procedural difficulties faced by field agencies because of the variations in status and functions of these agencies, delay in release of grants, inadequacy of trained staff due to paucity of funds, and the reluctance of State Governments to take over the responsibility. For example, 13 States and 3 Union Territories agreed to accept the responsibility for Family and Child Welfare Projects at the end of the Fourth Plan Period; and in the six States which have not so agreed, the continuation of ongoing projects is uncertain and it is proposed to absorb them in the new programme for Integrated Child Development. The CSWB feels that these changes in the nomenclature and the contents of the programmes and their transfer to State Governments without ensuring their continuity, only tends to confuse the rural population, and affects results.

Recommendations

We will now conclude this chapter with a brief enumeration of our major recommendations.

Health and family planning. In our opinion, over-concentration on efforts for family planning has led not only to the neglect of maternity and child health services and general public health services, but also defeated the ultimate objective of the family planning programme itself. We therefore welcome the proposed integration of family planning with other health services and recommend that:

1. The rank of the Chief Executive for the integrated maternity and child health services, including family planning, should be upgraded to at least Additional Commissioner, so that this service does not again become subordinate to family planning. This procedure should be adopted at all levels of the administration at the Centre and in the States.

2. A separate budget head for maternity and child health services should be created, drawing on the provisions now made for family planning and the general health services since programmes for immunization and nutrition of infants yields better results when they form a part of general maternity and child health services, we see no difficulty in increasing the allocation for these services.

3. At the level of the primary health centres, the maternity and child health services should be separated, for purposes of administrative provision, medical personnel, and budget as this will ensure greater priority of treatment. Facilities in the way of maternity beds, equipment for immunization of children, and family planning for women could be allocated to the MCH Unit. The PHC could be made responsible for sterilization operations for men along with other general health services. The MCH Unite could co-ordinate the nutrition and immunization measures which form a basic component of the integrated child development programme.

4. Each MCH centre should collect and maintain fertility and morbidity data which should be studied and evaluated at the district level by persons with the

necessary competence. This will call for a health statistics Section at the district level.

5. The present practice of providing financial incentives to promoters of family planning should be abolished. Incentives to women who accept family planning should be in the shape of a token or certificate to ensure them greater priority in health care facilities for both the mothers and their children. Compensation for loss of wages during sterilization operations should, however, be paid to daily wage labourers. Others should be given paid leave for this purpose.

6. The qualifications prescribed for recruitment of personnel for these services in rural areas need to be gradually raised. Attempts should also be made to obtain the services of older and mature women for these services in the rural areas.

7. Research in the field of female disorders; *e.g.*, puerperal psychosis and effects of family planning methods, should be promoted.

8. The denial of maternity benefits to women in Government service after three children (as adopted by some State Governments*) should be rescinded.

9. Mass compaigns for family planning should also aim to correct prevailing social attitudes regarding fertility and metabolic hereditary disorders and the sex of the child for which the woman is generally blamed. Correct information in these matters would go a long way to improve the status of women.

Changes Needed in the Medical Termination of PregnanayAct

1. According to Section 4(a) of the Act, consent of a minor girl is not required for this operation while in other surgical operations of children above 12, such consent is necessary. In our view this distinction is

**e.g.*, Maharashtra and Kerala.

uncalled for and may lead to guardians compelling young girls to undergo this operation even when they do not want it. The consent of the patient should be essential. In the case of a minor girl nearing majority, if the doctor and the patient are in agreement, the consent of the guardian may be dispensed with. In all such cases, greater discretion should be permitted to the doctor.

2. Section 8 of the Act provides an overriding precaution to the doctor for any damage caused by the operation. This seems unnecessary and may lead to negligence. It should be deleted.

3. While we appreciate the ethical considerations which make many doctors reluctant to perform this operation, we feel that it is a woman's right to have control over the size of her family. At the same time it is important that doctors should have the authority to discourage such operations when they pose definite risk to the health of a patient. The condition being imposed in many hospitals that abortion will only be performed if the patient agrees to sterilizaiion, should not be compulsive. It would be far better to adopt methods of persuasion through expert counselling.
4. The procedure and paper work involved in these operations need to be simplified. It is also necessary to extent facilities for authorized termination of pregnancies, particularly in the rural areas.

5. Many hospitals continue to insist on the husband's consent before performing these operations though this is not required by the law. A special effort needs to be made to convince the medical profession of the social value of this law from the point of view of both individuals and society.

6. Most doctors are reluctant to perform these operations in the case of unmarried girls. It is necessary to clarify the point that rape is not the only ground to justify

termination in cases of unmarried girls, nor is there any legal obligation on the doctor to inform the Police of an operation done in a rape case.

Welfare and Development

1. In order to prevent any ambiguity in the understanding of what constitutes women's welfare and to prevent the development of policies that sometimes go against the basic objectives, Government of India should evolve a national policy on women's development in the light of the constitutional directives and pledges made to the women of this country and to the international community from time to time.
2. The Central and State Social Welfare Boards should be reorganized as a statutory and autonomous specialized agency for planning, coordination, and management of welfare and development programmes for women and children.

Constitution of special commissions at the centre and in the states: One important reason for the failure of various laws and administrative programmes to make the desired impact, is the absence of any single agency, which could co-ordinate and examine these measures and provide expert a dvice on methods of implementation. We therefore recommend the constitution of statutory, autonomous Commissions at the Centre and the States with the following functions:

1. *Collection of information*: For this function, these Commissions should be empowered to call for information on different matters from the concerned agencies of Government and suggest improved methods of data collection.

2. *Evaluation of existing policies, programmes, and laws* that have a bearing on the status of women with powers (1) to censure non-implementation of these measures and (2) to point out lacunae or deficiencies and to suggest amendments or improvements. The comments and suggestions of the Commis-

sion, made in consultation with the concerned Government Department, should be placed before Parliament or State legislature in the form of a report and should be answered by the Government concerned within a stipulated period.

3. Authority to recommend, to Parliament or to the State legislatures, new laws, policies, or programmes with a view to implementing the stated objectives and policies. The Government concerned should be responsible to consider such recommendations for action or to explain their non-acceptance.

4. *Redress of grievances* in cases of actual violation of existing laws.

In view of the functions visualized for the Commissions, their compositon has to be broadbased and representative. One group of members may be drawn from representatives of leading women's organizations, trade unions, legislative and local bodies, and employers from both public and private sectors. The second group should be drawn from experts in the fields of law, health, education, social research, and adminstration. The Commissions should be empowered to co-opt one or two members from sectors which are unrepresented.

The Chairman should be a full-time non-official woman. The majority of the members should be women and the Commissions should be empowered to appoint their secratariat.

We also recommend the establishment of Special Tribunals, for all violations of human rights, discrimination aginst women, violation or evasion of the existing laws and policies for the protection of women's rights in society.

6

Industrial Training Facilities and Women

Provision of tuition free education and stipends, free and subsidised hostels, books and stationery, reservation of seats in institutions, relaxation in admission criterion, job reservation are some of the measures taken by the Central and State Governments over the past quarter of a century to enable the traditionally disadvantaged sections take advantage of various educational and training facilities which have been expanded substantially since Independence.

Considering the special importance of industrial training facilities for the scheduled castes and scheduled tribes students those who are admitted to the Industrial Training Institutes, are giving not only free training but also a stipend of Rs. 45 per month. Besides, books, equipment and two work uniforms are supplied free to all the scheduled students. The facility of free or subsidised hostels is also available at places. Most important, seats have been reserved by trades for these category of students in the ITIs and if the sufficient number of candidates are not available with required marks there is further relaxation in marks so that the reserved quota could be filled. In case students from one scheduled groups are not available, priority is given to students of other scheduled groups. Further, in order to motivate more and more members of these groups avail of the facilities, reservation of seats in jobs and in apprenticeship training have been made for them. It is expected that the above facilities will motivate ever larger number of students of disadvantaged groups avail of the facilities.

In the selected states all these incentives and facilities have been made available to the scheduled categories in varying degrees. While a detailed analysis incentives and facilities will be attempted in a later chapter, this chapter will be confined to the extent the reservation policy for the deprived has been implemented in the selected states. This will be followed by an analysis of the relative competition for seats among the scheduled castes, scheduled tribes and others. The analysis will throw light on the popularity of this training. More importantly, it will bring out whether sufficient number of qualified candidates seek admission in various trades in the ITIs from amongst the two scheduled groups.

In the last section an attempt will be made to focus on inter caste variations among the scheduled categories with a view to see if new inequalities are creeping in.

SECTION I
RESERVATION POLICY IN GENERAL ITIs

Though in principle, the reservation ought to be in accordance with the proportion of the particular group in the population of the state, in practice the policy of reservation in the ITIs is not uniform in all the states. For example, in Andhra Pradesh, 14 per cent reservation for the scheduled castes and 4 per cent reservation for the scheduled tribes is provided uniformly throughout the state. This is roughly in proportion to their strength in the population of the state which is 13.3 per cent for scheduled castes and 3.8 per cent for scheduled tribes. In Madhya Pradesh the reservation for the scheduled castes and scheduled tribes is 14 per cent and 18 per cent respectively while their share in states population is 13.1 per cent and 20.1 per cent. The reservation of seats for the scheduled castes in Bihar is 14 per cent of the intake capacity but for the scheduled tribes the reservation varies from area to area. Areas with higher concentration of scheduled tribes have higher reservation while areas with lower proportion of the scheduled tribes population have much lower quota for them.

In Gujarat while reservation for the scheduled castes is 12.5 per cent (with their proportion in total population as 6.8 per cent) for the schedule tribes the reservation of seats varies from institution from 5 per cent to 20 per cent. Thus, while in the ITIs located at Baroda, Godhala, Palanpur and Surat only 12.5 per cent seats are reserved for scheduled tribes at Bilimoria and Surendranagar the reservation is only 5 per cent.

Maharashtra has reserved 13 per cent seafs for the scheduled castes and 7 per cent for the scheduled tribes. This is quite in variance with their proportionate share in the states population which is 6.0 per cent for the scheduled castes and 5.9 per cent for the scheduled tribes. Further, in Dhule, Nasik and Thane district the reservation for the scheduled tribeds is 22 per cent while in Chandrapur and Yevatmal it is only 15 per cent respectively. Maharashtra also provides an additional 10 per cent reservation to Vimukta Jati and Nomadic tribes (VJNT). The reservation for servicemen is 5 per cent.

It may be noted that in Gujarat and Maharashtra reservation for the scheduled castes is quite disproportionate to their share in the population while for the scheduled tribes it is more or less in accordance with their proportion in total population.

Reservation Policy in Special ITIs

Special ITIs were started in the tribal areas by the government with a view to help the tribal youth acquire necessary skills needed for the newly developing industries in those areas. The aim is to reach the benefits of industrialisation to the people in the area through substantial employment of tribals in the up coming industries. In these ITIs most of the seats are reserved for the scheduled tribes or scheduled castes. Such ITIs are available in all the states surveyed by us.

In Andhra Pradesh on ITI was started at Upper Sileru with 50 per cent reservation for the scheduled tribes and 35 per cent for scheduled castes. The remaining fifteen per cent seats are reserved for non-scheduled categories. The Ranchi ITI at Ranchi in Bihar reserves 54 per cent of the seats for the scheduled tribes.

In Madhya Pradesh there are four institutions exclusively started for the scheduled tribes by the Tribal Welfare Department besides the three started by the Labour Department. These are at Dhammod, Betul, Shahdol, Ambikapur, Nandia, Korba and Bastar. The ITI at Bastar, selected for the study, was started exclusively for the tribals with 100 per cent seats reserved for them. The Gujarat government has started an ITI at Ahwa in Dangs district exclusively for the scheduled tribes.

In Maharashtra there are ITIs specially for scheduled tribes at Manik Dhor in Poona District, and at Jalgaon in Jalgoan District.

Relative Competition for Seats in the ITIs by the Scheduled Castes Scheduled Tribes and Others

Several studies have pointed out the fact that reserved quota has seldom been fully utilised by the scheduled groups and the most common explanation is that not enough qualified candidates are available for the seats. To test the validity of this explanation, statistics have been worked out of the number of applicants per seat separately for the scheduled castes, scheduled tribes and others in the selected ITIs (Table 6.1).

Overall one can easily see that competition for seats is more in Andhra Pradesh compared to Gujarat and Madhya Pradesh. There were 54 applicants for one seat in Andhra Pradesh while there are only 9 applicants per seat in Gujarat and Madhya Pradesh. This means Industrial training is more popular in Andhra Pradesh as compared to Gujarat or Madhya Pradesh. Same trend is evident with regard to number of applicants per seat among the scheduled castes and scheduled tribes. One specially notices that competition for seats is very high among scheduled castes in Andhra Pradesh compared to Gujarat and Madhya Pradesh. In contrast, there is very little competition among the tribals in all the 3 selected states. In Gujarat specially, there are lesser number of applicants among the scheduled tribes than the seats for them.

TABLE 6.1

Relative Competetion for Seats Among the Scheduled Castes, Scheduled Tribes and others in the Selected States 1980-81

States	*Number of Applicants per Seat*		
	Scheduled Castes	*Scheduled Tribes*	*Others*
Andhra Pradesh	26	4	54
Gujarat	7	0.2	9
Madhya Pradesh	6	3	9

Note: Number of Applicants are not available for Bihar and Maharashtra.

From the above one can conclude that though much more efforts are needed to get eligible candidates of the scheduled tribes as compared to non-scheduled groups, for the scheduled castes the situation is more or less comparable with non-scheduled groups in the ITIs in all the three states for which data are available.

SECTION II
UTILISATION OF INTAKE CAPACITY

(a) Utilisation of Intake Capacity in the General ITIs

While the data on competition for seats by the scheduled castes, scheduled tribes and others helps in understanding the relative chances of these groups in getting admission to the ITIs, the percentage utilisation of intake capacity helps in understanding if the facilities are being optimally utilised by the different groups. Percentage utilisation of seating capacity is defined as:

$$\text{Percentage Utilisation} = \frac{\text{Actual Enrolment}}{\text{Intake Capacity}} \times 100$$

Table 6.2 gives the percentage utilisation of seating capacity for the selected states (based on statistics of selected Institutions) separately for the scheduled castes, scheduled tribes and others.

TABLE 6.2

Percentage Utilisation of Intake Capacity (ITIs) 1980-81

Sl. No.	*State*	*S.C.*	*S.T.*	*NSC/ST*
1.	Andhra Pradesh	107	109	100
2.	Gujarat	97	14	98
3.	Madhya Pradesh	76	7	107
4.	Maharashtra	167	47	85

Note: The data for Bihar as provided by the Project Director/is not amendable for the above analysis.

There was full utilisation of the intake capacity in Andhra Pradesh by the non-scheduled groups. While there was over utilisation by the scheduled castes and scheduled tribes.

In Gujarat while there was near full utilisation by the non-scheduled and scheduled castes, the seats were highly under-utilized by the scheduled tribes.

Similarly in Madhya Pradesh, whereas utilisation by the non-scheduled castes and tribes was full or near full, the utilisation by the scheduled tribes was extremely low since only 7 per cent of seats earmarked for them were utilized in 1980-81.

In Maharashtra the over-utilisation of seats by the scheduled castes is very high while the scheduled tribes could utilise less than half the seats reserved for them. Non-schedule castes scheduled tribes also utilised only 85 per cent of the seats available to them.

Gross under-utilisation of seating capacity by the tribals in Gujarat and Madhya Pradesh apparently is a matter of great concern. However, one needs to note that tribals are concentrated in certain areas in the states, and it will not be fair to generalise on the basis of general ITIs. In fact in both the states there are special ITIs for the tribes located in tribal areas where all or most of the seats are reserved for them. Infact considering the uneven nature of tribal distribution, in Gujarat the reservation quota for the scheduled tribes differs from district to district from 5 per cent to 20 per cent.

Considering the peculiar nature of tribals distribution in different districts, and the fact that ITIs are generally district phenomenon, it will be but fair to prescribe district wise reservation of seats for the tribals in all the states. This should be based on percentage population of the tribals in the district. This way one can hope to have a more rational and equitable distribution of facilities for the scheduled tribeds.

(b) Utilisation of Intake Capacity in the Special ITIs

In the tribal ITI of Vishakhapatnam district in Andhra Pradesh there were a total of 155 seats. Out of these 78 are reserved for the scheduled tribes and 54 for the scheduled castes, the remaining 33 seats were open. As against this during 1980-81, there were 80 scheduled tribes students. 53 scheduled castes students and rest were non-scheduled students. As the institute was started only in 1980-81 the data for earlier years were not available. One can see that quota were full for each of the social categories in this institution which is in keeping with the general ITIs that we had discussed in the previous section. One can, therefore, say that in Andhra Pradesh there is no cause of special concern for the scheduled castes and scheduled tribes from the viewpoint of their intake in the ITIs.

In Madhya Pradesh, as already indicated, there were seven

ITIs specially started for the tribes either by the Tribal Welfare Department or by the Labour Ministry. For the purpose of our study the ITI at Bastar was selected. This ITI was exclusively started for the tribals. The ITI had a seating capacity of 203 in 1980-81 but only 185 students were enrolled, thus giving 91 per cent utilisation of the seating capacity. Even among the students enrolled, there were 163 scheduled tribes and the rest were scheduled castes implying about 20 per cent under-utilisation by the scheduled tribes.

In Gujarat, the ITI at Ahwa in Dangs is a special ITI for the scheduled tribes with 100 per cent seats reserved for them. It had an intake capacity of 76 of which only 56 to 60 per cent was utilized in 1980-81. Even among the enrolled the scheduled tribes constituted just 40 per cent which is about 25 per cent of the intake capacity. It may be noted that while in absolute terms the number of the scheduled tribes in the ITI was almost constant over the years at 17 or 16, in percentage term one notices that while in 1977-78 the scheduled tribes constituted 47 per cent of the total enrolment, their percentage share gradually declined to 37 in 1980-81. (Appendix Table A.1). It was lowest in 1979-80 being only 25 per cent of the total enrolment. This matter needs a deeper probe because instead of increase in the proportion there has been gradual decline in the

TABLE A.1

Total Enrolment of Scheduled Tribes in Ahwa ITI, 1977-78—1980-81

Year	*Enrolment*			*Enrolment of ST. as percentage of total Enrolment*
	Total	*S.C.*	*S.T.*	
1	*2*	*3*	*4*	*5*
1977-78	36	1	17	47.22
1978-79	38	—	16	42.11
1979-80	48	—	12	25.00
1980-81	43	1	16	37.21

proportionate enrolment of the scheduled tribes in this institution which is wholly meant for them. As it is, in other ITIs also, enrolment of the scheduled tribes is very insignificant in Gujarat.

ITI at Manik Doho in Pune district had total intake capacity of 162 students out of which 114 seats were reserved for the scheduled tribes and 20 for the scheduled cates. There was a total utilisation of 159 seats in 1980-81 of which 61 seats were utilized by the scheduled tribes, 22 seats by the scheduled castes, and 76 by others. Proportionately, the scheduled tribes utilisation was only 53.5 per cent of the reserved seats, whereas the enrolment of the scheduled castes was 110 per cent and that of non-scheduled category 151 per cent.

Looking at the data on utilisation of the intake capacity in the general ITIs and special ITIs in the selected states one can conclude that while the enrolment of the non-scheduled groups is generally more than the number of seats earmarked for them, the situation in the case of tribes is quite dismal not only in general ITIs but also in special ITIs except in Andhra Pradesh. The scheduled castes situation in the ITIs was however, satisfactory since they were also utilising more seats than reserved for them. In Maharashtra they were using more seats than reserved for them even though the reserved quota itself was more than twice the proportion of the scheduled castes in the total population.

Tradewise Utilisation of Facilities by the Scheduled Castes and Scheduled Tribes

In order that the scheduled castes and the scheduled tribes are able to take as much advantage of the middle level technical vocational training as the non-scheduled groups, it is essential that they are represented fully in those trades where employment opportunities are comparatively better. From this viewpoint one expects two-year engineering trades to be more popular than one-year engineering trades or non-engineering trades. Similarly, one year engineering trades should be more popular than the non-engineering trades. However, some of the earlier studies relating to higher technical education have pointed out that the scheduled castes and scheduled tribes enrolment is comparatively lower in highly prestigious courses like the engineering courses at degree level or the medical courses but they have higher enrolment in general arts and science degree courses. Further when the courses are allotted in particular institution, whether engineering or medicine the scheduled groups are largely given least preferred courses. Considering the fact that the two-year engineering trades generally require educational background at the high school level and they take double the time in the ITIs than the one-year programmes, we hypothesized that the enrolment of the scheduled groups in the two-year trades will be lower compared to one year trade. The hypothesis is examined below on the basis of micro-level data at hand. Besides, an attempt has also been made to compare the enrolment of the scheduled groups with the non-scheduled groups in some of the more popular trades.

It was observed that engineering trades accounted for 95 per cent of the total enrolment of the ITIs. Among the two year engineering trades the most popular at all India level were the trades of electrician, fitter, machinist, motor vehicle mechanic, turner and wireman accounting for about 78 per cent of total enrolment in two year engineering trades. As regards the one year engineering trades the most popular were blacksmith, carpenter, mechanic, moulder, welder, sheet metal worker. These trades accounted for 92 per cent of total enrolment in one year engineering trade. Among the non-engineering trades stenography was the most popular followed by cutting, hand composing, book-binding and printing machine operator. These four trades covered more than 95 per cent of the total enrolment of non-engineering trades.

The tradewise utilisation of training facilities by the scheduled castes and scheduled tribes in the selected institutions of the selected states has been analysed by examining the respective distribution in the two-year engineering trades, in one-year engineering trades and in the non-engineering trades.

Taking the data from the selected institutions of Andhra Pradesh for 1980-81 it was observed that scheduled castes had over-utilised the seats in all the three types of trades. For example, against 145 seats reserved for them in the two-year engineering courses 157 were admitted, similarly against 42 seats in one year engineering trades 44 were admitted. In one year non-engineering trades also 22 scheduled castes were enrolled against 21 seats.

Scheduled tribes had also over-utilised the seats in engineering trades (two-year and one-year duration). However, in one year non-engineering trades the utilisation was about 67 per cent.

As regards the popular trades the scheduled castes were quite well represented in all except motor mechanic, welder and stenography. Scheduled tribes were best represented in fitter, welder and stenography but very poorly in draftsman (civil) and carpentary trades.

In the selected ITIs in Bihar, the two-year engineering trades were more popular than one year engineering or non-engineering trades. Among the two-year engineering trades the highest enrolment of both the scheduled castes and scheduled tribes was in fitter trade. Next in popularity among the scheduled castes was electrician while with the scheduled tribes turner was the second most popular trade being closely followed by electrician trade. Wiremen and machinist were less popular among both the scheduled groups as compared to electrician, fitter and turner. Among one-year engineering trade welder had the highest enrolment followed by moulder and sheet metal worker. Among the non-engineering trades blacksmith was the only popular trade.

Tradewise enrolment in Gujarat varied from region to region. Here also two-year trades were more popular than one-year trades. Of the total enrolment in the ITIs, 83 per cent were enrolled in the two-year engineering trades.

In Palanpur ITI the scheduled castes trainees on roll

exceeded the number of seats reserved for them. For trades of fitter and stenography (Gujarati) trades the scheduled castes trainees on rollwe re twice the number of seats reserved for them (Appendix Table A.2). Only for diesel mechanic the under-utilisation was very high *i.e.*, out of 36 seats only 12 were filled.

TABLE A.2

Tradewise Utilisation of Seats by Scheduled Caste Trainees in Palanpur ITI. Oct. 1981

Trade	*Sanctioned Seats*	*Trainees on Roll*	*Per cent of (3) to (2)*
1	*2*	*3*	*4*
Electrician	6	7	116.67
Fitter	7	14	200.00
Gen. Mechanic	2	3	150.00
Draftsman Civil	2	3	150.00
Engg. cum Electrician Mech	4	6	150.00
Machinist	3	4	133.33
Motor Mechanic	6	11	133.33
Turner	5	6	120.00
Wireman	6	10	166.67
Diesel Mechanic	36	12	33.33
Stenography (Guj.)	2	4	200.00
Water	3	3	100.00
Total	52	83	159.62

Note : Tradewise sanctioned seats are calculated on the assumption that tradewise share of SC/ST is 12.5 per cent as it is for all trades.

Ahmedabad ITI which is very big in size had 16 two-year trades and 14 one-year trades. Here the scheduled castes were over-represented *i.e.*, as against 88 seats reserved for them, 99 students were enrolled. They were slightly under represented in two-year trades while they were highly over-represented in one-year trades (Appendix Table A.3). In one-year non-engineering trades ten students belonging to the scheduled castes were enrolled as against two seats reserved for them. In contrast the scheduled tribes were grossly under-represented. There were in all six scheduled tribes as against 43 seats reserved for them.

TABLE A.3

Inter-Tribal and Inter-Caste Differencies in the Utilisation of Facilities in Selected ITIs of Maharashtra

Name of Caste	*Eng. 1 Yr.*	*Eng. 2 Yrs.*	*Non-Eng.*	*N.M.*	*Total 1 Yr.*
1	2	3	4	5	6
Scheduled Castes					
Mahar	156	153	39	3	351
Chamar	55	96	14	2	167
Mang	58	71	14	1	144
Nav-Boudha	42	12	2	—	56
Dhor	5	10	3	—	18
Khatik	1	1	0	—	2
Matang	0	2	0	—	2
Linghadher	0	1	0	1	2
Others	—	—	—	—	30
Not mentioned	—	—	—	—	8
Total	317	346	72	7	780
Scheduled Tribes					
Mahadeo Koli	28	85	5	2	120
Thakur	4	10	0	—	14
Others	—	—	—	—	14
Not mentioned	—	—	—	—	2
Total	32	95	5	2	150

Note : Data for Nagpur ITI not included in the table.

Scheduled castes made full use of the newly introduced trades of electrician, diesel mechanic and stenography (Gujarati). Scheduled tribes were also enrolled almost in proportion to the seats reserved for them in electrician and stenography trades.

In Surandranagar ITI both the scheduled castes and scheduled tribes were highly under-represented. In 1980-81 only 6.2 per cent of the total enrolment was of the scheduled castes and 0.35 per cent of the scheduled tribes. In the two-year engineering trades the scheduled castes were enroled to the extent of 50 per cent of the seats reserved for them while in the one-year engineering trades, it was about 122 per cent, overall utilisation being about 60 per cent of their quota. Scheduled castes were very poorly represented in electrician trade (only 1 student as against 8 seats reserved for them). Scheduled castes were over-represented in general mechanic trade (6 against 2 seats) and welder trade (5 against 3 seats).

In Madhya Pradesh also the enrolment in trades varied from region to region. In Ujjain ITI the most popular trades were mechanics and electronics. Stenography and printing and composing were the two newly introduced trades. Carpentry was generally given very low priority. Automobile mechanic was on wane. In the Indore ITI while there was good demand for the newly introduced trade of instrument mechanic, the demand for the tractor mechanic was low. This trade was therefore discontinued. Stenography was also a popular trade in Indore.

In Maharashtra, engineering trades (both two-year and one-year) were more popular than non-engineering trades. Not only there were substantially higher number of seats in engineering trades, but their utilisation was also more than 100 per cent in 1980-81. In contrast, in the non-engineering trades about 10 per cent seats remained vacant in that year.

Scheduled castes and other backward classes overutilised their share in all the popular engineering and non-engineering trades while scheduled tribes, VJNT and the general category people used lesser number of seats than allotted to them. Under-utilisation was very marked in the case of the scheduled tribes specially in one-year engineering trades and non-engineering trades. There was special need to pay more attention to increase scheduled tribes enrolment in these instititutions.

The analysis of the data on tradewise enrolment for Andhra Pradesh, Gujarat and Maharashtra does not bring out any clear differentials in the enrolment of the scheduled castes and the scheduled tribes in two-year engineering, one-year engineering and non-engineering trades *vis-a-vis* the non-scheduled groups. The enrolment of the scheduled tribes was found below their reserved quota in almost all trades. The scheduled castes enrolment was somewhat lower in two-year engineering trades in Ahmedabad and Surendranagar ITIs with a higher enrolment in one-year trades but, in other ITIs, the enrolment of the seheduled castes in the two year engineering trades was higher than their quota. Further the scheduled castes are found to be well represented in most of the popular trades.

Special ITIs

In the special ITI in Andhra Pradesh, there was over utilisation of seats by scheduled tribes in fitter, motor mechanic, welder and plumber trades and 100 per cent utilisation in stenography course during 1980-81. In draftsman (civil) trade only one scheduled tribe candidate joined against 10 seats. There was under-utilisation to the extent of 60 per cent in the electrician trade. Carpentry also did not impress the candidates as only three candidates chose to pursue it against 10 seats available to the scheduled tribes students. The scheduled castes candidates filled the seats in draftsman (civil) trade which were not filled by the scheduled tribes. There is over-utilisation of seats by the scheduled castes in electrician and carpentry trades, but there is under-utilisation of capacity by them in fitter and motor mechanic trade.

In the Ranchi ITI, scheduled tribes were well represented in all the five-two-year engineering trades while their enrolment was highest in fitter trade. Over the last five years 573 scheduled tribes were enrolled in fitter trades, 266 in turner and 238 in electrician trade. The corresponding number of the scheduled castes for these trades was 118, 45 and 46 respectively.

Welder was the most popular trade among the one year engineering trades with a total enrolment of 106 in a period of five year. The scheduled castes enrolment was 26. In black-smith 38 scheduled tribes trainees were enrolled during the same period. The number for scheduled castes was, however, only 8 for the whole period.

Ranchi ITI was enrolling a very large number of scheduled tribes students. Here an important question is as to how many of them completed the respective courses? This would be examined in the next chapter for the selected ITIs.

Even though there appeared to be full utilisation of seats as a whole in all the trades in Ahwa ITI, there was very low utilisation by scheduled tribes for whom this ITI was started. Only 40 per cent of the enrolment was of the scheduled tribes. The under-utilisation was around 30 per cent in wiremen trade and about 60 per cent in fitter and welder trades. One of the important reasons for the under-utilisation was the shortfall in the number of scheduled tribes applicants in relation to the seats reserved for them.

In the ITI at Bastar, the most popular trades were of fitter, tractor mechanic and welder. These seemed to be good scope for carpentary but it is generally not liked and the capacity was not fully utilised.

In the special ITI at Manik Doho in Pune, Maharashtra, there were in all three trades namely, carpentry, fitter and wireman. In each of these trades 22 seats were reserved for the scheduled tribes and 4 seats for the scheduled castes. In

1981-82 while the scheduled castes utilised 50 per cent of their quota in carpentry and fitter trades in wireman trade they utilised only 25 per cent of the seats. The scheduled tribes, in contrast were better represented in the fitter trade (12 out of 22 seats reserved for them) compared to carpentry and wireman where only 7 were enrolled in each of the trade. The seats not filled by the scheduled castes and scheduled tribes were utilised by the other backward classes and general category students.

SECTION III

UTILISATION OF FACILITIES BY SUB-CASTES AND SUB-TRIBES

Uptill now the scheduled castes and scheduled tribes have been discussed as two groups. However, this merely gives a broad indication. Several studies have indicated inter-caste and inter-tribe variations with respect to their economic and educational progress. In each of the studies it has been found that a few progressive castes/tribes have been making use of various facilities and incentives much more than others. These caste groups are not necessarily the numerically preponderant groups. In contrast, there are many other very poor and needy castes/tribes which are not really able to take benefit of the available training facilities for various reasons. Keeping this in view, it was hypothesised that there will be caste/tribe wise differences in the use of ITI facilities also.

Data were to be collected by all the Project Directors on the sub-castes/sub-tribes of each of the trainee who was enrolled in the selected institutions for the last five years. The office records of the institutions did not however, mention the sub-castes/sub-tribes of the students except in Bihar. It was therefore, decided to collect such data from the present trainees. Project Directors in Andhra Pradesh and Madhya Pradesh were however not able to get the sub-castes/sub-tribes datawise even for the present trainees. Therefore, our analysis in this section relates only to Bihar, Gujarat and Maharashtra.

The caste and tribe wise distribution of enrolment in Bihar for the years 1976-77 to 1980-81 for the selected institutions located in Patna, Ranchi, Monghyr and Purnea districts is presented in Appendix Table A.4.

TABLE A.4

Inter-Caste and Inter-Tribe Differences in the Utilisation of Facilities in Selected ITIs of Bihar

Castes/Tribes	*Years*				
	1976-77	*1977-78*	*1978-79*	*1979-80*	*1980-81*
Scheduled Castes					
Chamar	101	113	122	117	109
Dusadh	83	72	97	86	78
Dhobi	26	43	39	58	73
Bhuyia	30	38	54	35	56
Pasi	45	28	33	49	54
Total	285	294	335	345	370
Scheduled Tribes					
Santhal	38	47	55	49	36
Oraon	112	119	132	151	162
Munda	96	98	113	127	140
Ho	57	54	33	29	24
Kharwar	35	22	28	17	16
Bhumij	12	16	8	113	15
Total	350	356	369	386	393

Among the scheduled castes in Bihar, Chamaras had utilised these facilities more than any other group. They were followed by Dusadha and Dhobi. If may be seen that Dhobis had improved their enrolments substantially between 1976-77 and 1980-81 from a more 26 to 72. Bhuyrias and Passis enrolment was lower than others but it increased gradually over the years. If one looks at the population of these scheduled groups in Bihar, one can say that their representation in the enrolment was quite in proportion to their population in the State.

Among the scheduled tribes in Bihar, Oraons and Mundas were the greatest beneficiaries of industrial training. Santhals who are numerically the largest groups in Bihar were least represented in the selected ITIs.

In Gujarat, among the scheduled castes, Parmars had made the greatest use of facilities in the selected ITIs. Vankars, Vaghelas and Chamars were the other three groups having an enrolment of 97 in all (Vankars 38, Vaghelas 32 and Chamars 27). Enrolment of all other sub-castes was less than 20 in the three ITIs. There were numerous scheduled castes groups that were not at all represented in the ITIs.

Tribes were poorly represented in the ITIs selected in Gujarat for the study. In the three general ITIs, including Ahmedabad ITI, their total enrolment in 1980-81 was 41 only. Patel, Vasura, Bil and Nayak accounted for half the enrolment. Only one person was enrolled from the remaining tribes. Some of the tribes were totally unrepresented.

In Maharashtra 57.1 per cent of the reserved seats for the scheduled castes were used by Mahars alone and 21.4 per cent by Chamars, while Mangs could use only 18.5 of the seats. Together these three groups accounted for 97 per cent of the enrolment against the seats reserved for the scheduled castes in the ITIs.

Among the tribes in Maharashtra Mahadev Koli alone constituted about 80 per cent of the total enrolment of the tribals in the selected ITIs. It may be noted that this is the most civilised and settled group among all the hill tribes.

Summary and Conclusions

On the basis of data relating to Andhra Pradesh, Bihar, Gujarat, Madhya Pradesh and Maharashtra, it was noted that the states did not follow any uniform policies with respect to the reservation of seats for the scheduled castes and the scheduled tribes in their ITIs. In Andhra Pradesh, Bihar and Madhya Pradesh, the reservation of seats for the scheduled castes was according to their proportion in the states' population but in Gujarat and Maharashtra proportionately more seats were reserved for the scheduled castes than their proportion in the respective populations. Reservation for the scheduled tribes was uniform in all the ITIs in some states but it varied from district to district in Bihar and Gujarat depending on the tribal concentration in various districts.

Utilisation of seats by the scheduled castes, the scheduled tribes and the non-scheduled groups varied greatly from state to state. Whereas, the non-scheduled groups generally over-utilised the seats by having excess enrolment than the number of seats meant for them, the scheduled tribes mostly under-utilised their quota. The scheduled castes fall in between the two but their enrolment in Gujarat and Maharashtra was well beyond the quota set out for them. In fact, as stated above even the quota was almost double the share of the scheduled castes population in these two states. These data reveal that if a certain effort is made by the concerned authorities, the capacity of the ITIs can be fully utilised very easily, specially by the scheduled castes. The study did not reveal substantial differences in the use of facilities tradewise by the scheduled and non-scheduled groups.

The analysis presented in this chapter also points towards the need for fixing quota for the scheduled tribes on the basis of their share in the district's population since, it was observed that in the Iustitutes located in non-tribal areas, hardly any tribal students sought admission in various trades.

The competition for seats in the ITIs could be analysed on the basis of data relating to Andhra Pradesh, Gujarat and Madhya Pradesh alone. It was observed that competion was quite tough in Andhra Pradesh but was nominal in Gujarat and Madhya Pradesh. In fact, in Gujarat, there was only one scheduled tribes applicant for every five seats meant for them.

This under-utilisation of seats and only a nominal competition among the scheduled tribes should be matter of great concern for the authorities.

Our analysis also indicates that there are only a few scheduled castes and scheduled tribes among the various castes and tribes that had made greatest use of ITI training facilities. These have not been necessarily the most-preponderant castes/tribes. It is probably the progressive character of these castes/tribes which have helped them in taking greater advantage of the available facilities.

7

Dropout and Its Causes and Women

While under-utilisation of existing facilities by the disadvantaged groups reflects one aspect of deprivation, the higher failure and dropout rate of the disadvantaged, reflects the other aspect of their educational backwardness. The previous chapter had clearly shown that under-utilisation of the facilities was highest in respect of the scheduled tribes in all the states followed by the scheduled castes. This chapter will present an analysis of the comparative dropout rates for the scheduled castes, scheduled tribes and others. Causes of dropouts among the scheduled castes and the scheduled tribes as perceived either by the students themselves or by their teachers and heads of the Institutions would also be analysed here.

Dropout is a universal phenomenon in Indian educational system at all the levels which results is considerable wastage of resources. Dropout is most serious at primary school level. A number of studies have shown that dropout is higher in case of disadvantaged poor students. The major reason given usually being that the children are an economic asset to the parents. In the case of ITIs, it was hypothesised that droupout rate would be higher among the scheduled castes and the scheduled tribes-students than the non-scheduled students because of their comparatively poor economic status.

To understand the phenomenon of droupt among the ITI students this chapter examines first the extent and nature of dropout of the scheduled castes and the scheduled tribes as compared to others. The reasons for dropouts are discussed next, and, finally, the chapter makes some suggestions for reducing dropouts from the Industrial Training Courses.

Ordinarily, a dropout is defined as a person who withdraws from a programme of study before completing the same. It differs from wastage where a student takes longer time to complete a course than the prescribed one. For example, at the primary level all those children who are admitted to class I and who do not complete class IV or V, are taker as dropouts. In the case of ITIs all those students who join a particular trade but do not complete the same because they leave the programme before the final examination, or after failing in it should, similarly, be regarded as dropouts. The actual situation in the ITIs is, however, somewhat different from the primary schools since many of the students who seek admission the ITIs simultancously apply for other programmes of studies in other institutions, the results of which usually get delayed. Some of these students who get admission in certain other preferred courses leave the ITIs as soon as they learn about it. Such cases mostly occur within the first month itself. Therefore, most of those students who leave the ITIs in the first month may not be regarded as dropouts. However, the institutes seldom come to know the exact reason for dropout.

To compute dropouts on yearly basis, the number of dropouts can be obtained by substracting the enrolment in the next higher class a year later from the number enrolled in a class in a particular year and those who are the repeaters in this class. Under this concept, the dropout rate can be defined as:

$$DOR_t = \frac{E_t^c - \left(E^{c+1}_{t+1} + E_{t+1} \right)}{E^c_t}$$

DOR_t=Dropout rate for a particular class 'c' in year t.

E^c_t=Enrolment in class 'c' in year t.

E^{c+1}_{t+1}=Enrolment in the next higher class one year later.

E_{t+1}=Repeaters in class 'c' in year t+1.

As data on repeaters are usually not available, the above formula is simplified into

$$DOR_t = \frac{E_t^c - E^{c+1}_{t+1}}{E_t^c}$$

which, of course, over-estimates dropout rate to the extent of repeater rate for the year t for class 'c'.

In the ITIs or other similar institutions, when the course is of one-year duration, there is no subsequent class. Here the dropout can be computed by subtracting the number of the successful completers from those who were admitted to the particular course. As some of those students who fail in an examination, complete the course in the next year or in a subsequent year, their number should be ascertained before computing drop out rate. It was, however, not feasible to ascertain their number. Hence in this investigation dropouts have been defined as those persons who left the course between their enrolment and final examination. As this definition of dropouts includes those persons also who left the course in the first mouth to join some other preferred nourses, it leads to somewhat over-estimation of dropouts.

With the above limitations, we shall examine extent of dropout for the scheduled castes, scheduled tribes and otbers in each of the states and then give an over all picture of dropout in all the five states.

Extent of Dropouts

In Andhra Pradesh dropout rate for the scheduled castes and the scheduled tribes (compiled on the basis of data for the years 1976-77 to 1980-81) were, on an average, 5.7 per cent and 7.4

per cent respectively. For the scheduled castes the rate ranged from 2.5 per cent in 1976-77 to 8.7 per cent in 1979-80. Among the scheduled tribes the lowest dropout rate (3.5 per cent) was in 1980-81 and highest (13.6 per cent) was in 1979-80. Thus, Andhra Pradesh had dropout rates of less than 10 per cent which can be regarded as quite low.

On the other hand the completion rates for the scheduled castes and the scheduled tribes were also comparatively low, the average completion rate for the period 1976-77 to 1980-81 for the scheduled castes being 72 per cent and for the scheduled tribes 62 per cent. Thus while dropout rates were not a matter of concern, the completion rates for the two depeived groups in Andhra Pradesh need to be viewed seriously.

In Bihar the dropout rates varied between 20 to 30 per cent in different trades. The highest dropout rates for both the scheduled castes and the scheduled tribes were in black-smith trade while for non-scheduled group the highest dropout rates were among sheet metal workers (21.4 per cent) followed by blacksmiths (19.9 per cent). In the non-scheduled group, the lowest dropout was in wireman trade. Dropout rates among the scheduled castes and the scheduled tribes was about the same-around one-fourth of the enrolment. Among the non-scheduled group the dropout rate was about 16 per cent which was considered low in comparison to that for the scheduled group.

In Bihar the completion rates of the scheduled castes and the scheduled tribes were very low being only about 50 per cent in two-year engineering trades and still lower in one-year engineering trade.

In Gujarat dropout rates differed greatly from institute to institute. In Surendranagar ITI the dropout rate was 25 per cent while in Palanpur it was just 7 per cent. In Palanpur eight trades did not have any dropout at all. Dropout rates among the scheduled tribes were higher than non-scheduled group in all the selected ITIs. In Surendranagar ITI the dropout rate of the scheduled castes was 40 per cent as against 25 per cent for others. In Palanpur ITI it was 13 per cent for the scheduled castes as against 7 per cent for others. In Ahmedabad ITI, dropout rate for the scheduled castes was little less than 10 per cent and the completion rate was about 75 per cent. In Ahwa ITI dropout rate for the scheduled tribes was just 14 per cent and their completion rate was 86 per cent.

Dropout rates were worked out in Madhya Pradesh only for Bastar ITI which was predominantly tribal ITI. For the three cohorts of 1976-77, 1977-78, 1978-79 the dropout rates were 29, 35 and 38 per cent respectively which was a matter of great concern since the dropout rates were not only high but they increased over the years.

Dropout rate in the selected ITIs of Maharashtra was about 19 per cent while the failure was about 25 per cent. Dropout rates were high for the scheduled tribes (26 per cent) while they were lowest for non-scheduled groups (18 per cent). The dropout rate of the scheduled castes was 19 per cent though their failure rate was the highest (40 per cent as against 20 per cent for others). Dropout rate in non-engineering trades at 22 per cent was higher in comparison to one-year engineering trades where it was only about 12 per cent.

Analysing the dropout rate for all the states together one finds that these were mostly between 20 to 30 per cent. The rates were higher for the scheduled castes and the scheduled tribes compared to non-scheduled groups. No tradewise pattern in dropout rate emerged although it was generally lower in two-year engineering trades as compared to other trades.

Reasons for Dropout

An attempt was made to examine the office records to collect information on the reasons for dropout. This was seldom mentioned and, if at all, did not reveal much. On talking to the principals it was found that as the ITI students do not require a transfer certificate to go in any other course or when they take up any job in private sector, the incomplete ITI training seldom matters to them. Therefore, they do not come to the Institute to report that they are leaving the course. Instead, they just absent themselves indefinitely and finally, their names are struck off. In the attendance register we very often found the world 'personal reasons' or 'absconder' (who continually keeps himself absent). Therefore, the causes of dropout given in this section are mainly based on the interviews with the principals or teachers who sometimes came to know of the cause directly on meeting the dropout himself, but more often, indirectly from some acquaintance of the dropout. Among the selected states Andhra Pradesh did not collect any data on the reasons for dropout.

In Bihar, dropout during the first month was only about 2 to 3 per cent for all the three group, namely, scheduled castes, scheduled tribes and others. Dropout rates increased substantially between 3-6 month period. The office records did not give any reason for the dropout.

The main reason given by the principals was poor academic record of the trainees. They felt that the students found it difficult to cope up with the subjects and were not able to concentrate on the practicals. As the pressure of the course taught in the various trades in these Institutes went one increasing, they found it incrersingly difficult to cope with. The second reason given by the principals and teachers was that some of the trainees were able to get job before the completion of the course.

According to the students, responsibility for the dropout lay with the teachers who did not teach well. Students were not able to understand what was being taught and therefore they left the course. Another reason mentioned by the student was their poor economic background, this was specially the case with the scheduled castes and the scheduled tribes. A stipend of

Rs. 45 p.m. was hardly sufficient. Therefore, as soon as the students got a job, they left the training.

In Bihar both academic and financial reasons were given as causes for dropout by both the groups—principals and teachers on the one hand and the students on the other hand.

The time of dropout was compiled for Surendranagar ITI in Gujarat. The two-year data for this ITI indicated that major dropout among the students belonging to the scheduled castes as well as the non-scheduled groups occured during the first month. The dropout rates in the first month as percentage of total dropout during the year were, however, higher for the scheduled castes compared to others—the proportion was 69.6 per cent in 1974 and 81.3 per cent in 1980 as against 65.8 per cent and 76.5 per cent respectively for the non-scheduled students.

A systematic study of the reasons for dropouts for the last five years are available for 22 dropouts for Ahwa ITI. Out of the 17 non-scheduled tribe dropouts six were from fitter trade, 6 from wireman trade and 5 from other trades. From fitter trade three left the training since they got employment, one got apprenticeship and one gave personal reason for leaving the training. One student dropped because he was short of attendance. Among the dropouts from wireman trade only one joined father's profession the rest five gave personal reasons for dropping out. Three of the trainees from other trades got transferred to other ITIs. No information was avallable for the remaining two.

Of the five scheduled tribes dropouts from this ITI three got job, one left because of health problem and the remaining one dropped because of accommodation problem (Ahwa ITI had no hostel).

Overall the most important reason for dropout is getting employment which explains about one-third of the dropouts in this ITI. Among personal reasons the reasons mentioned were poor health accommodation problem and shortage of attendance.

As regards other ITIs in Gujarat, office records did not specifically give the reasons of discontinuance. Against the dropout column; the only remarks reported were 'fee recovered' 'returned' or 'refunded' which meant nothing since the training is free for all in all the ITIs. These words very clearly indicated that no one was concerned as to why the students left the course their only worry seemed to justify the audit.

Principals and teachers of the surveyed ITIs is Gujarat felt that the most important reason for dropout was employment. Wrong choice of subject and consequent inability to pursue the course was also given as reason for leaving the course. Several students left the course when they realised that the training was too tough for them. There is a week wise programme and three tests in a year. Lxaminations are interstate. Training is rigorous and any complecency on the part of the students is at a high cost to them. If a student misses a few weeks programme, it becomes almost impossible for him to make up and cousequently he is forced to leave it in between.

A very common feeling expressed by the principals and teachers about the reason for dropout of the scheduled castes and scheduled tribes students was that they joined the course only for stipend and that they were not interested in training. This feeling did not seem to be wholly correct if one looks at the expressed aspirations of scheduled groups students who mostly looked for government jobs which they could get only after completion of the training.

In Madhya Pradesh the maximum dropout occured during the first few months probably bccause ITI training was least preferred programme for many students. As soon as pupils got admission in traditional general courses they left the training. Getting another job even before completion of the training was reason for dropout among the scheduled group students.

In Maharashtra also the highest dropout was reported in the beginning of the session, reason being the same as in Madhya Pradesh, that is, getting some job. Dropout in the middle of the course was ascribed to poor conditions and agricultural background of most of the trainees. Whenever additional manpower was required at home they went back and remained absent for long spells. After some time the institutions struck off their names. Some of the trainees had to undertake some small jobs for the family, hence they could not concentrate on their studies. As a result they were unable to cope up with the prescribed training. Some of them, therefore, left the programme midway while others left it after failing in the examination.

Several students left the training because their economic conditions compelled them to take up any type of work even with low wages. Poor economic condition of the trainee was given as an important cause of dropout by the teachers. In some rare cases an alternate good job also resulted in the dropout of the trainees. Economic reason was given as the most compelling reason for dropout in Maharashtra, even low performance and failure was ascribed to the poor background of students which interfered with their studies in several ways.

Although the responses from all the states regarding reasons for dropout were not as comprehensive as one would wish them yet it is possible to say that economic reasons turned out to be the most important one. This was reflected either in taking up of a job which, in most cases, were low paid ones, or in lack of concentration and absenteeism.

Academic failure largely resulted from poor background. It was incorrect to say that the scheduled castes and scheduled tribes joined the ITI courses only for stipend and that they were basically not interested in them. Stipend may be a motivating force for continuing in the courses, this does not seem to be explaining their disinterestedness since most of the scheduled group aspire for Government job which can come to them only after completing the training. If stipend was at all responsible for the dropout, it was because the amount was so meagre that they prefarred to give up the training as soon as they got even a low paid job.

While dealing with causes of dropout one should not overlook academic reasons because a large number of dropouts seemed to be among the failures. Punctuality and rigour so essential in training and its good feature but for genuine cases of absenteeism, there is need to make some provision to help them overcome their academic defficiencies.

Summary

Dropout is a universal phenomenon in Indian educational system which results in considerable wastage. A dropout has been defined here as one who having enrolled in a particular trade either leaves it mid-way or leaves after failing in the final examination.

While dropout rates in Andhra Pradesh were low they were about 20 to 30 per cent in other states. The survey revealed that dropout rates were higher among the scheduled castes and the scheduled tribes. Completion rates for scheduled castes and scheduled tribes were only about 50 per cent in Bihar. There the dropout during the first month was minimal (2 to 3 per cent), while in Gujarut and Maharashtra the major dropout occurred during the first month. One may say that first month dropout is not a cause of great concern in the case of ITI students since most of them go in for alternative courses.

Economic reason appeared to the most important cause for dropout. Generally the students took up a job and in most cases a low paid one as soon as it was available, otherwise there was lack of concentration on studies or absenteeism due to poor economic background. Even academic failure largely resulted from poor background. It is not correct to say that the scheduled castes and scheduled tribes students joined the ITI courses just for stipend and that basically they were not interested in studies. Stipend might be strong motivating force for joining the ITI training but it does not explain their disinterestedness since most of the scheduled groups students aspired for government job which they could get only after completing the training. If stipend is at all responsible for the dropout, it is because the amount was so low that it did not meet even their minimum needs, and as soon as a student got even a low paid job he gave up the ITI training. It is quite possible to minimise dropout by raising stipend amount.

While dealing with causes of dropout one should not overlook academic reason since a large number of dropouts were the failures in the programme. Punctuality and rigour so essential in training are its good features but for genuine cases of absenteeism, there is need to make some provision to help them overcome their academic deficiencies by making arrangements for some remedial teaching.

8

Employment Pattern of Extrainees and Women

Technical and vocational education, unlike liberal education, has a special place in an economy which is on the path of industrialization. The expansion of technical education is supposed to meet manpower requirements of the industries. In this sense, the expenditure on it, whether by the government or by private individuals, is an investment expenditure.

The effectiveness of the investment in training can be judged on the basis of several indicators which are given below:

— Percentage of trainees who are able to get jobs soon after their training.

— Extent to which employment is related to the skills acquired in the training.

— Proportion of trainees who are able to get self-employment.

— Differentials between the job performance of the pre-service ITI trainees and those trained on the job.

— Extent to which emoluments are commensurate with the training.

— Extent to job satisfaction of the trainees.

— Employer's assessment of the performance of ITI trainees.

In this study effort were made to obtain information on the employment status, waiting time for the job, sector and tenure of employment, emoluments, and the extent of job satisfaction from the extrainees belonging to the three social groups-scheduled castes, scheduled tribes and others. A special proforma addressed to the extrainees was prepared to collect information on these items.

Considering the availability of time and resources, only a small number of extrainees could be covered. From each of the selected institutions, 25 extrainees were to be selected from the ones enrolled between 1977 and 1981. It was decided to select 5 extrainees from scheduled castes 5 from non-scheduled category. These were to be contacted at their residential address as given in the office records.

After the completion of the training some extrainees migrated to other places for jobs; some others who came to a particular place for training went back to their own district after acquiring the training. As the institutions did not maintain complete records of the extrainees they did not have their present residential addresses. Consequently, state level Project Directors devised different methods of contacting them. The response rate, therefore, varies from about 75 per cent in Gujarat, 65 per cent in Maharashtra and 40 per cent in Bihar to 18 per cent in Andhra Pradesh and 13 per cent in Madhya Pradesh (Table A.1). In Bihar and Gujarat only locally available extrainees *i.e.*, at the place of selected ITIs, were contacted. In Madhya Pradesh 16 extrainees were contacted locally. Of the 50 questionnaries mailed in Madhya Pradesh 20 came back filled; 11 were returned unfilled and there was no response from the remainining 19. In Andhra Pradesh, addresses of only 56 extrainees could be obtained and postcards were sent to them requesting them to meet the concerned Project Director. For the remaining extrainees, their addresses were not available.

Majority of the extrainees selected belonged to the recent three years 1979, 1980 and 1981. They accounted for 88 per cent of the actual respondents in Maharashtra, 78 per cent in Andhra Pradesh, 65 per cent in Madhya Pradesh and 55 per cent in Gujarat. Extrainees of 1981 alone formed 61 per cent of the respondents in Andhara Pradesh, and 48 per cent in Maharashtra, but only about 20 to 25 per cent in Bihar, Gujarat and Madhya Pradesh. This is probably explained by easy access to recent racords.

According to our plan categorywise breakup of extrainees should have been 20 per cent for the scheduled castes, 20 per cent for the scheduled tribes and 60 per cent for the others. But the actual proportions of extrainees contacted hardly conformed to the above pattern. Scheduled tribes were under-represented in three out of five states—the proportion rangining from 4.0 per cent in Andhra Pradesh, 7.4. per cent in Gujarat to 11.0 per cent in Maharashtra. The sample conformed to the designed proportion in Bihar but it was three times (62.5 per cent) in Madhya Pradesh.. The proportion of the scheduled castes was comparatively bettter in all the states—16 per cent in Maharashtra, 19 per cent in Gujarat and 25 per cent in Madhya Pradesh, but 34 per cent in Bihar. Their share among extrainees in Andhra Pradesh was, however, thrice the prescribed level. Around three-fourth of the extrainees in Gujarat and Maharashtra belong to non-scheduled group which conforms to the pattern of enrolment noted previously among the present trainees. In Bihar their share was 44 per cent, in Andhra Pradesh the share of non-scheduled groups extrainees was 35 per cent whereas in Madhya Pradesh it was just 12.5 per cent. Their share in total enrolment in 1981-82 around four-fifthts in Andhra Pradesh.

Analysis of tradewise enrolment in ITIs had shown that the two-year trades were more popular in comparison to one-year trades. The representativeness of our sample could also be judged by classifying extrainees by the duration of their courses.

In Gujarat nearly three-fourths of the scheduled castes and non-scheduled groups and nine-tenths of the scheduled tribes extrainees contacted had completed training in two-year trades. Another 11 per cent (STs) and 21 per cent (SCs & other) had opted for one-year engineering trades. Andhra Pradesh and Madhya Pradesh largely present a similar picture, the proportion of extrainees with trainining in two-year trades was 74 per cent and 50 per cent respectively. In Maharashtra, the corresponding share of extrainees of two-year trade was 42 per cent while that of one-year trade was 53.5 per cent. Even categorywise in both the states-Andhra Pradesh and Madhya Pradesh-the share of scheduled castes, scheduled tribes and other extrainees' in two-year trades exceeded that in one-year trades. Only Maharashtra was an exception.

Although the shares of the scheduled castes, scheduled tribes and others in the total number of extrainees did not conform to the prescribed pattern, their shares in relation to the total enrolment and total population and two and one-year trades indicated that extrainees in the sample were fairly representative of the extrainees as a whole.

It may be mentioned here that the initial sample by itself was quite small which got further reduced during the data collection phase. In view of this it would be hazardous to make any generalization regarding the extrainees. Analysis at best can be taken as indicative of direction. Moreover, it also provides certain comparisons between scheduled and non-scheduled categories.

In what follows an attempt has been made to study the employment status, waiting time for job, sector and tenure of job and the emoluments for the scheduled and non-scheduled categories. Other indicators have not been presented because the necessary data for them could not be obtained for various reasons.

Employment Status of the Extrainees

After completion of the ITI training, the alumnee either go for apprenticeship or take up one job or the other. Getting apprenticeship or a job, therefore, is one way of finding out the effectiveness of training. Another important aim of this training as emphasised by various Commissions and Committees is to prepare the trainees for self-employment. Effectiveness of the training can therefore also be judged from the extent of self-employment among the extrainees.

It was hypothesized earlier that, because of reservation in jobs and in apprenticeship training in the factories, a large percentage of the scheduled castes and scheduled tribes as compared to others will be able to get employment. It was also hypothesized that self-employment would be comparatively lesser among the scheduled groups because of their poor economic situation and lack of connections to start their own work units.

In this section the above two hypothesis would be tested first with the help of combined data for the four selected states (data for Madhya Pradesh is not available by social groups) and then separately for Bihar, Gujarat, and Maharashtra (since Andhra Pradesh sample is too small for separate analysis).

Activity Status of Extrainees

Extrainees have been classified into employees, self-employed, apprentices and unemployed. Out a total sample of 249 ins the four states 41 per cent are reported to be working a apprentices, 37 per cent as employees, and about 10 per cent as unemployed. It is noteworthy that a little over 8 per cent of extrainees are self-employed. (Appendix Table A.2).

Comparing the employment status of the scheduled castes and scheduled tribes with the non-scheduled groups, it was found that both among the scheduled castes and the scheduled tribes the apprenticeship rates were the same as for non-scheduled groups (about 41 per cent). However, there were substantial differences in the percentage of employed, self-employed and the unemployed among the three groups. The proportion of employees was highest among the scheduled castes (41 per cent) but very low among the scheduled tribes

(28 per cent). Self-employment was higher among the non-scheduled groups as compared to the scheduled castes and the scheduled tribes. Unemployment rates were highest for the scheduled tribes (21 per cent) while these are lowest for non-scheduled people (7 per cent).

On taking each state separately it was observed that in Bihar a little more than half the extrainees 'were employed, the employment ratès were same for the three groups. A higher percentage of scheduled castes were working as apprentices compared to the non-scheduled or the scheduled tribes. One-fifth of the total extrainees were unemployed. The unemployment was more among the scheduled castes and scheduled tribes as compased to non-scheduled groups. All the five extrainees who were reported as self-employed were from the non-scheduled categories (Appendix Table A.3).

In Gujarat, as in Bihar, about half the extrainees were employed, and one-forth were working as apprentices. Unemployment rate in Gujarat was 10 per cent. Here also it was highest for the scheduled tribes and lowest for the non-scheduled categories. Self-employment was about 15 per cent in Gujarat. Two-trainees each from the scheduled castes and the scheduled tribes were reported as self-employed, their number being ten for the non-scheduled extrainees.

In Maharashtra of the extrainees contacted about 70 per cent were apprentices. Nine per cent did not report their activity status. Only 5 of the 81 extrainees were reported as unemployed. As regards self-employed there were only two cases-one from the scheduled and the other from the non-scheduled category.

Reviewing the results from the employment status of the extrainees in the selected states one can say that the first hypothesis regarding the comparative employment status of the scheduled and non-scheduled group was not confirmed by the data at hand. Apprenticeship rates were more or less same for all the three groups. Unemployment rates, however, were higher for scheduled groups as compared to the non-scheduled group. This was inspite of the reservation quota.

As regards the hypothesis of higher self-employment among the non-scheduled groups as compared to the scheduled groups, the same stands confirmed by our data though the sample of self-employed was too small to arrive at any definite conclusion. As pointed out earlier, keeping in view the sample size as well as the procedure of sample selection followed by different project Directors, the results of the present enquiry enable us only to know the direction. These conclusions, therefore, need to be taken cautiously.

Waiting Time for Jobs

There is some waiting time for all categories of jobs because the number of students who complete a particular training is generally greater than the jobs available for them. However, considering the lower enrolment of scheduled groups than their quotas and reservation of jobs for them according to their population proportion, that the waiting time for the scheduled castes and scheduled tribes will be shorter than others.

Data for the waiting time was available for three states—Bihar, Gujarat and Maharashtra. Out of the 226 extrainees in these states only 132 trainees replied to the questions relating to waiting time. From the remaining a majority were apprentices while some were unemployed (Appendix Table A.4).

The data for 132 extrainees indicated that only 54 per cent were able to get a job within less than 9 months while 46 per cent had to wait for more than nine months to get a job. Waiting time was longest for the scheduled tribes trainees. For the non-scheduled grops also it was almost the same as for the scheduled tribes. For scheduled castes it was however, the least. Less than 35 per cent of the scheduled castes extrainees had to wait for more than 9 months as compared to about 50 per cent for the scheduled tribes and the non-scheduled categories.

The waiting time for all categories of trainees in Bihar was very high as for none of the 26 trainees for whom data were available, it was less than nine months. In fact, for more than half of the extrainees, it was more than a year.

In Gujarat, out of 96 extrainees 68 gave information on the waiting time. Of these 54 per cent got job in less than 9 months, while the rest had to wait for more than 9 months. Here waiting time for the scheduled castes was less than that for the scheduled tribes or others. More than 80 per cent of the scheduled castes got the job within first 9 months while only 50 per cent of scheduled tribes and only 48 per cent of the non-scheduled were able to get a job in this period.

In Maharashtra 38 out of 81 trainees replied to the questions relating to waiting time. Two-thirds of the extrainees were able to get a job in less than 9 months. In Maharashtra, as in Gujarat, the waiting time for the scheduled castes was lesser than that for the scheduled tribes or the non-scheduled groups.

In all the three states, the waiting time for a job was somewhat longer for the non-scheduled group, which lends support to our hypothesis that waiting time should be less for the scheduled categories. However, the scheduled tribes did not differ from the non-scheduled groups. This could be either due to low holding power of the scheduled casts because of which, they took the very first job that came to them, or because the reservation quota enabled them to get the job faster than others. The importance of the first factor can be determined from the comparative status of jobs or the comparative emoluments got by the scheduled groups and the non-scheduled groups. Unfortunately no data were available in this regard.

Sector of Employment and Job Tenure

ITI training generally equips a person to work in the manufacturing units either as fulfledged employees or as apprentices in the first instance. These units can either be in the public sectors or in the private sector. There is reservation for the scheduled castes and scheduled tribes in factories and plants both in the public and private sector. However, there is a feeling in the public that private sector employers generally do not adhere to the reservation. Accordingly it was hypothesised that a higher percentage of scheduled groups trainees will be found in public sector as compared to private sector. Further, as more jobs in public sector are likely to be permanent, more of the scheduled group trainees should be in permanent jobs as compared to non-scheduled trainees.

The data for testing the above hypothesis were available for Bihar and Gujarat alone. In Bihar more than half of the employees were in public sector. In contrast, in Gujarat the private sector employed almost 60 per cent of the trainees. In addition, about 19 per cent were self-employed. Public sector employment in Gujarat accounted for only 14 per cent of the total employed. Not a single scheduled castes extrainees was reported working in the public sector undertaking while among the non-scheduled 11 persons were employed in the public sector. Fourteen out of 16 scheduled castes employees and 6 out of 7 scheduled tribes employees in Gujarat were in the private sector.

As regards the job tenure, more than half the extrainees in Bihar were in permanent employment among all the three groups. There was no difference in temporary and casual no employees in the three categories. In Gujarat, 37 per cent of the employees did not report their job tenure. Forty-five per cent of the employees were either in temporary or casual employment. This was in keeping with the sector of employment reported in the two states.

The data regarding sector and tenure of employment were too scanty to arrive at any meaningful conclusion. All that one can say is that there were no marked groupwise differences in these respects.

Emoluments

One of the aims of ITI training is to improve productivity of the workers and their emoluments. It was however, hypothesised that the earnings of the scheduled groups will be lower than others. Data were collected on the income levels of the employed extrainees in five categories and were tabulated separately for the scheduled castes, scheduled tribes and others. (Appendix Table A.5)

In Bihar a little over 50 per cent of the extrainees got monthly emoluments of more than Rs. 500. In fact, none of the extrainee was getting less than Rs. 300 p.m. There were no noticeable differences in the salaries of the scheduled castes, scheduled tribes and others. While among the non-scheduled category, the salary of exactly half the extrainee was above Rs. 500 p.m., amomg the scheduled castes and scheduled tribes also a little over 50 per cent were getting emoluments of more than Rs. 500 p.m. In Gujarat 25 per cent of the ex-trainees did not give information regarding emoluments. From the remaining 64 employees, 24 reported that they were getting a salary of less than Rs. 200 p.m. This was probably due to the fact that the sample included 23 apprentices whose stipend was a maximum of Rs. 200 p.m. Only 10 per cent of the extrainees were getting emoluments exceeding Rs. 500 p.m. while another 9 per cent were getting between Rs. 400-500 p.m. The rest had a salary between Rs. 200 to Rs. 400 p.m. It is noteworthy that while among the scheduled castes and scheduled tribes half their number was drawing a salary of more than Rs. 400 p.m. among others this percentage was just 22.

In Maharashtra, 93 per cent of the respondents got a salary of less than Rs. 200 p.m. while the remaining 7 per cent got a salary of more than Rs. 500 p.m. It may be recalled here that 56 employees in Maharashtra were working as apprentices. Only 13 were reported as employee or self-employed. These figures implied that about half of the employees also got a salary of less than Rs. 200 which was very low by any standards.

Taking an overview of the emoluments pattern for the three states one notices that the one-fifth of the extrainees had an income of more than Rs. 500 p.m. while a little more than 70 per cent were in the income bracket of Rs. 100 to Rs. 399 p.m. This was because, out of 99 extrainees, 79 getting less than Rs. 200 p.m. were working as apprentices. It is worth noting that a higher percentage of the scheduled castes and scheduled tribes extrainees were drawing an income of more than Rs. 500 per month.

Place of Employment

Considering spatial mobility essential for improving the prospects for better job, information was collected on the place of work for the extrainees under three categories *i.e.*,

1. Within the district
2. Outside the district but in the state, and
3. Outside the state.

We had hypothesised that mobility will be less among the scheduled groups extrainees compared to the non-scheduled groups.

The survey data indicated that while 80 per cent of the extrainees from all the categories were employed within the district, the other 20 per cent were employed outside the district but within the state (Appendix Table A.6). There was only marginal difference of two percentage points in this respect among the scheduled castes and scheduled tribes and others. It would however, be futile to generalize on the basis of the limited sample of this project. It is quite possible that in some cases the ITI may be nearer the other district than the farthest place in the same district. Moreover, as noted earlier, many of the extrainees in the ITIs came from nearby districts. Possibly, many of them took a job in their district of origin.

Summary and Conclusion

To examine the effectiveness of the investment on the training provided by the ITIs, information was collected from the extrainees regarding their employment status, sector and tenure of employment, waiting time for the job, emoluments and the extent of job satisfaction. It was decided to select 25 extrainees from each institution 5 belonging to the scheduled castes, 5 to scheduled tribes and 15 to non-scheduled groups from among these who had completed their training over a five year period from 1976-77 to 1980-81. The Project Directors in the selected states, however, could not get complete lists of addresses of the extrainees and, hence, the samples taken by them were largely from more recent cohorts. Moreover, the method of selection of the sample differed from state to state and, sometimes, even from institution to institution. Among the selected extrainees a large proportion happened to be apprentices whose stipend was generally upto Rs. 200 only. In view of these considerations, the findings of this chapter are only tentative.

Keeping in view that there is reservation for the scheduled castes and scheduled tribes in job it was hypothesized that these categories will get jobs faster than others and will be employed in greater proportions. Our data did not sustain either of these hypothesises although the proportions of the scheduled castes who took more than nine months to get a job was somewhat lower than others. According to our expectation, the self-employment among the scheduled castes and the scheduled tribes extrainees was, however, lesser compared to the non-scheduled extrainees.

The data on the sector of employment of the extrainees that is, public sector or private sector, were two scanty to arrive at any meaningful conclusion. Whereas in Bihar, more that half the extrainees were employees in public sector undertakings, in Gujarat, particularly in Ahmedabad, almost three-fifths were employed by private sector. In the latter case, public sector employment was only about 14 per cent.

As indicated earlier, a large number of extrainees contacted for their employment status were apprentices. Although we had hypothesized that the scheduled castes and scheduled tribes extrainees will be getting somewhat lower wages because they have little holding power and would therefore take any job at the first available opportunity, but this did not seem to be true as no such differences were observed from the data relating to Bihar, Gujarat and Maharashtra.

APPENDIX

TABLE A.1

Sample of Extrainees form the Selected States

Selected States	Number approached				Number responded			
	Scheduled Castes	Scheduled Tribes	Others	Total	Scheduled Castes	Scheduled Tribes	Others	Total
1	2	3	4	5	6	7	8	9
Andhra Pradesh	27	16	13	56	14	1	8	23
Bihar	25	12	25	62	17	10	22	49
Gujarat	—	—	—	100	19	9	68	96
Madhya Pradesh	—	—	—	66 (16+50)	—	—	—	—
Maharashtra	—	—	—	125	13	9	59	81
Total	—	—	—	409	63	29	157	249

In Andhra Pradesh 14 trainees (10SC, 1ST, & 3 others) completed the training in 1981.

In Maharashra 40 trainees (7SC, 5ST, & 28 others) completed their training in 1981 and another 27 (3SC, 1ST, 23 others) in 1980.

TABLE A.2

Activity Status of the ITI Extrainees by Social Categories for Selected States

Activity Status	*Scheduled Castes*	*Scheduled Tribes*	*Others*	*Total*
1. Employees	26 (41.27)	8 (27.58)	58 (36.94)	92 (36.95)
2. Self-employed	3 (4.76)	2 (6.90)	16 (10.19)	21 (8.43)
3. Apprentice	26 (41.26)	12 (41.38)	65 (41.40)	103 (41.36)
4. Unemployed	8 (12.70)	6 (20.69)	11 (7.01)	25 (10.04)
5. N.R.	(—)	1 (3.45)	7 (4.46)	8 (3.21)
Total	63	29	157	249

TABLE A.3

Activity Status of Extrainees in Andhra Pradesh, Bihar Gujarat and Maharashtra

	A.P.				*Bihar*			
	S.C.	*S.T.*	*Others*	*Total*	*S.C.*	*S.T.*	*Others*	*Total*
1	*2*	*3*	*4*	*5*	*6*	*7*	*8*	*9*
1. Employed	2	—	5	7	9	5	12	26
2. Self-employee	—	—	—	0	—	—	5	5
3. Apprentice	12	1	3	16	4	1	3	8
4. Unemployed	—	—	—	0	4	4	2	10
5. No Response	—	—	—	0	—	—	—	0
Total	14	1	8	23	17	10	22	49

(Contd.)

TABLE A.3 (*Contd.*)

	Gujarat				*Maharashtra*			
	S.C.	*S.T.*	*Others*	*Total*	*S.C.*	*S.T.*	*Others*	*Total*
1	*10*	*11*	*12*	*13*	*14*	*15*	*16*	*17*
1. Employed	12	3	33	48	3	—	8	11
2. Self-Employee	2	2	10	14	1	—	1	2
3. Apprentice	2	2	19	23	8	8	40	56
4. Unemployed	3	2	5	10	1	—	4	5
5. No response	—	—	1	1	—	1	6	7
Total	19	9	68	96	13	9	59	81

TABLE A.4

Waiting Time for Jobs by States

	A.P.				Bihar			
	S.C.	S.T.	Others	Total	S.C.	S.T.	Others	Total
1	2	3	4	5	6	7	8	9
1. Less than 3 months	—	—	—	—	2	—	4	6
2. 3—6 months	—	—	—	—	2	2	11	15
3. 6—9 months	3	2	4	9	6	2	8	16
4. 9+months	6	3	8	17	2	4	25	31
	8	5	10	23	7	1	20	28
Total	17	10	22	49	19	9	68	96

(*Contd.*)

TABLE A.4 (*Contd.*)

	Gujarat				*Maharashtra*			
	S.C.	*S.T.*	*Others*	*Total*	*S.C.*	*S.T.*	*Others*	*Total*
1	*10*	*11*	*12*	*13*	*14*	*15*	*16*	*17*
1. Less than 3 months	6	2	11	19	8 (27.59)	2 (11.11)	15 (17.65)	25 (18.94)
2. 3—6 months	—	—	4	4	2 (6.90)	2 (11.11)	15 (17.65)	19 (14.39)
3. 6—9 months	—	1	1	2	9 (31.03)	5 (27.77)	13 (15.29)	27 (20.45)
4. 9+months	2	2	9	13	10 (43.48)	9 (50.00)	42 (49.41)	61 (46.21)
	5	4	34	43	20	10	64	94
Total	13	9	59	81	49	28	149	226

TABLE A.5

Emoluments for Extrainees by States

Emoluments	A.P.				Bihar			
Rs.	S.C.	S.T.	Others	Total	S.C.	S.T.	Others	Total
1	2	3	4	5	6	7	8	9
1. 109—199	—	—	—	—	2	1	21	24
2. 200—299	—	—	—	—	4	1	17	22
3. 300—399	2	1	1	4	—	—	—	—
4. 400—499	2	1	5	8	2	1	3	6
5. 500+	5	3	6	14	3	1	8	12
6. N.A.	—	—	—	—	5	3	14	22
Total	9	5	12	26	16	7	63	86

(Contd.)

TABLE A.5 (Contd.)

Emolument	Gujarat				Maharashtra			
Rs.	S.C.	S.T.	Others	Total	S.C.	S.T.	Others	Total
1	10	11	12	13	14	15	16	17
1. 100—199	10	9	56	75	12	10	77	99
2. 200—299	—	—	—	—	4	1	17	22
3. 200—399	—	—	—	—	2	1	1	4
4. 400—499	—	—	—	—	4	2	8	14
5. 500+	3	—	3	6	11	4	17	32
6. N.A.	—	—	—	—	5	3	14	22
Total	13	9	59	81	38	21	134	193

TABLE A.6

Distribution of Employed Extrainees Place of Employment by States

Place of Employment	*A.P.*				*Bihar*			
	S.C.	*S.T.*	*Others*	*Total*	*S.C.*	*S.T.*	*Others*	*Total*
1	*2*	*3*	*4*	*5*	*6*	*7*	*8*	*9*
1. Within District	6	4	6	16	16	7	63	86
2. Outside District	3	1	5	9	—	—	—	—
3. Outside State	—	—	1	1	—	—	—	—
4. No Response	—	—	—	—	—	—	—	—
Total	9	5	12	26	16	7	63	86

(Contd.)

TABLE A.6 (*Contd.*)

Place of	*Gujarat*				*Maharashtra*			
Employment	*S.C.*	*S.T.*	*Others*	*Total*	*S.C.*	*S.T.*	*Others*	*Total*
1	*10*	*11*	*12*	*13*	*14*	*15*	*16*	*17*
1. Within District	10	6	29	45	32	17	98	147
2. Outside District	3	2	21	26	6	3	26	35 (19.12)
3. Outside State	—	—	—	—	—	—	—	1 (0.5)
4. No Response	—	1	9	10	—	1	9	10
Total	13	9	59	81	38	21	134	193

9

Industrialisation and Women

Prof. Arnold Toynbee, the noted historian of the age, has rightly declared that the twentieth century will be recalled in history not for its wars and atom bombs but for having been the first stage, since the dawn of civilization, in which it became practicable to make the benefits of civilization available to the whole human nation. Iadustrialisation, which is roughly a synonym for economic development, is the agency to realise that goal.

In the eighteenth century, when industrialisation started in England, workers protested by destroying machines. In the mid-twentieth century workers and for that matter people do not destroy machines. The protest of today is more in favour of industrialisation than against it. Thus, with the passing of time, people's attitude towards industrialisation has completely changed.

The poeples of the world to-day are everywhere on the march towards industrialisation for it is a means to conquer poverty. Industrialisation refers to the actual course of transition from the traditional society towards industrialism.

Industrialisation may be defined "as a process in which

changes of a series of strategical production functions are taking place." It involves those basic changes that accompany the mechanisation of an enterprise, the building of new industry, the opening of a new market and the exploitation of a new territory. That is, in a way, a process of deepening as well as widening of capital. It is true to say that high productivity produces industrialisation and that industrialisation produces high productivity. Industrialisation is also treated as a process in which the economic gains of industrial progress, mainly in the nature of increasing returns, are continuously created and wholly or partially realised.

Industrialisation may be individual or private initiated, Stateinitiated or jointly initiated (termed as mixed economy). The U.S.A., France and U K. may be grouped in the first type Russia and China in the second and India and Japan come in the third.

The New Approach

The problem of industrialisation and economic growth of the relatively underdeveloped areas has in the recent past attracted the attention of economists. We can distinguish different types of forces which helped to build up a strong theory of industrialisation. To begin with, the adoption of an employment and income approach in the study of the basic problems of underdeveloped economies provided a new stimulus towards industrialisation. Moreover, the industrialised countries are realising that a high level of employment in the poorer countries is essential for the continued prosperity of the world as a whole and for the maintenance of a high and stable level of employment in the developed countries themselves. The second important force which provided a stimulus towards industrialisation all over the underdeveloped world in the 30's (except (USSR, of course,) was the pressure on the balance of payments caused by the depression. 'Most of the underdeveloped countries in Australia, Asia and Latin America and in Eastern Europe—had been heavy borrowers in the past. The depression and the re-agrarianisation of industrial countries which started near about this time, combined to reduce the volume and money value of the export surplus which such countries required to meet their debt charges and the pressure of this situation created a strong stimulus towards industrialisation'. Thirdly, a positive encouragement has been given by the theoretical analysis developed in the last few years in respect of the problems of growth and also by the tools that have been developed for the study of inter-industry relations. Fourthly, the high standard of living enjoyed by the people of the developed world as well as the achievements of socialist countries in attaining a high rate of economic growth have also added to the dcsire for rapid development which is a synonym for industrialisation. 'The main form which the new approach has taken in these countries is a strong advocacy for industrialisation and more generally, for increasing the capital intensity of all production.'

Even if we are satisfied that industrialisation is the goal towards which our efforts should be directed, we have to offer a satisfactory answer to those who believe that in a world of perfect territorial division of labour, the function of agricultural countries would be produce goods in which their comparative efficiency appeared to be the greatest, *i.e.* goods which were labour-intensive and land-intensive rather than capital-intensive. Next, a definite economic answer is necessary in our own interest. It is not possible to pursue an industrial policy on sound lines unless we are clear as to why and for what purpose we really want to industrialise India.

Every country has certain advantages over others. They may be natural or acquired. It is natural for a country to develop along the lines indicated by such advantages. The India has always been an important agricultural country. The fertility of her soil, the variety of climates together with the inherited skill of her farmers made her a first rate agricultural country.

Dr. A. K. Dasgupta has pointed out that the classical theory of international trade is based on static comparative cost conditions ; It does not take account of the possibility of changes in these conditions that a push towards economic development may entail, A country may have comparative advantage in agriculture under given circumstances ; and if these circumstances are allowed to persist, the peculiar comparative advantage also persists, resulting in its continued specialisation in agriculture. But if steps are taken to shift resources from agriculture to industry, certain developments may take place in the country which alter the entire comparative cost configuration. And it often does pay the country to take these steps as transition measures. Therefore, it is not necessary, that a country which has special advantages in agriculture should be totally unfit for manufacturing industries. Manufacture is not the monopoly of one nation. Our country has always made remarkable progress in this direction also since the attainment of independence in 1947.

The Report of the Industrial Commission contains sufficient material to prove the industrial supremacy of India in the days gone by. It was only after the Industrial Revolution in the West that India began to lose her poition and the erroneous idea that tropical countries with their naturally fertile land and trying climate were suited to the production of raw materials rather than to manufactures began to spread. India therefore, possessed at least in those earlier days all that was necessary for a healthy development alone industrial line. Nor is there any reason why what was possible once should be impossible now. Provided that factors of production are sufficiently mobile or labour can be trained and capitul imported, a country can develop almost may industry within certain limits. Given the favourable conitions there is no reason why India should not once more be able to take her place along with other industrial countries of the world.

Relationship Between Agriculture and Industry

In the short run, agricultural development and industrialisation might be conflicting as one sector of the economy grows at the expense of other sectors; in the short-run each sector competes for limited resources against all others, But in the long run the relationship is not competitive but complementary and growth in one sector may not only raise the level of resources available generally but may also more directly promote growth in other sectors, 'In many countries in the past growth and improvement in ariculture have fostered and smoothed the way for the estalishment and growth of industry. The leading industrialised countries of today were once predominantly agicultural and economic historians have traced the various ways in which a prosperous and expanding agriculture formed the basis for the concurrent or subsequent establishment and expansion of manufacturing

Rationalisation agriculture and industrial advance are in reality parts of a single programme. 'One might consider industrialisation as one chapter of agrarian reconstruction or one might treat the improvement of agrarian production as one chapter of industrialisation, what matters is to remember that the two area inter-connected parts of one problem'.

Industrialisation and agricultural improvements are interrelated. Agriculture and industry feed each other. Improvement in the productivity of argiculture is one of the most important means of promoting industrialisation. Agriculture supplies labour, food and raw materials to industrie. Moreover, industrialisation does not begin in vacuum, it begins on the agricultural base. Therefore, agricultural surplus should be used to provide not merely working capital but also to finance the import of capital equipment. The development of agriculture of generates income and creates a growing internal demand for industrial goods. Unless agriculture is modernised, industrial expansion is an underdeveloped country is likely to proceed at a slow speed due to lack of purchasing power in the hands of the majority of population. In return, industry supplies agricultural inputs like means of irrigation, fertilizers, agricultural machinery, etc. which helps the growth of agriculture. Agricultural improvements cannot go far unless there is industrial development to take up the released man-power and to provide a solid technical base for the equipment and services essential for modernised argiculture. The develop-ment of argiculture simultaneously with manfacturing is needed to secure a balance between agriculture and industry. 'Over-rapid and unbalanced growth of the industrial sector, unaccom-panied by complementary changes in the agricultural sector give rise to phenomena which in the long run are likely to retard economic development—balance of payment difficulties, inflation, excessive urbanization and the disruption of accepted social patterns.'

Advocacy of Industrialisation

The argument for industrialisation that held the field for nearly four decades of the present century was mainly drawn from the doctrines of Friedric List; this helped to build up a strong nationalistic theory of industrialisation for bringing the country on a per with the other countries of the world for reducing the dependence on imports, for getting rid of foreign enterprise. During the first world war period there was begin-ing of dim realisation of the real importance of industrialisa-tion. The Montague-Chelmsford Report of 1917 recommend-ed a forward policy of industrialisation, to give India economic stability to satisfy the aspirations of her people to stand before the world as a well-poised, up-to-date country, to provide an outlet for the energies of her youngmen who are otherwise drawn exclusively to government service or to few overstocked professions. Let us sum up more positive arguments in favour of industrialisation.

There is no doubt that industrialisation offers large pro-spects of raising the appalling low standard of living the people. It is agreed that industrialisation is necessary to increase aver-age per capita incomes throughout India. 'With the far higher per capita productivity of labour in industrial and related activities, it is ebvious that a widespread development of factory and non-agricultural industry, which will absorb an increasing and eventually large proportion of the population, is necessary if Indian per capita incomes are to rise. In 1931-32, Prof. V.K.R.V. Rao, found per capita incomes in urban areas three times those in rural areas, in 1951 output per engaged person in the non-agricultural sector was above 150 per cent higher than in the agricultural sector. Colin Clark, W.E. Moore and others contend that 'a declining percentage of agricultural employment means a rising overall per capital income, a rising agricultural output per worker and also an increasing total of agricultural output. There can be strong assumption in favour of the conclusion that any predominantly agricultural occupation-structure is non-optimal'.

In the second place, industrialisation will develop a balanced economy. A more balanced economy providing a larger variety of occupation is to be preferred to an unbalanced one, so that there may be ample scope for the labour and capital of the country to shift from one occupation and trade to another, according to need. It is a wise policy not to put all the eggs in the same basket.

In the third place, it has to be noted that the demand for agricultural products is in general, less elastic than the demand for manufactured articles. When a country produces and is therefore able to offer only those goods the demand for which is not so elastic, it is at a disadvantage in bargaining with another country the production of which is not confined to commodities of such inelastic demand. If we want a larger quantity of cloth from a foreigner we shall have to offer a very much larger quantity of rice to induce him to accept the bargain. For his want of an extra quantity of rice is not so strong as our want for an extra quantity of cloth. The terms of trade are therefore most likely to be unfavourable to an agricultural country.

Fourthly, industrialisation is a means of achieving continuous economic growth. Whether carried on by small but potentially expanding firms or by relatively large organisations, it leads to the creation of an economic surplus in the hands of those firms. With the relatively high marginal propensity to save and invest of these industrial firms; this sector contributes significantly to the eventual achievement of a self-sustaining economic growth with continued high levels of investment and a rapid rate of increase in income and indnstrial employment.

Fifthly, the need for industrialisation of poor countries is felt for producing conditions conductive to change in the population trends. The specific fertility rates are almost always higher among the rural agricultural people than among the urban industrial class. In India the urban fertility rate in 1931 were about 32 per cent below the rural rates. A change in environments can very quickly change the whole attitude towards reproduction.

Sixthly, manufacturing industries which necessitate the use and repair of machines exercies a healthy educative influence on the people. They contribute to a fuller development of a man's personality not only by providing opportunities for the exercise of intellectual qualities, but also by creating in him a greater sense of responsibility towards his work.

Lastly, the development of industries helps the agriculture of the country in several ways, in the long run, by reducing the pressure of population on land and by increasing the purchasing power of the population. Thus, there would be a greater demand for agricultural products, higher prices, more profits and a smaller number of men to share this bigger profit.

The development of a more balanced economy will lead to increase of wealth and welfare in the country. Production will, on the whole, become less risky as manufacturing industries will not have to depend so much on an undependable climate and unemployment will decrease. And there will be a marked decrease in the unemployment among the educated classes as increasing demand for their services will be created by the development of industries. With the increase of wealth in the country, the revenue of the State will also increase. All this will mean an acceleration of the speed with which social and economic reforms can be introduced in a country. There are other non-economic reasons for industrial development—military power, independence from foreign influence and pride.

Basic Strategy of Industrialisation

At the beginning of industrialisation, the pioneering countries in the field produced consumer goods accounting for two-thirds or more of the total industrial output and the remaining one-third was producer goods, but as industrialisation proceeded the ratio between the two sectors was completely reversed. The history of industrialisation of the U.K., France, Germany, U.S.A., Japan and U.S.S.R. shows that producer goods expanded twice as fast as consumer goods in the initial stages of industrialisation and later the gap between the rates of growth of the two sectors narrows down.

Mr. S.P. Patel, emphasises that if the underdeveloped countries can attain an annual increment of 8-10 per cent in their industrial output in the coming 3 to 4 decades, the task of substantially narrowing the gap between the highly industrialised and non-industrialised countries will be realisable.

The countries which have completed Industrial Revolution are now economically and technologically mature and developed. The countries entering the race of industrialisation are looking ahead to catch up with them. Each successive country that has embarked on industrialisation has generally attained a higher rate of growth. To secure a higher rate of growth, governments of underdeveloped countries are organising and financing 'Big Push' programmes. This is necessary to 'take off' their economies within a short possible time.

The demand for rapid rate of industrialisation dictates that heavy industries should be given a priority. Industrial Revolution began with textile because heavy industry is the effect and not the cause of the (English) Industrial Revolution. But once a technological revolution has taken place its fruits are to be enjoyed. This is why the late-comers have invested more in the construction of heavy industries.

Mr. Patel demonstrates that heavy industry everywhere increased 1½ to 2 times as fast a light industry so that its share fell to a point where the initial relationship was totally reversed.

The study of recent growth models reveals that a more rapid growth of producer goods industries than consumer good industries is desirable for the developing nations. This approach should be treated as a purely technical requirement for rapid industrialisation.

Balanced Versus Unbalanced Growth

Almost all nations to-day are development-minded. The less developed countries are in a state of revolt against poverty, disease and ignorance. The developed countries likewise are committed to growth. 'This almost universal quest for forward movement is, in essence, a revolution which has no precedent in history. It is fired by rising aspirations for economic, social and political progress and it is based upon the optimistic conviction that man, in this century of science. can move forward by leaps instead of steps. The slogan of this world-wide revolution is development and like other revolutionary slogans, it has various meanings to different groups,' Ours is an underdeveloped economy and here development means industrialization. As students of economics, we are interested in economic growth because economists tend to equate development with economic growth.

The advocates of balanced growth suggest that in development programmes all sectors of the economy should grow simultaneously so as to keep a proper balance between different sectors. The alternative strategy is called unbalanced growth in which case one sector of the economy will grow faster than another. If capital goods sector grows at a faster rate, there will be a shortage of consumer goods bringing about unbalanced or inflationary growth.

The problem of an underdeveloped country is to make output grow faster than population; otherwise, at a low level of income, any increase in investment brings about a faster increase in population so that per capita income declines. Leibenstein calls this the 'low level equilibrium population trap'. Thus, overpopulation in underdeveloped countries seres asart trap and it becomes difficult for the economy to rise out of this low income trap. A 'minimum critical effort' or a 'big-push' to capital formation becomes imperative to pull the economy out of the trap. Various concepts such as take-off,' 'big-push,' 'great-spurt', 'break-through,' 'critical minimum effort' or 'the great leap forward' suggest that the early phases of growth may be critical and that only a fairly substantial change in the structure of the economy may lead the country from chronic poverty to chronic growth. "Growth should begin with a 'bang' and not with a 'whimper'." Nurkse advocates the theory that a wave of capital investments in different industries is required to break the vicious circie of poverty and to lift the underdeveloped economy out of the trap.

On the other hand, Hirschman advocates unbalanced investment for underdeveloped countries on the ground that these countries cannot afford to invest in too many different industries simultaneously, so that they have to select certain strategic sectors and make huge investments only in those sectors. Then will per capita income be pulled out of the population trap. When leading sectors of the economy achieve a high rate of growth they will sponsor development in other sectors as well.

Problems of Industrialisation

The main problems which a proposed programme of industrialisation raises are:

(i) the extent of the industrialisation,

(ii) the nature of the industries to be established,

(iii) the order of priority for the establishment of the industries if they cannot be established simultaneously,

(iv) the localisation of new industries,

(v) the pace of industrialisation, and

(vi) the relative emphasis on large-scale and small-scale industries.

The Extent and Pace of Industrialisation

The extent and rate of industrialisation would depend on the resources that could be spared from industries producing con-consumer goods and on foreign borrowing, In particular, the output of consumers' goods industries should at first be kept relatively low in order to permit as rapid a development of capital formation as possible. However, the output of consumer goods industries expands fairly quickly with the development of new industries. Consumer goods industries could also be expanded with resources which are not suitable for the development of capital goods industries. The pace of industrialisation cannot be left to be determined by the play of 'natural forces', is might be accelerated by planned Government intervention.

As compared with Europe at the start of the industrial revolution, the Asiatic countries are at a disadvantage in regard to rapid economic development, because of the much higher density of their population and the possibility that the forces which have tended to reduce the growth of population elsewhere will take a longer time to grow. In order to catch up with and outstrip the increase in population and to accelerate the working of forces tending to reduce the rate of its growth, economic development in India would have to be as rapid and as extensive as possible.

Order of Priority

The likelihood of quick returns is obviously an important consideration in determining the order of priority in which industries shauld be developed. It is true that the diversion of resources to capital investment redues the output of consumer goods for a time, but this period differs in duration with different types of investment. It is for the planning authorities in each country to determine in the light of local circumstances, the types of investment to be undertaken at each stage.

The improvement of productivity in agriculture is particularly important, having regard to its place in the economies of under developed countries including India and the fact that the former are the main source of labour supply for new industries. It may therefore well be that judicious investment in the improvement of soil fertility and farm equipment is the type of capital investment which will yield speedy returns. Should this be the case, high priority should be given to the production of fertilisers and farm tools and machinery as well as to the improvement of farm methods in general.

The farmer, however, will have no incentive to increase his output if he cannot be sure of being able to sell it. Improvements in transport and communications to enlarge the market for farm produce are, therefore, an essential part of any programme for the improvement of agriculture, and it is only through adequate and cheap transport that the products of the farms can be brought to consumers at prices within their means, thus helping to raise living stands for the people as a whole.

The development of electric power is also important. In most of the underdeveloped countries including India electric power is not sufficiently developed at the present time. Electricity is of special importance to modern industry and its contribution to the amenities of daily life need not be stressed. It should also be noted that the supply of power wiil influence the location and the nature of the industries to be developed as well as the extent and pace of urbanisation.

Relative Importance of Consumers' and Capital Goods

The arguments in favour of giving the production of capital goods priority over that of consumer's goods are as follows. If the formation of capital is accelerated it will lead to a more rapid rise in incomes inasmuch as the workers can be provided more quickly with larger supplies of the tools of production. As capital is scarce, it is necessary that considerable effort should be devoted to the early and rapid development of the capital goods industries. And as some of the capital has to be borrowed from abroad in the form of machines, the quick formation of capital at home will make a country more rapidly independent of foreign aid.

Relative Importance of Export and Domestic Industries

In general, it can be said that the division of labour should be extended as far as possible because such division leads to a rise in productivity and the standard of living. International extension of the division of labour means that each country tends to produce those goods which it can produce relatively cheaply. The export industries sell in competitive markets in which they enjoy no protection; for that reason alone they tend to be among the most efficient industries in any country. It is often preferable in order to make the best use of national resources, to import some goods and to pay for them by exports rather than to produce them less efficiently at home. To the extent that this is the case, the standard of living can be raised to higher levels by an early and vigorous development of export industries.

Countries in the process of development need a considerable volume of foreign exchange. This is required in part to service their foreign loans and in part to pay for necessary imports of capital equipment not available at home. As the total requirements of foreign exchange are likely to be very great, a substantial volume of exports will have to be maintained. Thus, in any programme of development, export industries should be given an important place.

Relative Importance of Large-scale and Small-scale Industries

The relative importance of large-scale and small-scale industries in a programme of economic development has also to be weighed. If productive efficiency is to be the sole criterion, there seems little doubt that in many types of production, large-scale industries are superior to small-scale industries. They are able to produce at lower costs per unit of output and consequently can afford to sell their products at lower prices and to pay the workers higher wages.

As against these advantages, there are some adverse social and economic consequences which may arise from the development of large-scale industries. The most serious is the risk of unemployment and impoverishment of workers engaged in rural and handicraft industries. The speed with which these workers can be transferred to more productive industries will depend largely on the rapidity of capital accumulation, the volume of modern business enterprise and the mobility of labour. Unless positive measures are taken to facilitate such transfers, establishment of large-scale industries will bring no immediate benefit to the working classes. Secondly, large industries are likely to be concentrated in a limited number of industrial centres. Because of the low mobility of labour, a large part of the labour force required by these industries will probably be drawn from the neighbouring rural areas, rather than from the ranks of handicraft workers who became unemployed in more distant parts of the country. Thirdly, the growth of large-scale indsstries may also lead to the concentration of economic power. Because of the high capital investment involved such industries frequently tend to be more or less monopolistic in character. As a result, the consuming public cannot get its full share in the fruits of economic progress and the gains of monopoly profits may accentuate the inequality in the distribution of income and wealth. Lastly, the rapid introduction of large-scale industries in an underdeveloped country like India may have serious disruptive effects on the traditional modes of living of the people. It will involve profound changes in social insitutions and in the scales of values by which the peoples of these countries have lived for centuties. It is true that the process of economic development is bound to involve a transformation from an agricultural into an industrial culture in these countries. But it is desirable to avoid the overwhelming impact of the sudden cultural change brought about by the introduction on a large-scale of radically different forms of economic organisation. The general welfare of the peaple would scarcely be promoted if economic gains were obtained at the sacrifice of a hermonious and integrated cultural social and emotional life. These considerations led many economists to conclude that 'in the conditions prevailing in many under-developed countries the development of small industry may be the most economic form of industrialisation; it may be more economic than either large-scale organised industry or cottage industry'.

The above mentioned consideration, however, do not suggest that large-scale industry is entirely unsuitable for an under-developed country. On the contray, there are certain industries, particularly the capital goods industries, which for technical and economic reasons, can be developed only on a large-scale basis.

Location of New Industries

The location of new industries is an important question in a plan of economic development. In the case of extractive industries, the location is determined by unalterable natural conditions. In the case of other industries, a considerable dispersion may be one of the objectives of any general plan. The tendency should be for the new industries to develop to a larger extent in the interior. The concentration of industries in a few cities to the neglect of other regions, has led to different standards of living in the country. It is desirable that the benefits of industrialisation are widely distributed all over the country and should not be monopolised by a few cities.

Choice of Technique

When an output can be produced by several alternative techniques, the planners will have to decide upon the most suitable technique. The differences in the techniques mainly arise from differences in the proportions in which inputs are combined to obtain the output. To economise the use of capital, a capital-poor underdeveloped country should concentrate on capital-light investments. Buchanan subscribes to the view that where investment funds are limited, investments having a high value of annual product relative to the outlay should have top priority. But this criterion is not necessarily the correct one for obtaining maximum return from limited investment resources. Capital is scarce in India and as a rule she should specialise in industries requiring a lower capital-labour ratios as compared to capitalrich countries like USA or UK. But it does not necessarily follow that in choosing between several possible lines of investments, those with the lowest capital-labour ratios should always be given the top priority. In most cases substitution of labour for capital would mean substitution of one type of disguised unemployment and inefficiency for another. As Mandelbaum' has observed, the problem of underemployment in one line of production would not be solved by employing labour in another line equally inefficiently. The allocation of investment to labour-intensive industries might be a social desideratum where surplus labour exist and employment regardless of output is the objective. But in the long run and when per capita output has to be looked upon as a criterion of economic development, the general validity of the argument in favour of investment to labour-intensive industries is questionable. Employment without the creation of output is really no employment at all.

From the above discussion it is clear that poor countries should not necessarily shun investments in capital-intensive industries. On grounds of technical superiority of one process of production to another and by reason of the inefficiency of complete substitution of labour for capital, there may be advatage in the heavier rather than in the lighter use of capital. 'Industrialisation typically means the establishment of capital-intensive industries. If the development of heavy industries is essential for building a basis for the economy of the country, they have to be brought into existence.'

Last but not least, the economies of underdeveloped contries have a high inflationary potential. If a rapid rise in the standard of living is to be achieved without generating inflationery pressures, attention should be devoted to the 'quick investment type' industries which have a short fruition lag'. The time-lag between the execution of the investment project and the flow of the consumer goods has to be relatively short, otherwise there will be dangerous inflationary pressures.

10

Women and Modernization

As we begin to unroll the scroll of Indian history, we notice that Indian society compared to other societies, has a very long past. Nearly all other civilizations of the ancient world were unable to stand the onslaught of time. They lie buried in the earth with their ruined cities. Indian civilization continues its existense in spite of vicissitudes.

Not only has India a living past, but in this long process of time people of India have come into contact with varieties of tribes, races, and cultures which lend a peculiar fascination to its study. As might be expected, Indian society did not remain static during this period. In different phases of its existence, it experienced changes in social organization, in social relations between its various component parts and also in ideology. The status of woman as a vital aspect of Indian society, also reflected similar changes.

As it is correctly said, the position of woman in any society is a significant pointer to the level of culture of that society. In our study of the past also we will find that position of woman has been affected by progressive or reactionary trend which prevailed in the society. When the former held ascendency, woman's position mproved, her status elevated, her subjection diminished and her rights extended. However, the study will reveal that on the whole the forces of reaction held sway and the positian of Indian woman increasingly deteriorated during the pre-British period. During this phase, woman sometimes is considered a goddess and at other times a slave but never a human being with a personality

In order to properly grasp the problems of the Indian woman which emerged in the British phase and also to comprehend the tasks confronting the modern woman, it is essential to study her position in ancient Indian society.

Really speaking, our study should begin with the life in times of Mohen-je-Daro and Harappa. But as history is the study of human past from written sources and as the script prevailing in the Indus Valley Civilization still remains undeciphered, we will began with the Vedic period.

Further even though the study of Indian history has attracted the attention of innumerable scholars, unfortunately there is no unanimity among them with regard to the chronology of its various phases. As wc are only interested in studying general trend of the development of woman's status we will not enter into thc controversy.

There is no doubt, however, to accept the continuity of Vedic traditions till the rise of Buddhism. The Dharmasutras reveal the process of change in the life of the Aryans that took place during a long period and Manu Samhita depicts the pattern of life which emerged became more or less fixed and was further conceived as the ideal for the Aryans. The Mahabharata, it must be noted, also indicates this process of change. Other Smruti writers contributed towards idealizing and giving fixity to the pattern. Buddhism, historically emerged as a powerful sacial revolt against the earlier Aryan pattern of society sought to be made immutable and eternal by lawgivers at an earlier stage. But the brave effort of the Buddha had a limited and short lived victory. This temporary progressive phase was followed by the reactionary orthodox traditions described in law books and the Puranas. The genius of Shankaracharya gave a final seal to the orthodox pattern. During this phase the social life though remainlng basically frozen became more and more decadent. There were number of reasons for such phenomenon, one of them being the advent of Islam. However, even in this dark phase also, the Bhaktas, the great humanists who initiated numerous Bhakti movements endeavoured to democratize the social relations including the woman's status but since no fundamental change occurred in the very foundations of social structure their influence too was temporary and limited. Hence the detriorated traditional orthodox attitude towards woman continued till the advent of the British in India.

We will now give a brief picture of the status of woman in different phase of the pre-British period.

The Position of Woman in the Vedic Society

The Vedic society was a patriarchal one, and hence father was the head of the family.[1] All efforts were therefore made to secure the birth of a son. The birth of a daughter was looked upon with disfavour.

Inspite of the attitude of indifference towards the female child and marked partiality for the male child, once born, the daughter was, it is very probable, entitled to all the privileges given to a son. In the matter of education the daughter was not distinguished from the son. No less than twenty women were among the composers of the Rig Vedic hymns. Gargi and Atreyi were the leadiog philpsophers of the times. We also find a class of women known as Brahmavadinis,[3] who continued their studies even for the whole lifetime.

It is to be noted that as the society was just evolving from a primitive stage and stood at the lower level of economic development, the nature and form of property during that period are still not quite clcar. But stray reference to gifts given to wife are made and also to the right of a brotherless daughter to property is established by Yaskacharya in Nirukta.

In the matter of religious life, which was all important and very absorbing aspect of the daily life of the people during this period, we are definitely informed that women actively participated in it. The Sama hymns were chanted by women. If the husband had gone on a journey, the wife was required to perform the sacrifices. Further, there are special sacrifices like Seetayagna, Rudrabali and Rudra yaga which were exclusively performed by women.

As regards the other aspects of woman's life, we are told that she used to move about freely in the public. There are references, in the Vedic texts, of women attending fairs, festivals, and meetings. The great popularity of the institution of "Samanas", an universal festival in which women participated, reveals that women enjoyed freedom of movement with men.

Even in the matter of selecting the partner, she seemed to exercise a good deal of influence. Marriages were entered into when girls were mature and evidently they must have been done with their consent. Evidences of previous courtship are well known. There are also references to marriages which were of gandharva form in which one's choice played an important part..

Moreover, a widow was allowed to contract a second marriage. The Atharvaveda alludes to the already remarried widows who, in consequence of their remarriage, obtained the flattering style of punerbhu—re-born, rejuvenated.

The practice of attaching a widow to a relative with a view to beget a son for the deceased, viz., Niyoga, was also known to the Vedic Aryans. According to S.C. Sarkar, in the Vedic society, Niyoga was not resorted to with the limited objective of getting a son, "but love, progeny and property generally; it is obvious that the main concern in this rite is a normal re-marriage of the widow, who oftener than not must have had borne sons already."

On the whole, in this period, within the framework of the patriarchal society the position of woman was high.

Post-Vedic Society

Regarding the first phase in the post-Vedic society, we cannot adequately describe the whole process of change since Manu Samhita and Mahabharata, the main available reference sources, were not the works of one writer written at one time. They were more or less, the works of a school and spread over centuries. One fact is, however, obvious that the society had already experienced a change in the direction of rigidification.

Manu invests the Brahmins with new privileges. He deprecates the Shudras and women and concedes to them an inferior status. He thus lays down a theoretical basis for the social and legal subordination of women. This theoretical degradation of women got strengthened ideologically whem in the Bhagvad-gita the new path of Bhakti was shown to be the way for liberation to the Vaishya, the Shudra and woman.

Marriage

According to the Hindu sages, there are eight forms of marriage. The first four are "Dharmya", *i.e.*, religiously sanctioned marriages. The idea behind them is the gift of the daughter by the father to a selected person. In other words it means the transfer of his domination over his daughter to that of another person selected and thought worthy of.

In the period of the Epics, Swayamvara form of marriage, *i.e.*, marriage based on free selection of the husband by a woman was popular among the royal families as evidenced in the case of Sita, Draupadi, Damayanti and others. But here the scope of selection was limited by the fact that the girl was married to one of those few invitees who could successfully perform the feat declared as the bait of marriage. Only, it seems, the girl would refuse, as Draupadi refused Karna, any person whom she did not like to participate in the feat. This form was thought appropriate only for the Kshtriya.

The scope of selection was narrowed down not only by giving religious sanction to the marriage but also by reducing the age at which marriage should take place to be a Dharmya marriage.

The lawgivers first emphasised that pre-puberty marriages are the ideal marriages. After establishing that, they fixed the age when the girl is supposed to reach puberty. Thus the age of marriage for the girl very much depended upon what the lawgivers considered the age at puberty. As observed by P.V. Kane, "about the beginning of the Christian era, it did not matter all if a girl was married a few months or a few years after puberty.

Even a rationalist like Kautilya in his Arthashastra interpretes the age of twelve years as that of maturity for the girl. The Manava Code prescribes that the wife should tender implicit obedience to her husband even though he be devoid of virtue, seeks pleasure outside home or beats her. The functions of wife as described by Manu are as follows:

> "Let the (husband employ his wife) in the collection of and expenditure of his wealth, in keeping (everything) clean in (the fulfilment of) religious duties, in the preparation of his food, and in looking after his household utensils."

But her fidelity was not to cease on the death of her husband. Therefore, Manu says, "A virtuous (Sadhvi) wife who after the death of her husband constantly remains chaste, reaches heaven, though she has no son, just like those chaste men."

The Manava Code attributes all wicked things to the widow who remarries and, further, ordains that a person marrying a widow should be excluded from the Shradha ceremony (the most vital ceremony in the life of the Hindus) along with the carrier of dead bodies. This reveals how unbearable the life of a remarried couple must have been. Manu however permits the remarriage of a widow whose marriage has not been consumated. Kautilya is however liberal and permits the remarriage to a childless widow. The widely prevalent practice of the Niyoga of the Vedic times is disapproved by Manu.

The story of Mahabharat is a clear illustration of the custom of levirite. Bhisma's refusal to Satyavati who asked him to beget children is not based on the ground that it is immoral, but because his action would involve the infringement of his vow of celibacy.

Though it is true that Manu Samhita add Arthashastra do not refer to the custom of Sati, three instances of Sati are recorded in Ramayana and one solitary instance in Mahabharata. This does not mean that the practice was widely prevalent; it only signified that in latter stages the trend had started.

While on the one hand woman was thus asked to be loyal to her husband, the latter was allowed to have more than one wife as the very concept of "Anuloma" marriage postulated hypergamy. Man was likewise asked to take another wife after the death of his first wife as he required a partner for the performance of sacrifice.

Only in Kautilya we find that conditions for divorce are mentioned. He however permits it only in the cases where marriages have taken place in the unapproved forms. Even a simple ground of mutual hatred can be the basis for divorce. He allows separation under certain conditions in the approved forms of marriage. Further, if the husband is unable to perform his material duties, the wife can remarry.

Manu on the contrary disfavours divorce. But even he prescribes definite periods of waiting after which perhaps she has freedom of action. He, no doubt, lays down that if the maintenance is provided, such an action is not valid. Jayaswal comments on this clause thus: 'The law was too well established to be ignored altogether. The Manaya therefore gave the law, but with an effective corrolary.

This dual standard of morality thus came into vogue and it paved way for the gradual deterioration of woman's position.

But this time the Hindu sages had formulated the theory of Sanskaras. As defined by Kane, "The Samskaras had been treated frcm very ancient times as necessay for unfolding the latent capacities of man for development and as being the outward symbols or signs of the inner change which would fit human being for corporate life and they also tended to confer a certain status on those who underwent them.

Naturally, when any person or section of the population is barred from the performance, his or her 'position in the society is low, to that extent. In the case of girls, it was laid down that except the marriage, other sanskars were to be performed without the Vedi e Mantras.'

Therefore, except the nuptial ceremony there is no religious life for woman according to Manu. The upanayana ceromony is not permitted in case of girls. This would result in indirectly terminating her education hence, in the elaborate chapter on studentship in Manu Samhita and that on the End of Sciences in Kautilya's Arthashastra there is no reference to girls' education.

The position of woman as regards property rights can be inferred from Manu's attitude in the matter. He says, "A wife, a son and a slave—these three are declared to have no property. The wealth which they earn is (acquired) of him to whom they belong."

Kautilya, however, continues to recognise the prior claim of a brotherless daughter. But Manu gives the daughter only the right of marriage expenses. Even according to Manu also the daughter's son gets greater importance if the son is non-existent.

The wife has only the right over *streedhan* which is defined by Manu as what was given to her before the nuptial fire in bridal procession in token of love and which she has received from brother, mother, father or husband.

The chaste widow can inherent the property of her husband but the remarried widow according to Kautilya keeps it only as the protector of the minors. Manu however debars the unchaste widow from any right to property.

As to the freedom enjoyed by woman in this phase of life, Kautilya does not permit woman to move alone and see spectacles. Manu advocates only domestic duties for her.

Much contradictory evidence is found regarding the degree of freedom enjoyed by woman in the period of the Epic. According to Miss Dharma, Gosha (veil) system was prevalent in the Ramayana period. The minute description of Zannanas (reference to the employment of female servants and such other items) suggests that the tendency among the royal families to keep woman in seclusion must have started during that period. Valmiki remarks that in times of distress, war, swayamwara, sacrificial ceremony and marriage festival, women are permitted to move freely. Indirectly their movement at other times was restricted.

Thus the freedom of movement which women enjoyed during the Vedic period was steadily and increasingly suppressed.

This study of the position of woman may be concluded with a reference to the reflections which the writers of the period made in respect to woman's character. The contradicrory statements about glorifying and condemning women are to be found. However, on the whole, they depreciate them.

Manu observes, "It is the nature of women in this world to

cause the seduction of man, for which reason the wise are never unguarded in the company of a female. A female indeed is able to driven from the right path in this life not a fool, but even a sage and can lead him in subjection to desire or to wrath." No amount of protection is able to save her from destruction because by nature she is heartless and of ficklessness of temper.

To sum up, Manu prepares a mental outlook for the future subordination of women. The steady lowering down of the age of marriage, the prohibition of remarriage and the increasing curtailment of her free life inevitably prepared the commentators to forge rigid chains for her subjection. That is why we have referred to this period as the formative period of women's subordination. The first step was taken; it was left to the writers of the second period to take the second and the last step in that direction. It must have been clear that Kautilya represents a progressive view and often differs with the pattern that was slowly evolving. The second important force which tried to deviate from the pattern was that of Buddhism.

Woman in Buddhist Society

Buddhism rose as a protest against the steadily rigidifying Brahmanism. In the post-Vedic period the dominance of rituals increasingly grew, thereby giving indomitable power to the Brahmins, Buddhism emphasised the superfluity of any intermediary between God and man and further opened the portals of religion to all human beings without any distinction. The sparead of Buddhism, was mainly restricted to the eastern zones of India in the first phase of its advance, but during the first centuries of the Christian era, its influence had considerably extended to other zones of the country also.

Buddhism, is in its essence, a religion of self-culture and self-restraint. One who is able to develop these two qualities, whether man or woman, can have access to Nirvana. Hence if a woman is able to achieve this she also is entitled to attain Nirvana. Thus after a long period, since the dissolution of the

Vedic society, the doors of religion were once again opened to woman and her right to salvation proclaimed. Only six years after the establishment of the Buddhist Order, women were admitted to it.

Though woman, according to Buddhism, can reach the highest state, she is however considered inferior in status to a male Bhikkhu. In spite of this distinction in the status of the Bhikkhu and that of the Bhikkhuni, Buddhism brought great freedom and equality for women in the sphere of religion, till now a closed circle for the elite. Now any woman could enter it. Even the prostitutes were admitted in the Buddhist Order and, therefore. Amrapali decided to join the Order rather than live the life of a courtesan of the whole city.

It is difficult to conjecture the main reasons which prompted women to joint the Order. B.C. Law thinks that it might be either due to the influence of Buddha's Dharma or it might be an easier method to escape the sufferings to which women were condemned in the Hindu society.

As far as lay women were concerned, their lot was also not bad when Buddhism was dominant in India. There are references which show that the birth of a daughter was not regarded a calamity. The education of women was also well looked after. The religious harangues of Sakka and the philosophical discussions of Khema and Dhammadinny reveal what high intellectual capacities women can manifest when given freedom and opportunity for development.

The age of marriage is generally believed to be between sixteen and twenty, The relation of the husband and wife is that of mutual respect though the status of the former is superior. If the unmarried daughter wishes to join the Order, the consent of both parents is necessary. This is a very significant right given to the mother who now gets a privilege to opine on the most vital matter in the life of her daughter. The right of divorce was given under certain conditions.

The presence or sight of a widow was not regarded as inauspicious. Through only one instance of widow remarriage has been recorded, this might be due possibly to the fact that widows used to join the Order and so had no need to remarry.

Summing up, it can be said that in the initial stages when corruption had not crept in the religious world of Buddhism, it worked as a powerful democratic force against the narrow outlook of the Brahmanic culture pattern that was slowly emerging. The right of admission to the religious order generated self confidence among women. "With the growing perception that their life was worth as an end in itself there was liberated a spirit of independence in women and for women."

Position of Woman in the Puranic Hindu Society

In the second period, the pattern got easily stabilised and all attempts were made to make it sacrosanct.

The Puranas were composed, it is believed, for securing the recognition of the Brahmins as the highest caste group carrying with them supreme authority in the pyramid of the Hindu society. The growing influence of Buddhism and Jainism which declared that between God and man there need not be any intermediary and that even a woman could join the religious order and become a nun, threatened the dominant position of the Brahmins in the Hindu society. They, therefore, started the movement "to re-establish the Varnashrama Dharma, the authority of the Vedas and moral rules among women, Shudras and those members of the upper three castes who, being influenced by the faiths other than Brahmanism, disregarded the Vedas and violated the rules of the Varnashrama Dharma." This resulted in the increasing rigidification of the Hindu society. Whatever mobility castes possessed was destroyed and rigidly demarcated castes with unequal rights were established. The position of woman became more aud more servile.

During the period, the Puranic writers contended that the husband is good for the woman and devotion to him is equivalent to man's devotion to God. She would derive the same benefits by worshipping her husband as he derives by worshipping God.

Even if the husband openly lives in a place of disrepute and is suffering from a deadly disease the wife should always look upon him as God and strive her best to please him. This was thus an era of the increasing subjection of woman. This enslavement of her to man was by a brutal irony of life glorified as "Pativrata Dharma." The transition from Kautilya to Puranic phase is very well described by Jayaswal: "It was not the wife of the time of Kautilya who would bring an action for defamation or assault and become a defendant in the court for beating her husband. It was not the wife of the time of Manava who regarded "Mutual fidelity" to be highest duty. It was the wife of Yajnavalkya's age permeated to the core like pickle . . . with the dharma of abject obedience and unnatural tolerance.

The religious life of woman was restricted to the observance of some "vratas" which more or less demanded blind faith from her. It is declared that "Women, Shudras and the mean twice born (Dwij Bandhu") are not entitled to hear the Vedas, it is only for their good that the Puranas have been written."

From about 200 A.D. onward, pre-puberty marriages become quite popular and prevalent. The writers of those days feel that even if an appropriate husband is not available to a girl, she should marry someone or other. By 1000 A.D. she was considered to reaeh the age of puberty when she was only ten years old with the result that girls were married even when they were less old. Brahmapurana even advocates the age of four years as the proper marriageable age for a girl.

P.V. Kane concludes that "the rule that brahmana girls were to be married between 8 to 10 years became general from about sixth or seventh century and continued down to modern times." When a girl is married at such a premature age, there cannot be any choice of a partner by her. Further, as the Puranas lay great stress on Grjhasthashrama, there cannot be any freedom for girls to choose to remain unmarried for the whole life. Society and religion of the period inexorably fixed a single life aim for her *viz.*, a domestic lifelong married existence.

Widow remarriage is prohibited during this period. Youan Chweng, a foreign traveller, records that during that period, in addition to the custom of marrying within the same caste. "A woman never contracts a second marriage." The lawgivers of the pre-Puranic phase at least showed sympathy towards the child widows, for, they permitted them a second marriage. Not only was widow remarriage prohibited during the Puranic period but the horrible practice of Sati was also more and more eulogised as an ideal, as Angiras and Harita did.

In the initial stage, it was recommended as second alternative. But in the latter phases the Kshatriy caste adopted it and turned Sati into a regular institution. The history of the community is crowded with episodes of Jauhar and Sati on a mass scale. Many instances of Sati are recorded in the Puranas also. With the emergence and spread of this custom, anti-climax was reached in the deterioration of the position of woman and her subjection. Where women voluntarily practised Sati, it proved their boundless spirit of self-sacrifice and love for their husbands. Where and in overwhelming cases it was forced on her, it proved the existence of barbarity of the extant Hindu society.

It was only in the matter of property rights that women were given some concessions which were really important.

As we saw, Manu developed the concept of Stridhana. According to Yajnavalkya along with the gifts from parents, brothers and husband, "presents to her on her husband's marriage to another wife and the rest (adya) is denominated Stridhana." The word *adya* led to quite a different interpretation at the hands of the commentators which led to the widening of the scope of Stridhana. Further Yajnavalkya gives her wide power over the Sridhana except when the husband utilizes it in the time of distress.

As for the rights in other kinds of property, Yajnavalkya and Vishnu are the first to recognize wife as the foremost heir if the person had no sons, though only the chaste widow is allowed to inherit. If the wife is deprived of her Stridhana, she gets a share equal to that of a son, according to Yajnavalkya.

The daughter comes fifth in the scheme of inheritance. She inherits the property in the absence of the mother.

To sum up, the position of woman before the advent of the Muslims, became worse. Child marriage became rampant, girls' education tended to be absolutely nil and the previous practice of widow remarriage declined, Further the custom of Sati increasingly became prevalent. The purdah system restricting woman to a secluded apartment in the residential premises came in vogue among the ruling and upper strata of society. Polygyny also spread among these strata.

Position of Woman in the Post-Puranic Phase

The invasion of the country by the Muslims brought about further deterioration of the position of woman. Restrictions on her rights and freedom and her resultant hardships were aggravated. One the one hand, the foreign Muslims conquerors attempted to impose their coercive norms on the conquered Hindu population; on the other hand, the Hindu society itself became more and more rigid curtailing thereby the rights and freedom of the lower castes and women. Due to this two-fold reason, the post-Puranic period—the third phase of development—is one of the darkest periods for woman in Indian history. The steady deterioration of her status continued till the 19th century.

Polygyny and the purdah were two of the most important social institutions of the Muslim conquerors of India. Under the purdah system, not only were women required to live in a secluded apartment in the house but also they had to dress in an apparel which completely covered their body excepting the eyes.

Most of the foreign travellers referred to the absence of the practice of the widow remarriage in the Hindu society. The widow was either burnt or lived the life complete self-denial. Before the Muslim conquest, the Brahmins had not followed the custom of Sati, but after it, instances of Brahmin women who practised Sati are also recorded. In the 15th century and after, the fereign chroniclers record, the Hindu widows who did not observe Sati were held in great dishonour. The practice of Sati was also extended to the southern parts of India.

The spectacle of the living widow consuming her body in fire was so gruesome that Ibn Batuta actually fainted when he witnessed one such instance. The widow in the case was persuaded to believe that her act of self-immolation was even more auspicious than the nuptial ceremony since it guaranteed the continual association with her husband in life after death.

As a stricter security measure, the prohibition of free movement of woman was advocated and the purdah with its elaborate form was also installed. Women participating in public discussions on vital social or philosophical problems or in popular festivals became only a memory of the past. Along with child marriage marital infidelity on the part of males became more common. Polygyny was a practice adopted frequently among upper classes and restrictions on or conditions laid down as necessary for the second marriage were also dropped.

Even during this darkest period when the black could of social reaction completely submerged the freedom of woman, a silver lining was visible. Some of the Mogul emperors through social reforms tried to relieve the hardships of women.

For, instance, as regards Sati, Akbar did not permit it in cases where there was the slightest disinclination on the part of the widow or when a young widow's marriage was not consummated.

Also some commentators attempted to improve the position of women. They strove to give a definite share of property to women. However in the total setting of complete subordination these meagre rights hardly brought any benefits to women.

During this period two schools of law emerged *viz.* Mitakshara and Dayabhaga, the exponents of these schools being Vignaneshwara and Jimutavahana respectively.

Stridhana, according to Mitakshara law, is "That which was given by the father, by the mother, by the husband or by a brother; and that which was presented by the maternal uncles and the rest at the time of wedding before the nuptial fire; and a gift on a second marriage or gratuity on account of supercession (and as indicated) by the word "adya" (and the rest); property obtained by (i) inheritance (ii) purchase (iii) partition (iv) seizure (v) finding. All this is Stridhana according to Manu and others. Thus he interprets the word "adya" of Yajnavalkya in a liberal manner and thus includes all property acquired in a legitimate manner by women. But Mitakshara law gives limited power over the Stridhana and further distinctions are also made between Saudayika and other property and hence his wide interpretation ultimately, as Jolly describes "is neutralised by her want of independence.

Jimutvahana, on the other hand, considers, "Stridhana is that property of a woman which she may give, sell or use independently of her husband's control.

As regards the other property rights, Mitakshara School gives right to the wife in separate property. She comes after the great grandson, the prior claimants being grandson and son while in the Dayabhaga the widow's right is recognized in the joint family property also. Of course, it is true that what the window inherits is technically known as "Widow's estate" *i.e.*, she has only limited power of the use of the property and further after her death it devolves to the next heir from whom inherited.

The daughter comes fifth according to both the schools. But the difference between the schools lies in the fact as to what kinds of daughters inherit. According to Mitakshara "first let the unmarried daughters take the paternal property; in their default the married daughters, amongst those also first the udprovided (poor) ones and on failure from the provided (wealthy) ones; all in the same predicament, however, take the property and divide it equally.

In the Dayabhaga scheme, after the unmarried daughter, all those married daughters who actually have or are likely to have male issue are given the property. As Jolly observes, "Barren daughters and those who have only brought forth female children do not inherit at all.

Thus a definite pattern of inheritance of property emerged during this phase which to some extent benefitted women.

The Hindus did not assimilate the customs like divorce, widow remarriage and a larger share of property for women, which governed the Muslim society. The Hindu society had become so static and rigidified that their contact with the Muslims, whose social relations were relatively democratic, did not prompt them to adopt the democratic elements of the Muslim society. The Hindu society continued its old pattern of life based on the principles and directives of Manu.

Resume

As we survey the history of pre-British Indian society we find that though it experienced periodic modifications it always retained certain fundamental characteristics. These persisted throughout its long period of existence commencing with the Vedic phase. We will now refer to these constant features.

The Indian society throughout this period remained a patriarchal society, with father at the helm of all domestic and social affairs. Within the family, the authority of the father was sacrosanct. Also the family being patriarchal woman's position was inferior. As time elapsed her position more and more deteriorated. This deterioration was reflected in the steady depreciation of what rights she possessed in the Vedic period in educational, social, religious and economic spheres. The Vedic society as we saw gave maximum freedom to woman at home and in society, though within the matrix of her basic subordination. After the Vedic phase ended, ccrtain tendencies making for the deterioration of women's position emerged and became more and more aggravated. Greater significance was being attached to the male child which finally resulted in polygyny and ill-assorted marriages. The child marriage also became a normal phenomenon. Further there took place an increasing curtailment of her religious privileges as evidenced by the conception of Sanskaras. Her freedom of movement bacame more and more restricted till in course of time she even lived for the most part in a secluded apartment at home and in purdah, hardly stirring out of the domestic premises.

Not only were direct conscious attempts made to keep women in an increasing subordinate position but also definite customs emerged during this epoch which further accentuated her subjection and robbed her of her freedom.

The rigid caste system with endogamy as its fundamental feature, the practice of Niyoga which treated women mainly as mere begetter of male children, the growing significance of the Shraddha ceremony signifying the importance of the male child, the denial of education through the exclusion of religious rites like UPANAYANA, the double stand and of morality which not only pardoned the lapses of the male but sometimes even approved of them, severely penalising the woman for even the slightest deviation from the legal and moral norms, the ideal of 'pativrata' which demanded one-sided fidelity and marital love and duty from the woman without imposing a counter-obligation on the part of the male, the sinister custom of deforming the widow through such compulsions as the removing of her hair and others so that she would look drab if not hideous and therefore not prove attractive to man, the branding of the mere presence of the widow as inauspicious, relegating her to the humiliating position of an unpaid lifelong domestic servant, socially shunned as a sight of ill-omen and excluded from all festivities and functions—all these contributed to the increasing subjection of the Indian women. With the emergence of the most inhuman custom of sati which forced a widow to ascend the pyre of her deceased husband and consume herself in fire, the oppression of the Indian women reached its climax.

All these forms of woman's subjection and oppression as we saw did not develop simultaneously but in course of the downward march of Indian society. As they emerged historically they were systematised by ideologues of social reaction into a visible body of principles which could not be infringed {and the observance of which was enforced by religious and secular sanctions.

Buddhism endeavoured to improve the position of woman by providing her with another alternative of life. But it itself subsequently deteriorated losing slowly its democratic features. This was inevitable since in absence of a fundamental change in the society (in its very foundations) such democratic socio-religious movements as Buddhism could only be short lived.

The Law-givers also sometimes in their own way made efforts to secure for women some part of inheritance but since the demand for such concession was not made in the name of any democratic principle, that of equality of man and woman, it could hardly yield stable and solid result, much less could result in any elevation of the general status and position of woman.

One more heroic effort to remove or at least substantially reduce the oppressive character of the Indian society and thereby also free the Indian woman from her subjection was made by the medieval saints. This attempt too proved futile in absence of any simultaneous fundamental change in the social structure. We have devoted a special chapter to study the various Bhakti movements (religious in form and democratic in content) started by the saints, assess their achievements, and analyse the reasons of their failure.

Dr. D.P. Mukerjee rightly describes such movements as mirror revolutions. For a fundamental change in the status of woman such patchwork was of no use. A basic transformation of economic and social relations was vital. This background was supplied by the British conquest.

Basic Problems on the Eve of British Rule

When the Indians came in vital contact with the British in the latter half of the eighteenth century, the position of the Indian woman had reached the maximum degree of deterioration. Ideologically woman was considered a completely inferior species, inferior to the male, having no significance, no personality; socially she was kept in a state of utter subjection, denied any right, suppressed and oppressed. She was further branded as basically lacking an ethical fibre.

The patriarchal joint family, the customs of polygyny and its concomitant koolinism, the purdah, the property structure, early marriage, self immolation of widows (sati) or a state of permanent widowhood, all these contributed to the smothering of the free development of woman.

Thus not only social institutions and customs thwarted the free growth of her personality, but the prevailing ideology also assigned the Indian woman an inferior status. She was denied independent personality. Her life, as Manu says, was to be associated with and subordinated to either the father, the husband or the son. In fact she had no personality of her own. She had no dreams of her own. She had no separate status as a member of the family or society. Her existence was taken for granted. Her opinion, her desires, her likes or dislikes were never to be considered. In short, the prevailing conception of woman, whether Hindu or Muslim, was basically feudal in character.

This leads us to the third side of the picture, *viz.*, moral. As regards her moral nature, woman was considered as a temptress, a being whose sole aim is to divert man from the right path. The daughter is considered by the father as a burden to be disposed off as quickly as possible through her marriage. For her husband she is an object for having male children.

She is further regarded unfit for participation in social, political or religious functions of any significance. She is not even worthy of receiving education.

We can conclude from this that she was virtually considered as a nonentity—a slave. Further in order that she may not rise in revolt against these customs, an institutional framework and an ideology were created, keeping her docile and in permanent subjection. As a result of this, the Indian woman on the eve of the British rule had not only lost her independence but her sense and urge for freedom and consciousness of independent personality. As Pandita Ramabai describes her position at that time, "She is forbidden to read the sacred scriptures. She has no right to pronounce a single syllable out of them. To appeal to her uncultivated low kind of desire by giving her ornaments, to adorn her person and by giving her dainty food together with an occasional bow which costs nothing are the highest honours to which a Hindu woman is entitled."

Naturally, in the midst of such a situation their only vocation was "to minister to men's physical pleasures and wants; they are considered incapable of developing any of those higher mental qualities which would make them more worthy of consideration and also more capable of playing an useful part in life."

In order to eliminate all the obstacles in form of the extant institutional complex as well as the prevailing ideology to the achievement of freedom for woman, a fundamental change in the very social structure was necessary. The feudal society based on the self-sufficient village economy, the caste and the joint family and authoritarian ideology was absolutely incapable for providing room for the liberation of woman within its framework. A new society based on new socio-economic relations and a new liberal democratic ideology was necessary for making woman conscious of her subjection, for realization of her real role in society, for the growth of woman's freedom movement in all spheres of life as also for a great advance in the direction of her complete freedom.

The British conquest of India resulted in the emergence of such an environment and ideology. Before surveying the impact of the British rule on the position of the Indian woman we will briefly review the role of the Bhakti movement in elevating her status in pre-British India.

11

Bhakti Movement and Indian Woman

The Hindu society as stated before was being steadily rigidified under the supremacy of the Brahmins. The first invasion of India by the Muslims took place during the period in which Shankaracharya lived, *viz.*, in the eighth century. The Hindu society with Shankaracharya as its great religious leader was evolving a technique of defence against the rapidly expanding Buddhism. To counteract the spread of the latter, Shankaracharya re-emphasized the supremacy of the Vedas and extolled Varnashram Dharma which implied the perpetuation of the social oppression of lower castes of the Hindu society as well as women whom traditional Hindu religion considered inferior to men. As we have seen, during the Puranic period women occupied a low status in society and it was believed that she could realize herself only through her husband.

India experienced a second Muslim invasion in the eleventh century when the Muslim hordes led by Muhhamad of Gazni swept over parts of India. It was during this period that Ramanujacharya, who funded the Bhakti cult and organized the first Bhakti Movement in India, lived.

The rigidification of the Hindu society was accentuated due

to the proselytising zeal of the Muslim invaders. Such rigidification could however only deepen the social oppression of the lower castes within the Hindu society. Since Islam promised social equality, the Hindu society was threatened with the danger of large scale desertion of downtrodden Hindu masses to Islam. The only means to effectively combat this danger was therefore a movement which would more or less democratiz the Hindu society, strike at the spiritual power of the Brahmins and declare and struggle for realizing the principle of human equality within the fold of the Hindu society. Such a liberal movement would soften social oppression and would arrest the tide of any mass conversion of depressed class Hindus to Islam.

Efforts were being made to bring about changes in traditional pattern to bring it in conformity with the contemporary ideas, both by orthodox as well as liberal sections. The former tried to give new life to the religious texts by learned commentories on the Vedas, and by introducing new laws by giving new interpretation to the old texts. As mentioned before, Shankaracharya also tried to awaken people by means of knowledge. In fact all efforts to save Hindu Society from destruction were attempted. "But", as Kshiti Mohan Sen describes. "The general mass of people were not much affected by these measures which were meant only for the learned."

The latter-liberals represented by the saints tried to slacken the rigidities and appealed to the mass of people. The Bhakti Movement was an attempt to introduce new trends in social life. Though it could not prevent Muslim expansion in the political field, it contributed to the saving of Hinduism and Hindu society.

The Bhakti Movement spread on an all-India scale. The exposition of Saguna Bhakti on scholastic lines by Ramanujacharya, was attracting the masses to this school. In Gujarat, Swami Madhavacharya was drawing many people towards the Dualistic Vaishnava cult. In the eastern part of the country, Jayadevji along with Cuckoo poet (Vidyapati) of Mithila throbbed the hearts of people with devotional love songs of Krishna. In Northern and Central India, Swami Ramanandji, (about 15th Century, A.D.) one of the followers of Ramanuj tradition, popularized the worship of Rama, who was considered as one of the incarnation of God Visihnu. On the other side, Swami Vallabhacharyaji spread among the people the worship of Krishna.

Numerous Movements of this type subsequently sprang up under the leadership of great religious teachers like Ramanuja, Madhva, Nimbarka and Chaitanya and also saint like Ramananda, Kabir, Nanak, Tulsi, Mira, Narsingh, Gnandeva, Namdeva, Tukaram and Ramdas. The Bhakti Movements led by the Saints exercised powerful influence over lower castes and women.

The striking feature of the movement is its deep humanism. Almost all saints preached against the rigidities of the caste system and against the social supremacy and religio-cultural monopoly of the Brahmin caste.

"Caste does not matter," says Tuka, "it is God's name that matters"

"According to Ramananda and bhakta taking shelter in God merges his previous identity in Him. Hence he is no longer different from his brother bhakta who might have come from a so-called higher caste."

Says, Kabir, "The Barber has sought God, the Washer-women and the Carpenter. Hindus and Muslims alike have achieved that End, where remains no mark of distinction."

The Bhaktas proclaimed that God could be worshipped not only through "Gnana" and "Karma" but also through "Bhakti". They maintained that one who was a devotee of God could get salvation through worshipping God directly. Unity with God could be achieved without the help of knowledge which was the monopoly of the Brahmins only. There was no need of any intermediary between God and the Worshipper nor the need of any rituals for attaining salvation. Such a view advanced by the Bhaktas led to significant progressive social consequences. Therein lies the progressive role of the Bhaktas and the Bhakti Movement. While describing the role of Maharashtra saints in shaping the culture of the people, Justice M.G. Ranade refers to some of their striking features. As most of these features are common to all Bhaktas, we shall briefly discuss them, here.

Leaders Spring from Various Castes

While religious teachers like Ramanuja, Vallabha, Gnanadeva, Eknath, Tulsidas and others sprang from the higher castes, many others belonged to the lowest classes as can be seen from the instances of Kabir, Raidas, Akho, Namdeva and others; they sprang from castes like weavers, cobblers, goldsmiths, and tailors respectively. Moreover the movements started by the latter wielded great influence over lower castes as well as women. Mirabai, Muktabai, a sister of Gnanadeva, Janabai, a maid-servant, Kanhopatra a dancing girl, two daughters of Dadu and two women relatives of Charandas are prominent women Bhakta leaders.

Saints Addressed Their Humanist Message to All

They preached their equalitarian ideas to all people irrespective of distinctions of caste, class or sex. Herein lies the democratic character of the movement. They for the first time opened the gates of their religious cult to all. As Prof. Patwardhan describes, "The gates of the Bhakti school were ever open . . . . Before Vithoba or Dattatraya or Naganath all were equal. Age and sex, caste and classes, breathed not in this equalising atmosphere." Thus Ramanand had two women followers; Kabir and Dadu preached their gospel to all classes, even to women. Narsingh Mehta visited the abode of untouchables even when reprimanded by the higher caste gentry.

Chaitanya also voiced the same feeling when he exhorted his two pupils whom he sent to Bengal to "teach the lesson of faith in Krishna to all men down to the Chandals and freely preach the lesson of devotion and love." Chaitanya and Eknath elevated prostitutes while Malopant did not discard his Mahar wife whom he only subsequently discovered to be belonging to the Mahar caste.

The well known book entitled "Base Bavan Vaishnavani Varta (The story of two hundred and fifty two Vaiŝhnavas) includes the tales of women bhaktas also. These women devotees sprang from the highest to the lowest strata of society. Among them there were Queens belonging to illustrious dynasties, women springing from labouring strata and even ex-prostitutes.

No Need of Ceremonials

The Bhaktas did not consider the living intermediary in the shape of a holy Brahmin or the inanimate intermediary in the shape of rites and ceremonies between man and God necessary for attaining salvation. They were the zealous exponents of the view that salvation could be achieved through Bhakti. Bhakti implies a pure, deep and sincere love for God, and therefore, there is neither any need of ceremonies nor of a priestly class for uniting man with God. They attacked the view that the Brahmins were a special creation of God whom the other castes should serve and worship.

Ramanand has said "Why do you any longer call me to go to the temples? Him, Omnipresent and All-pervading, I have met in the very temple of my heart."

Pilgrimages and observances of vows are vain according to Dadu and Namdeva.

The Bhaktas stressed the teaching of Moksha or Salvation from re-birth as the highest goal of man and therefore declared that every man and woman had the inalienable right to strive for it through deepest love for God. Regarding this right the saints eliminated the distinctions between the Hindus and the

Muslims. The right was a human right as D.P. Mukerji remarks, "Temples had no sanctity for them, the heart was the temple, and its keys were love and intuition. . . . Priest craft was sought to be avoided; it could have no place in a scheme of direct contact, unison and intuitive comprehension" Narsingh Mehta and Akho Bhagat exposed the futility of ceremonies, and referred to the vain attempt to reach God through rituals and pilgrimages.

The Saints also held the view that the householder's life was no impediment barring approach to God. Therefore, we find that most of these saints were living married lives and performed their daily secular duties.

Gave Impetus to Vernaculars

The saints did a yeomen's service to the development of vernaculars by preaching the gospel of Bhakti to the people in their own language. They knew that, as books on religion were written in Sanskrit, and as women and Shudras were not permitted to learn that sacred language, the latter sections of society were debarred from a direct access to religious knowlegde. Thus the saints struck at the monopoly of religious knowledge of the higher castes and brought the treasures of knowledge within the access of the common people as well as women through a vernacular literature which they themselves created. Thus a new era begins in literature also. K.M. Munshi depicts the amazing emergence of the vernacular literature manifested on all India scale thus; "Chandidas and Vidyapati in Bengal, Narsingh and Bhalan in Gujarat, Namdev and Tukaram in Maharashtra and Kabir, Surdas and Tulsidas in North India, inaugurated a new literary epoch. A new pattern of culture began to emerge in each one of these region."

Kabir once remarked that Sanskrit was like the water of wells, Bhasha was like a running brook Prof. Patwardhan describes the whole movement thus; "The partisans of Sanskrit were still very powerful and contempt for Marathi was still rank and rampant. But it was not for name and fame among the Pandits that Eknath wrote: It was for the diffusion of truth and light among the illiterates, among women, and Shudras that Eknath wrote."

Due to the conscious effort of the saints to write and sing in the language of the people, and resultant emergence of great vernacular literatures, religiophilosoyhical, and sociological teachings which constituted Indian culture, became accessible to common Indian people.

The Sakhis of Kabir, the Chopai of Tulsi, the Kirtan of Chaitanya, the morning songs of Narsingh the Abhanga of Gnanadeva and Tukaram and Bhajans of Mirabai and Surdas represent a precious literature of the Indian people. Thus religious and philosophical culture become accessible to down-trodden classes of the Indian society as well as to Indian woman, a culture which till then was the monopoly of Sanskrit knowing Pandits. Hence M.G. Ranade remarks. 'The Professors of the Sanskrit learning found for the first time, to their great surprise that the saints and prophets addressed the people in this own vernacular and boldly opened the hitherto hidden treasures to all and sundry, men and women, Brahmins and Shudras alike."

Bhakti Movement and Women

We have seen that the Bhaktas, in the field of religion stood for the right of women to religious worship. One, however, feels that their total conception of women's status was not quite free from the admixture of the then prevailing attitude to womanhood. It is true that they endorsed Grihasthashrama. However, many of them often declared that woman was a great obstruction in the way of achieving final beatitude. For instance, Eknath said "An aspirant must therefore keep himseif aloof from the influence of woman." Tukaram also expressed the same view when he declared "give me not the company of women.. for by them I forget God's worship and my mind goes beyond my control." Though such an evaluation of the role of woman is not made in the case of one's wife, even regarding her, saint Eknath remarked, "One should call and talk and speak to her only as much as is necessary. But we should never allow mind to be filled with the idea of even our own wife." It is said about Chaitanya that he refused to see the face of a man of his sect if he was habituated to talk with women. This is, inspite of the fact that he admitted women to his own sect. Shyamsunderdas, while editing the poems of Kabir wrote that the saints looked down upon women from a different angle. Their conception of women relates only to the sex-aspect of both man and woman.

Barthwal also describes the same feature as follows: "Women alone are a race injured by these saints. With a view to evoke detachment, which the Nirgunis also followed; Kabir calls the woman a hellish well. Palatu would not believe even a woman of eighty years.... It is a pity that they should have seen only the sex in women, and shut their eyes to her spiritual significance which they seemed quite near realizing when they conceived of themselves as wives of the eternal lover. No doubt they must have decried only the sex aspect in woman but the sex in her is not the whole of woman. They bore no ill-will to womsn as a person, for according to them, like man she is also a creature of God."

In short, the attitude of the saints towards woman as a personality was not at all different from the prevailing one, which might perhaps be due to the fact that they considered Moksha as the basic objective of life and called on men to eschew whatever obstructed the attainment of that objective. Inspite of this limitation the new opportunities gave a different purpose to the life of woman.

Unlocked the Gate of Religion to Women

With the method of approaching God through Bhakti, women also could worship God and attain Moksha. Such a right conceded to women made it possible for them to achieve freedom from the torment of rebirth, the cardinal conception of Hindu religious philosophy. The Smruti and Puranic ideal contemplated that they could secure Moksha only if they, as subservient wives (Pativrata), obeyed and ideally served their husbands. Now in contrast to this even a prostitute or a deserted woman could attain salvation through pure devotion to God. Thus equality of man and women in the religious field was once again re-asserted due to the rise of the Bhakti Movement.

Women Saints

It was only because of the crusade of the Bhaktas to secure this right of freedom of direct worship of God and thereby attain salvation for women, that a galaxy of women saints appeared in the Hindu social world, during the phase of the Bhakti movement. In every province of India, women saints leading a life of deep devotion to God emerged. Incidentally, these very women saints were great women poets which India produced in her history. During this period of the dominance of the Bhakti movement women, married and unmarried, beautiful as well as ugly, Hindu as well as Muslim, all women in fact, secured the opportunity to propitate the deity, and express their boundless love to God in literary creation. Mira, who refused to live a married family life, could not have been the leader of a religious mass movement but for the environs and freedom created for women, by the Bhakti movement. Same is true for other women saints like Jani and Muktabai, Ksema and Gangubhai.

Social Freedom and Uplift of Women

Since the saints stood and struggled for equal rights of man and woman in the religious sphere as an outcome of it women secured certain social freedom also. Amardas, a third prominent follower of Nanak, abolished the practice of purdah among his disciples. As "Kathas" and "Kirtans" were methods adopted by the Bhaktas to propagate their message, women also attended and participated in them. The Kirtans of Chaitanya were organized from street to stseet and attracted the mass of men, women and children who participated in them. This contributed to the demolishing of caste and sex barriers as also freed women from the circumscribed domestic life. As previously stated, the saints did not ask the people to renounce family life hence their movement bringing new freedom to women only increased the importance of women. In fact, the saints valued highly "Grihasthashrama". One striking feature of the Bhakti Movement was that no saint was permitted to take Sanyasta without the consent of his wife. This implied giving a very important right to woman. Gnanadeva's father, because of this, had to return to the wordly life which the had renounced without the wife's consent. Besides, this, if the wife after giving her consent expressed desire to accompany the husband in his new life, she had a right to do so. The necessity of such a consent from wife as well as the necessity to permit her to accompany him if she so desired is a further proof of the religious equality stressed by the Bhaktas. The Puranic emphasis on "Grihasthashrama" as the most significant stage for woman was also considerably modified by this new emphasis by Bhaktas. Further, it also implied that women had the right to co-operate not only in the mundane life but also in the struggle to attain "Moksha". When Pipa refused his queens to accompany him "Ramananda however interposed and said that Pipa had no right to refuse them permission to accompany him if the queens were ready to renounce their royal splendour and to follow him in ordinary life. The younger queen did accompany him.

Since the time of Manu, women were increasingly being debarred from the right to any education. But as the saints used the vernacular, the language of the people, as the medium of spreading their teachings amongst the common people, and even produced enormous literature in vernaculars, the Indian culture became accessible to women also. The sect of Ramanuja is known as Shri Sampradaya and the chief deity it worships is Narayan with Lakshmi, Nimbarka, the originator of Dwaitadwait" philosoby, introduced the worship of Krishna and Radha. Madhavacharya also extolled the worship of Vishnu and Lakshmi, Chaitanya and Vallabhacharya preached in an extensive pare of India a deeply emotional worship of

Krishna and Radha. The feminine counter-part of the deity indirectly helped elevate the status of women.

Evaluation of Their Role

These are the main achievements of the Bhaktas in the field of improvement of the status of women. They gave a new life to women. They provided women with a literature they could read. The Bhakti Movement raised the status of women, especially in the religious field.

One problem arises. *viz.*, how it was that, inspite of the great democratic Bhakti Movement which swept all over India during pre-British period and which attacked the caste system and elevated the position of women, India's social life as well as status of women at the time of British advent, stood on a low level?

A number of thinkers have attempted to discover the cause of the retrogression. One thinker explains the degeneration by stating that the Indian society by that time had exhausted all its creative power and hence the advance achieved by the Bhakti Movement did not last long. He remarks that while the Bhakti Movement successfully introduced democracy and equality in the religious field, the society was too rigidly stratified to be liberalized. Hence the efforts of the saints could not create a new spirit to oppose all obstacles.

D.P. Mukerji holds the view that since there was no fundamental change in the economic structure of Indian society, any attempt to change society radically were bound to fail. The social structure continued to remain on self-sufficient village economy. If was not possible to destroy caste completely until this economic basis of caste was undermined by such a force as Industrial Revolution. Hence he remarks. "The mystic revolution, in the absence of a fundamental change of the Indian social economy, was bound to be a mirror-revolution." He also remarks further, "So within the social system of their work they were active revolutionaries but not dynamic ones.

They had to wait for Western commerce and capital for more substantial changes."[25]

The programme of the Bhakti Movement had primarily religio-reformist content. It basically struggled to establish democracy in the religious sphere. It did not advance a critique from the democratic standpoint of the foundations of Indian society, of its basic institutions like family, property relations and others. Even its attack on the undemocratic caste system was motivated by the urge, viz., that of freedom to worship God and strive for Moksha for all irrespective of caste and creed distinctions. The socio-reformist programme subserved a religious objective.

Secondly, inspite of their profound love for mankind, they had, however, no alternative programme of social and economic re-organization of Indian society. When they declared that the caste system should be removed they had only a vague conception of social equality. They lacked any theory of society and social development. They did not expound that society should be based on the principle of functional division and not on a social hierarchy. Hence Tukaram and Ramdas, subsequently, said that if the Brahmins discharged their function properly, they should be restored to their superior status. In fact their appeal was emotional rather than rational. They felt the unreality of caste and they appealed to the people for equality in their emotional songs, but they could not argue it out on rational principles.

As the Bhaktas lacked a social theory it led to the third limitation of the Movement, *viz*,, that though the saints denounced social injustices, they could not build up any national institution to fight against them. Since they lacked a social theory andl therefore. a positive social programme, the whole struggle became individual and not a collective opposition to the status quo. Narsingh Mehta or Tukaram or Chaitanya might be ready to immolate his life in defence of the right of religious worship for all but there was no organized mass movement to enforce this right.

Inspite of the fact that the Bhakti movement was an all India movement, it was split into various sects some of which, subsequently, even degenerated. The Hindu-Muslim distinctions still survived in the sect; new forms of ceremonies emerged and the emotion of pure Bhakti took erotic form as in the case of the Vaishnava Maharajas. The freedom movement of the oppressed and downtrodden classes completely deteriorated. The necessity of an United All-India Movement was only later on recognized, *viz.*, in the case of Guru Govind Singh and Ramdas.

With all these limitations, it must, however, be admitted that, during the period when the Hindu society was rigid and callous to lower castes and women, the Bhaktas voiced the first protest against the prevailing inequalities and injustices. The Bhakti Movement did advance even for a brief duration the position of the oppressed lower castes and women.

Justice Ranade, narrates their achievements thus:

"It modified the strictness of the old spirit of caste exclusiveness. It raised the Shudra classes to a position of spiritual power and social importance almost equal to that of the Brahmins. It gave sanctity to family relations and raised the status of women. It made the nation more human at the same time more prone to hold together by mutual toleration. It suggested and partly carried out a plan of reconciliation with the Mahomedans. It subordinated the importance of rites and ceremonies and of pilgrimages and fasts and of learning add contemplation to the higher excellence of worship by means of love and faith. It checked the excesses of polytheism."[26]

REFERENCES

1, Padmapuranam 41 Adhyaya 15th Verse.

2. San Kshiti Mohan, Medieval Mysticism of India pp. 42-43.

3. Shukla Ramachandra Hindi Sahitayaka Itihasa, p. 76.

4. Belvalkar S.K. and Rande R.D., 'History of Indian Philosophy, Vol. II, p.326.

5. Sen K., Medieval Mysticism of India, p. 73.

6. Tagore Rabindranath (Ed.) One Hundred Poems of Kabir, pp. 1-2.

7. Quoted by Belvalkar and Ranade. History of Indian Philosophy, Vol. II, p. 209. Also refer to Ranade M.G. Rise of the Maratha Power, p. 146. Shastri Durgashsnkar K., Vaishnava Dharma No Sankshipta Itihasa, p. 209. Munshi K.M., Gujarat and Its Literature, p. 138.

8. Ishwariprasad, History of Kedieval India, 568.

9. Ranade M.G., Rise of the Maratha Power, p. 156.

10. Sen K., Medieval Mysticism of India, p. 73.

11. Mukerjee D.P., Modern Indian Culture, pp. 20-21.

12. Majmudar Manjulal, (ed.) Sahityakar Akho, p. 8.

13. Munshi K.M., Thodak Rasdarshano, p. 144.

14. Munshi K.M., Gujarat and Its Literature, pp. 115-116.

15. Quoted by Belvalkar and Ranade, History of Indian Philosophy, Vol. II, p. 257.

16. Ranade M.G., The Rise of the Maratha Power, p. 159.

17. Belvalkar and Ranade, History of Indian Philosophy, Vol. II, p. 242.

18. *Ibid*, p. 352.

19. *Ibid*, p. 266.

20. Shyam Sunderdas Kabir Granthawali, p. 14.

21. Barthwal, Nirguna School of Hindi Poetry, p. 182.

22. Shri Ramakrishna Centenary Memorial., The Cultural Heritage of India, Vol. II, p. 225.

23. Ref. to "Urmi and Navrachna", May June and Aug., 1950 series entitled "Sarvodaya ke Samyavad"—Vasubandhu".

24. Mukerjee D.P. Modern Indian Culture, p. 28.

25. *Ibid*, p. 20.

26. Ranade M.G. The Rise of the Maratha Power. pp. 171-172.

12

Far-Reaching Effects of the British Rule and Culture on Indian Society

Indian contact with modern West in general and Great Britain in particular was and event of decisive significance for her future development. It was a veritable point of departure in the historical development of Indian society.

There were sporadic, episodic contacts between India and some western countries in the past. However, when Vasco-de-Gama anchored his ships in the Indian waters and landed on the Indian shore, a phase of continuous contact with the western world was inaugurated.

Though, since the historic event, Indian society began to feel the impact of the western world; it experienced a far-reaching transformation in political, economic as well as cultural fields only when Britain extended its conquest and rule over India, particularly when, at the end of the eighteenth century, Britain organized and established in India well-ramified administrative system penetrating even the remotest village and influencing the social economic and cultural life of the Indian people.

Prior to the British rule, India had experienced frequent military invasions by foreigners from the North. These invaders, however, departed after plundering the people or even when they settled in the country as political conquerors and rulers, they did not alter the existing socio-economic structure based on the self-sufficient village, the caste system and the joint family which "persisted inspite of recurring invasions from without and constant revolution within" It was only during the period of the British Rule and its accompanying economic and cultural forces that the self-sufficient village-economy and the resultant communal village life were destroyed, and social institutions like the caste system and the joint family began slowly but steadily to experience first attacks on their hitherto stable foundations.

In order to properly evaluate the effects of the Brisish impact on Indian society, it is vitally necessary to know what economic system and culture the British conquerors and rulers of India represented.

Europe in the Nineteenth Century

Since the beginning of the fifteenth century Britain had been experiencing a far reaching technical, economic, social, political and cultutal transformation. This tranformation was a part of the transformation which the whole of Europe had been undergoing. The Industrial Revolution which took place in the eighteenth century in the England was the culmination of the revolutionizing process in the techno-economic field which led to momentous social, political and cultural consequences in that country.

This was the period of great geographical discoveries with resultant expansion of trade between Europe and other continents and social, economic and political strenthening of the new historically progressive class of the bourgeoisie. It was the period when the feudal economy based on serfdom increasingly disintegrated resulting in the decline of the social, economic and political power of the dominant class of feudal

Barons. The exigencies of development of trade and manufacture gave momentum to the development of natural resources and technology. It was the period of Enlightenment, of the growth of scientific knowledge, of the emergence, also, of democratic ideas. The invention of the printing press in Europe helped to bring democratic conceptions such as those of individual liberty, sovereignty of the people, the antithesis of the concept of the Divine Right of Kings on which the feudal state rested, nationalism which had for its objective the national integration of the ununited feudal principalities and national consolidation of the ununited feudal communities ruled by a multitude of feudal lords. It was also the period when great scientists, philosophers, and sociologists, the pioneers of scientific rationalism and humanist modern culture like Bacon, Locke, Hume, Rousseau, Voltaire, Helvetius, Diderot and others, flourished. There were the ideological leaders of the movement which transferred European feudal society into modern society based on such progressive conceptions as democracy, nationalism, rationalism and others.

The movement accomplished revolutionary changes in the life of the European people. In the economic field, it resulted in the overthrow of the feudal economic system based on serfdom and establishment of the capitalist economic system based on free wage labour and production for profit, and market. In the political field the structure of the state based on the conception of the Divine Right of Kings was superseded by the modern national state based on democratic conceptions such as the sovereignty of the people, individual liberty, equality of citizens and representative instiutions. In the ideological field, the philosophy of liberalism with its basic tenets such as equality of all men, respect for human personality, recognition of individuality of every human being and reason as the supreme criterion to judge social institutions and actions of men. became the dominant philosophy,

Capitalism in the economic field, democracy in the social and political spheres and liberalism in the ideological domain—

there were the principal features of the new society which was being established mainly in the West European countries.

When Britain came in decisive contact with India, she had undergone transformation to an appreciable extent from a feudal to a liberal capitalist basis.

The conquest of India by Britain was that of a disunited feudal people by a modern liberal capitalist nation, This vital fact determined the specfic line of development of the Indian people during the period of thc British rule.

Tenets of Liberal Philosophy

Liberalism substituted the principle of contract in place of the doctrine of status. In feudal society the life of the individual was determined by the accident of birth. Contract freely entered into by individuals was the juridical foundation of the new society based on the liberal philosophy. It is true that this feedom became restricted in practice in the new capitalist society since the capitalist class which commanded economic power could impose its will on other sections of society who were economically dependent on it for livelihood. Nevertheless even this formal freedom implied a historical advance over feudal society which tied the serf to the feudal lord in Europe and prevented a Hindu in India to take to any vocation other than that presued by the caste into which he was born. Liberalism attacked all privileges and disabilities based on birth.

Rationalism was the second principle of the Liberal philosophy. It declared as valid only that which was endorsed by reason. Institutions ideas which could not stand the critical test of reason had to be repudiated and discarded even though they may have been existing for ages.

The social life in all its aspects, political, economic and intellectual, according to this philosophy, should be recorganized on the basis of the principle of reason.

Liberalism, further, asserted the right to challenge the authority which wields power. The acceptance of a particular thing should depend not "because authority accepted it, but because its inherent validity, secures for it the free consent of others."

Lastly the Liberal philosophy stood for the iiberation of the individual from all shackles. As Laski describes, "the essence of the revolution that occurred is thus' in a real sense. the emancipation of the individual." Uptil now the individual had no existence apart from the social life which governed all his behaviour; with the new philosophy arrived individual responsibility. Religion now began to be considered as individual affair. The respect for individual's personality, and individuality became the slogans of the new era. It is on this basis that Mill takes up the problem of women's emancipation. He, while respresenting the case for women's franchise maintains, "workmen need other protection than that of their employers, and women other protection than that of their men."

In actual life these principles took the form of rights through which they could be realized. According to Hobhouse rights of personal liberty, social liberty, economic liberty, domestic liberty and political liberty are the most important among these. The struggle for these rights engaged all fighter for human freedom during the late eighteenth and nineteenth centuries. Thomas Paine passionately demanded a democratic government for the people and respect for the individual in his outstanding book "Rights of Man." It was during this period that the movement for universal suffrage was launched by Bentham. His utilitarian philosophy cleared the path for democratic individualism and laissez faire. This constituted the essential core of the culture of the British nation at the time when Britain extended its domination over India.

As Dr. Ghurye describes, "It was the period of Supreme reign of laissez faire and individualism. Individual liberty and freedom became the centre of their doctrine. It is also the age when new womanhood emerged; as as result partially of Mill's advocacy, partially as a result of now industry which opened a new scope, and partially due to free education. By the end of the century (19th) the liberated woman was exhibiting the freedom by becoming more athletic as pointed out by Trevelyn, the bicycle opened up the countryside to her either alone or in the company of complimentary sex."

An adequate idea of England of that period is given by Sir N.J. Chandavarka, who describes it thus: "It was an age of splendour when humanity seemed to stand at the start of a quickened life with promise of a bright future for modern civilization. In politics it was the age of reform bills, of Free Trade, of the abolition of slavery, of statesmen of towering personality like Palmerston, Peel, Gladstone, Disraelli, Cobden, Bright, Clarkson, and Wilberforce. In social reforms it was the age of the emancipation of women, of Elizabeth Fry and Florence Nightingale. In literature which for the period reflects its currents and character and the ideas of the people, it was the age of Wordsworth, Tennyson, Browning reflecting through them the might hopes that make us men."

India in the Nineteenth Century

Prior to the advent of Britain, India's economic system "was based on the village community, which was a more or less self sufficient unit combining agriculture and handicrafts, production was everywhere on a small scale and for consumption rather than for exchange. Technology was backward, communications were poor, money was scarcely needed and everything moved in narrow, well-worn grooves fixed by custom. It was in short a pre-capitalist economy."

This backward economy of India came in contact with the slowly developing capitalist economy of England. The impact of the latter on the former had the following results.

Industrial England felt increasing need of raw materials for her expanding industries. Indian agriculture which was hitherto producing for meeting the needs of self sufficient village communities, here-after began to produce for market providing requisite raw materials for British industries. Subsequently it also produced for the world market. Thus the village agricultural economy became an integral part of world capitalist economy no longer producting for meeting the needs of the village population. This Indian agricultural production was commercialized and subject to the vicissitudes of the world market.

British conquest of and rule over India brought about also a transformation of land relations. The British ruler created two types of private property in land, the Ryotwari and the Zamindari, thereby suppressing the traditional communal ownership of village land in India. Land which became now privately owned thereby became "heritable, transferable and marketable." It is, however, important to note that the creation of the individual ownership of land by the British did not, unlike in Britain and some other western countries, lead to any appreciable growth of capitalist agriculture in India. This was mainly due to the fact that while in the western countries the introduction of capitalist relations in agriculture was acompanied by the creation of compact farms as units of agriculture, in India. Britan did not initiate such reorganization of land. The maintenance of land fragmentation and the open field system proved a powerful obstacle to the growth of capilalist farming in India.

In addition to the emergence of a single unified national economy and the resultant economic unification of the Indian people, British conquest of India led to the political unification of the ununited Indian people under a single centralized state. Monarchs like Ashoka, Samudragupta and Akbar had conceived the dream of a politically integrated Indian people. They did not, however, succeed in achieving this grand dream because of the feucal and hence weak Indian economy and transport and hence on the eve of British advent in India, the country was divided into a multitude of principalities.

British could bring the entire Indian people under a single political rule primarily due to the facilities provided by the new modern means of communications such as railways, and postal and telegraph services which she established in India. The introduction of railways brought the scattered groups comprising the Indian people together and increasing their points of contact. It broadened their outlook and made possible the cooperation of the Indian people on an all Indian scale in social, political, economic and cultural spheres. It helped to build and develop a collective national life. The extensive social contact among the people which railways made possible contributed to relax, to a certain extent, caste, communal and provincial prejudices. Great social reform movements including that of the emancipation of the Indian women on all-India basis became possible because of the facilities provided by the railways.

Britain enunciated the principle of 'equality of all citizens' before law. The introduction of a new legal system based on this principle brought a change in the legal relationships between the Indians. It also substituted a uniform reign of law in place of custom. It introduced the principle of contract in place of that of status based on birth. In addition to these changes in objective conditions, British contact resulted in the spread of the great liberal philosophy of modern Europe among the Indian intelligentsia. As O'Malley observes; "In the great majority of cases the impact of western influences has been due to impersonal factors particularly the systems of government and law, the importation of technical developments and material of European civilization and the invisible import of ideas."

The new economic system and administrative machinery required a new type of educated personnel. Britain consequently, established a network of educational institutions in India which imparted modern western education. A new class of educated Indians trained in modern western sciences and culture as a result evolved. It was a section of this class which became the vanguard of all progressive movements in India.

While introducing these progressive changes in Indian society, it must be however noted that they were basically adapted to the requirments of Britain for economic exploitation and political domination over India and were therefore, partial and distorted. For example, when in the initial stage, Britain did not require educated Indians, she maintained and encouraged oriental studies. It was Raja Ram Mohan Roy who at that time agitated for the spread of English education and modern western culture among the Indians. Even in the economic sphere though the rulers destroyed the old Indian economy they did not build up nor permit the development of a modern capitalist economy. Consequently, the development of the the Indian economy was lop-sided and insufficient. Indian economy became a colonial adjunct of British economy primarily subserving the needs of the latter.

The introduction of the new economic system as well as education by Britain in India, though limited, created new social forces in Indian society. The restriction on the free development of Indian economy was one of the main economic motives of the rise of the Indian National Political movement.

When Britain was increasingly transforming Indian society, an increasing group of enlightened Indians felt animated with nationalist and democratic urges. They studied the democratic ideology of modern Europe, assimilated its liberal principles and followed with deep interest the great struggle of the contemporary European nations for national freedom, democratic social relations and scientific culture.

In fact, England and other Europen countries, in the first half of the ninteenth century were feeling the repercussions of the great French Revolution. They were stirred with the individualistic liberatarian ideas of Rousseau and Voltaire. They were astir with the inspiring nationalist ideas of Mazzini. They were hotbeds of struggle against medieval superstition under the influence of the philosophies, of Comte, of Encyclopaedists and others.

The study of contemporary European history and culture inspired the enlightened Jndians to evoluate critically the extant Indian conditions and institutions. They came in contact with novel conceptions like "freedom of Speech and the pen, criticism of authority, the questioning of accepted dogmas, the insistence on the rights of man as opposed to his duties. The growing familiarity with these has brought a new spirit into Indian life, the stirrings of scepticism, instead of a stagnant authoritarianism, a glimmering if not the forerunner of what we in Europe call democracy."

The enlightened Indians imbibed ideas like those of equality and progress, liberty and nationality, reason as the basis of thought process, applied them to the conditions previlling in Indian society, and organised struggles to transform the extant conditions in the spirit of those ideas.

As Ranade declared in the twelfth Session of the Indian National Social Conference, "that issue is not this or that particular reform about which people have so much controversy but the general spirit of parity, justic, equality, temperance and mercy which should be infused into our minds and which should illuminate our hearts."

Dr. Bhandarkar voices the same feeling. "The question now is whether with our minds liberalised by English education and contacts with European civilization we shall still continue to worship custom and be its slaves, and allow our moral sentiments to remain dead and unjust and cruel social practices to flourish...No...our social institutions must improve and become more rational and just... ."

Mr. C. Shankaran Nair, also declared, "to break down the isolation of Hindu religion, to remove the barriers which now prevent free social intercourse and unity of action, to extend the blessings of education to the lower classes, to improve the position of women to one of equality to men, we require the continuance of a strictly secular government in through sympathy with liberal thouht and progress."

To sum up, the genesis and growth of the movement for the emancipation of Indian Women was the result of the impact of advanced democratic civilization on the Medieval India. Britain established the modern capitalist economic system and modern state based on principles of liberty, equality and others. The new economic background became a breeding ground of changing the social relation in Indian society and of liberal urges among the Indian people. These urges and yearnings became articulate through the enlightened Indians, the social reformers who assimilated the liberal ideology of the West. These liberals became the pioneers of all progressive democratic movements, social, political, economic and cultural.

They, therefare, became pioneers of the movement for the freedom of Indian women, thereby extending the liberal principle to the status of Indian women also.

APPENDIX I

State-wise Coverage of World Bank Assisted Projects For Technician Education. (polytechnics)

(*Rs. in Crores*)

States	*Project Base Cost* ***	*No. of Schemes*	*Proposed No. of Institutions to be covered*	*Annual Plan 90-91 Budgeted Outlay*	*Annual Plan 90-91 Actual Expdr.*	*Annual Plan 91-92 Budgeted Outlay*	*Annual Plan 91-92 Anticipated Expdr.*	*8th Plan (1992-97) Recommd. Outlay*
1	*2*	*3*	*4*	*5*	*6*	*7*	*8*	*9*
Phase—I								
Bihar	88.08	21	26	11.97	1.07	20.16	20.54	79.05
Gujarat	65.08	21	32	9.76	0.52	16.27	16.27**	50.00
Karnataka	52.78	21	43	6.00	1.00	7.50	7.50**	42.50
Kerala	34.10	21	24	5.20	0.58	10.60	10.60	36.67
Madhya Pradesh	100.13	21	49	10.29	8.56	16.90	16.90**	74.50
Orissa	56.79	21	13	8.15	8.14	7.00	7.00	43.93
Rajasthan	44.61	21	23	3.80	2.88	8.17	8.17	41.10
Uttar Pradesh	200.00	21	86	6.58	0.65	45.00	45.00	188.00
Sub-Total	641,57	168	296	61.75	23.4	131.60	131.98	555.75

Phase II								
Andhra Pradesh	79.55	21	59	—	—	9.70	5.90	74.04
Assam	30.00	21	9	—	—	2.86	1.00	29.00
Haryana	80.87	21	18	—	—	10.00	10.00	72.00
Himachal Pradesh	20.24	21	5	—	—	2.10	2.10	21.43
Maharashtra	122.68	21	54	—	—	30.00	0.30	120.00
Punjab	79.48	21	19	—	—	12.31	12.31**	75.81
Tamil Nadu	68.00	21	55	—	—	19.96	2.00	76.00
West Bengal	85.16	21	34	—	—	6.00	6.00**	80.00
UT of Delhi	23.60	21	9	—	—	3.20	3.20**	23.00
Sub-Total	590.58	189	262	0	0	96.13	42.81	571.88
Total	1232.15	357	558	61.75	23.40	227.73	174.79	1127.63

Notes: 1. Does not include 10 new Women's Wings to be converted Polytechnics in both phases.

2. Does not include the central component of Rs. 40.00 Crores.

3. Out of Rs. 1892 Crores (US $ 745 million), the world Bank Assistance would be Rs. 1318 Crores (US $ 518.88 million).

**Represents budgeted outlay as anticipated expenditure not specified.

***The Base Cost excludes the price escalation due to inflation and increase due to physical contingencies.

Source: Deptt. of Education, Government of India and Plan documents of States/UTs.

APPENDIX II

Health and Family Welfare

Health of the people is not only a desirable goal but is also an essential investment in human resources. The National Health Policy (1983) reiterated India's commitment to attain "Health for All (HFA) by 2000 A.D.". Primary health care has been accepted as the main instrument for achieving this goal. Accordingly, a vast network of institutions at primary, secondary and tertiary levels have been established. Control of communicable diseases through national programmes and development of trained health manpower have received special attention.

Many spectacular successes have been achieved in the country in the area of health. Small-pox stands eradicated and plague is no longer a problem. Morbidity and mortality on account of malaria, cholera and various other diseases bave declined. The Crude Brith Rate and Infant Mortlity Rate (IMR) have declined to 29.9 and 80 (1990 SRS data) as compared to 37 and 129 respectively in 1971. Life expectancy has risen from a mere 32 years in 1947 to 58 years in 1990. However, HFA, is a long way off. Disease, disability and deaths on account of several communicable diseases are still unacceptably high. Meanwhile, several non-communicable diseases have emerged as new public health problem. Rural health services for delivery of primary health care are still not fully operationalised.

Urban health services, particularly for urban slums, require urgent attention due to changing urban morphology.

Programme Thrusts in the Eighth Plan

It is towards human development that health and population control are listed as two of the six priority objectives of this Plan. Health facilities must reach the entire population by the end of the Eighth Plan. The Health for All (HFA) paradigm must take into account not only high risk vulnerable groups. *i.e.*, mothers and children, but must also focus sharply on the under-priviledged segments within the vulnerable groups. Within the HFA strategy "Health for underpriviledged" will be promoted consciously and consistently. This can only be done through emphasising the community based systems reflected in our planning of infrastructure, with about 30,000 population as the basic unit for primary health care.

Minimum Needs Programme (MNP)

Rural Health Programme

Development and strengthening of rural health infrastructure through a three tier system of Sub-centre Primary Health Ceutres (PHCs) and Community Health Centres (CHCs) for delivery of health and family welfare services to the rural commnnity was continued during the Seventh Plan. But, lack of buildings, shortage of manpower and inadequate provision of drugs, supplies and equipments constituted major impediments to full operationalisation of these units.

The achievements and the present situation for health infrastructure under the MNP and availability of building and manpower are given in Annexures 12 1, 12.2 and 12.3.

The approach and strategy for rural health during the Eighth Plan would be:

(i) Consolidation and operationalisation, rather than major expansion, of the network of Sub-centres, PHCs and

CHCs so that their performance is optimised. This would be achieved through:

(a) strengthening of physical facilities including completion of building of the centres and staff quarters;

(b) provision of essential equipments as per the standard list;

(c) filling up of all vacant posts within a defined time frame and in-service training of staff;

(d) ensuring supply of essential drugs, dressings and other material.

(ii) To monitor the progress of implementation of MNP at the District, State and National levels, a health information management system will be developed and used.

(iii) The targets regarding setting up of Sub-centre, PHC and CHC on the basis of population norm are indicative only. The States will be given flexibility in establising these units as per the local needs depending on geographical and population considerations, resources, manpower availability, etc. In opening new centres the needs of tribal population and communities living in difficult and inaccessible areas will be given first priority.

(iv) The rural hospitals and dispensaries will be suitably modified, equipped and staffed to convert them into Sub-centres, PHC, CHC as the case may be, thereby integrating them into primary health care system.

(v) The backlog of Sub-centres, PHCs and CHCs in many States is staggering and the resources required to meet the targets are astronmical and as such unachievable in near future. In view of this the entire policy of establishment of Sub-centre, PHC and CHC with the present norms will be reviewed and new policy options developed to make the primary health care accessible, and affordable to all. Re-organisation of the Indian Systems of Medicine and Homoeopathy (ISM&H) dispensaries/hospitals in rural areas to create ISM&H health centres is one such option. This would be in line with the Government's accepted policy of promoting ISM&H.' Reorientation of existing personnel of these dispensaries/hospitals, provision of additional facilities and/or staff, redefining the roles and responsibilities would be some of the pre-requisites to put the concept of ISM&H Primary Health Centres and Sub-centres in an operational mode.

(vi) Mechanism will be developed to make the rural health services responsive to the needs of the rural masses and accountable to the community. Panchayati Raj system would become an effective instrument for eliciting community participation in the health programme and providing supervision and support primary health care infrastructure.

(vii) Linkages will be developed with the sub-divisional and district hospital to provide referral back-up.

Urban Health S ervices

More than one quarter of the population in the country now lives in urban areas. In metropolitan and large cities about 40-50 per cent of the urban dwellers are estimated to be living in slum areas where the health status of the people is as bad as, if not worse than, in rural areas. But infrastructure for primary health care in urban areas hardly exists. Serious attempts will be made to develop urban health services as per the recommendations of Krishnan Committee. Organic linkages will be forged with the urban development schemes including Urban Basic Services for a comprehensive development of health and welfare services. Local hospitals will be made responsible to run these centres and treat them as their extension counters for providing health services to the community. Voluntary organisation and local bodies would be enconraged to develop partnership and ultimately taking full responsibility for carrying out these programmes. Health system research to develop a model of urban primary health care services will be undertaken.

Secondary and Tertiary Care Services

Alongwith the empaasis on consolidation of primary health care, the strengthening of secondary care services and optimisation of tertiary care services would be key objectives of the Eighth Plan.

The sub-divisional and district hospitals which are the secondary level medical care institutions, lack adequate manpower and facilities, to be able to discharge their reponsibilities satisfactorily. In view of the resource constraints, there is need for raising resources to maintain the quality of care and meet rising expectations of the people. It is time that the concept of free medical care is reviewed and people are required to pay, even if partially for the services. The system can be so designed that the truly indigent population are able to get free/highly subsidised medical care. Innovative approaches/practices to this end and a system of medical audit will be developed during the Plan. Maximum cost-effective utilisation of existing services will be another item on the agenda.

In accordance with the new policy of the Government to encourage private initiatives, private hospitals/clinics will be supported subject to maintenance of minimum standard and suitable returns for the tax incentives. Norms for minimal facilities and accredition of private hospitals/clinics would be developed to maintain quality of patient care.

The medical college hospitals and specialised hospitals have to be used exclusively as tertiary care centres and for health manpower development. Important pre-requisities for this would be improvement in the facilities and standards of race available at secondary care level and development of strong referral system.

A conscious decision has to be taken to enforce a balanced

development of primary, secondary and tertiary care services in the country with priority for primary health care. Otherwise there is a distinct risk of the paradigm of primary health care as a tool for "Health for All" being overrun by the mechanism of "All for a few". This tendency and trend can be halted only with scientific arguments for which sound epidemiological, health management and health financing data is needed and hence the need for health systems research.

Health Man-power Development and Training

As much as approximately two thirds of the total expenditure on health services is spent on personnel. Yet, health manpower planning, production and management, which constitute key elements for effective implementation of health programme, have not received enough attention.

While the States have been more than anxious to start new medical colleges, their efforts to develop institutions for training of para medical staff have been entirely suboptimal. This has resulted in a considerable mismatch between the requirement and avilability of health personnel of different categories. Ideally, the doctor-nurse ratio should be 1 : 3 but currentl there are less than 3,00,000 registered nurses against 4,00 registered medical graduates. Similarly, there is a shortage pharmacists, laboratory technicians, radiographers, dental surgeons, etc., in the country.

The National Health Policy affirmed that the effective delivery of health care services would depend very largely on the nature of education, training and appropriate orientation towards community health of all categories of medical and health personnel. It is, therefore, of crucial importance that the entire basis and approach towards manpower development in terms of national needs and priorities are reviewed and training programmes restructured accordingly. Besides there is an urgent need to asess appropriate health manpower mix to deliver health services at primary, secondary and tertiary level and for the purpose of training and research.

The approach and strategy for health manpower development during the Eighth Plan would be:

(i) A National Policy on Education in Health Sciences which when formulated may form the basis of new initatives in manpower development.

(ii) The existing situation regarding health manpower supply, demand and projection and facilities for training of different categories will be reviewed.

(iii) Appropriate steps will be taken for bridging the critical gaps in the manpower requirement for primary health care and the higher levels and for training and research needs. Starting vocational courses as part of vocationalisation of general education at the + 2 level of the 10+2 system will be supported to expeditiously bridge the gap in the supply of paramedical personnel.

(iv) The distortions created in the past on account of over-emphasis on training of doctors, often at the cost of other categories of personnel, and also the undue emphasis on specialisation/super specialisation will be checked.

(v) Continuing education for all categories of staff will be given high priority. For this, district and regional level training institutions will be suitably strengthened. Medical colleges and other institutions including professional bodies like Indian Medical Association (IMA) will continue to play an important role, in coordination with the National Academy of Medical Sciences (NAMS), which has been identified as the nodal agency for this purpose.

(vi) The existing facilities for training of medical graduates has outstepped the needs. No new medical college or an increase in the admission capacity of the existing colleges will, therefore, be supported during the Eighth Plan. Instead, resources will be used to strengthen the hospitals, laboratories and libraries of the existing medical colleges so that the standards of training are maintained.

(vii) For ensuring uniform standards of medical and para-professional education, need for establishment of universities of medical and health sciences at regional level has been recognised. Necessary support will be provided as and when a policy decision in the matter is taken.

(viii) Statutory councils will be strengthened and new councils for para-professionals, where they are needed, will be created so that standards of training and education can be laid down and enforced. The proposed Education Commission in Health Sciences will promote and co-ordinate all educational activities for all categories of health manpower at all levels.

(ix) Training facilities for epidemiology and health management, the two disciplines which contribute to the maximum extent to efficient functioning of health services including hospitals, will be augmented in medical colleges and created in specialiised institutions where training of teachers can be undertaken.

(x) Training of doctors of ISM and H will also be reviewed and re-oriented to make it congruent with the needs of national health programmes and primary health care.

(xi) Efforts for re-orientation of medical education, started during the earlier plans, will be pursued vigorously with emphasis on faculty development through workshops. for the teachers to make them conversant with the health needs of the country, national policies and programmes, advances in educational technology, and make them appreciate the need for re-direction and retargetting of medical education, relavent to contemporary and futuristic needs.

Programmes for Control of Communicable Diseases

A number of national programmes for eradication/

control of communicable diseases have been initiated in the country since the early years of planning. Most of the control/ eradication programmes for communicable diseases have been in operation since last several plans at huge financial cost. With a few exceptions, however, no national level comprehensive review/evaluation of these programmes have been undertaken. During the Eighth Plan the following strategies will be followed for control of communicable disease:

(i) National level review of the ongoing control/eradication programme to assess the current strategies nd their impact on the disease status.

(ii) Ensuring sufficient supplies and logistic support including mobility for carrying out the programmes.

(iii) Establishment of epidemiological-cumsueveillance centres at district/regional levels and improvement of health management information system for continuous monitoring of the disease situation and taking appropriate and prompt action.

(iv) Intersectoral coordination will be strengthened with departments of public health engineering, local bodies like municipalities. Ministries of Information and Broadcasting, Women and Child Welfare, Water Resources, etc., for control of vector borne and other diseases.

(v) The Information, Education and Communication (IEC) activities within each programme would be given special attention for enlisting community participation, which constitutes one of the weakest links, for carrying out the disease control programmes.

(vi) Strategy of training of staff at horizontal level, both within the primary health care and higher level, is essential.

(vii) Training in epidemiology is woefully inadequate in the country. Unless this situation is rectified decisions regarding control of communicable diseases and its implementation will be handled by the group of professionals and para-professionals who are not sufficiently equipped to do so with its attendant consequences. Specialised institutions/departments to cary out both pre-service and in-service training in epidemiology for different category of staff will be created and the existing ones strengthened.

Programme-wise strategies are briefiy outlined hereunder:

Vector Borne Diseases

Malaria Eradication

As a result of introduction of modified plan of operation in 1976 the incidence of malaria has come down from about 6.5 million cases in 1976 to about 1.89 million cases in 1990. The problem of drug resistance of P. falciparum malaria in several States is a cause for concern. Several operational problems and non-availability of matching funds from States to this 5 per cent Centrally Sponsored Scheme (CSS) has resulted in shortfalls in spray operations, decline in blood slide collections and incomplete treatment of cases. Irrigation projects without adequate strategies for management of water resources and floating labour population to cities and major project sites has also contributed to the increased incidence of malaria. Since 30% of all malaria cases and 60 per cent of the more dangerous P. falciparum infections are in the tribal areas, a major intensification of efforts would be directed towards these areas.

Kala-azar and Japanese Encephalitis

Kala-azar and Japanese Encephalitis (JE) have emerged as major public health problems in recent years. For control Kala-azar in twin approach of:

(i) vector control by insecticide spraying and

(ii) case detection and treatment at PHC and referral hospitals was adopted.

The reported cases and deaths due to JE in the affected States viz. Andhra Pradesh, West Bengal, U.P. Tamil Nadu and Assam have shown considerable decline during the Seventh Plan with the use of indigenously produced vaccine.

The existing guidelines for Vector-borne disease control include:

(i) Residual indoor spraying with appropriate insecticide in areas with population having API 2 and above in any of the last 3 years.

(ii) Spraying of BHC in districts reporting 100 or more cases of JE in any one of the years during the past decade.

(iii) DDT spraying in PHCs reporting 10 or more cases of Kala-azar in any one of the last three years.

(iv) Continuation of the anti-larval operations; and.

(v) Malathion fogging/ULV spraying to be undertaken as a contingency measure in out-break of JE and Malaria.

These conventional approaches of use of inceticides and chemicals would have to be supplemented or replaced, depending upon the local situation, by newer strategies such as biodegradeable inceticides, biocides, bioenvironmental improvement and preventive measures like impregnated bed nets. Finally, the surveillance activities would need to be strenghened so as to improve case detection and case management, resulting in a break in the chain of infection transmission.

Leprosy Eradication

The approach under this 100 per cent Centrally Sponsored Scheme has been early case detection and domiciliary treatment and health education. Multi Drugs Therapy (MDT) has been introduced in all 201 endemic districts and 41 low endemic districts (till March 1991) for case treatment. The programme has shown steady progress in achieving its objectives during the Seventh Plan.

Within the Leprosy Eradication Programme the following activities will be pursued:

(i) Creation of additional physical facilities in all the endemic districts.

(ii) Extention of MDT to remaining endemic districts and in low endemic district in phases.

(iii) Training of the PHC staff in leprosy eradication activities, both in endemic and low endemic district, with the aim of preparing them to take over the responsibility of leprosy eradication activities following reduction in the prevalance and incidence of the disease.

(vi) Creation of vocational and rehabilitation facilities for the patients declared cured in those districts which have been under MDT for more than 5 years.

Tuberculosis Control

Early case detection and treatment have formed the strategy for control of Tubeculosis (TB) under a CSS with 50 per cent Central funding. A major achievement of the programme during the Seventh Plan was the sucessful introduction of short course chemo-therapy in 212 districts, thereby reducing the treatment duration from 18—24 months to 6—8 months. However, the programme has suffered from poor case holding leading to treatment default. Problem of drug resistance is yet another cause for concern.

During the Eighth Plan, the TB Control Programme will be further expanded and strengthened by opening District Tuberculosis Centres (DTCs) in those districts where these do not exist. Short course cheme-therapy will also be introduced and supply of drugs ensured, in all the remaining districts of the country under the Programme. The DTCs will be strengthened by providing necessary equipments like X-ray machines and maintaining essential supplies like drugs, X-ray films etc.

Blindness Control Programme

This programme which was launched in 1976 as a 100 per

cent CSS aims at reducing blindness prevalence from 1.4 per cent in 1980-81 to 0.3 per cent by 2000 AD. Cataract is the cause of more than 80 per cent of blindness. Demographic shift leading to larger old age population has increased the prevalence of cataract in recent decades. So far the main strategy has been to provide access to opthalmic services through eye camps and mobile units. While this has succeeded to some extent, it has fallen short of the requirements. Besides the inherent limitation of the camp approach, the magnitude of the problem demands creation of permanent eye care infrastructure operational throughout the year and within easy reach of the people.

These initiatives will be combined with an intensification of efforts aimed at ophthalmic manpower development with the ultimate objective of improving the outreach and quality of ophthalmic care at primary, intermediate and tertiary levels.

Guinea Worm Eradication

This programme was launched during 1983-84 with the objective of achieving zero incidence of guinea worm by 1990-91. Althouh the estimated number of cases has come down from 39,790 in 1983-84 to about 20,000 in 1990-91 the objective of "Zero Guinea worm" still remains unachieved. Total eradication of the disease through better surveillance system and improvement cf drinking water supply in the endemic areas will be achieved during the Plan.

AIDS Control Programme

Acquired Immuno Deficiency Syndrome (AIDS) has emerged as a new public health problem in the country. The AIDS Control Programme was launched in 1986 as a Central Sector Scheme. Establishment of surveillance centres, testing of cases for infection, training of personnel and mass health education formed the main activities within the programme. But, the incidence of the disease has shown an increase from 137 seropositives among 41,000 tested up to May 1987 to 7272 seropositives among 13,49 lakhs persons tested by April 1, 1992.

Inadequate surveillance system and absence of facilities for examination of blood and blood products and the growing menace of intravenous drug abuse contributed to his upsurge in infection.

For the prevention and the control of AIDS a national programme will be launched during the Eighth Plan. The strategy to be adopted for AIDS control would comprise of:

(i) Surveillance of the population with special emphasis on high risk behaviour groups for detection of infection;

(ii) Strengthening of the blood banks and blood safety measures with priorities on special areas and metropolitan and large cities to start with.

(iii) Area specific strategy for mounting control of infection and target specific IEC activities based on epidemiological data;

(iv) Integration of the control programme with the activities of the departments like Social Welfare, Youth and Sporte, etc. and other Government and non-government organisations; and

(v) Strenghening of STD Programme and training of staff.

Diarrhoeal Disease

Diarrhoeal Disease Control Programme which was initiated durtng the Sixth Plan was strengthened and included as a part of maternal and child health activities in the Seventh Plan Under the programme, a large number of professionals and para-professionals were trained for the programme implementation and support besides intensifying IEC efforts. Oral rehydration salt for prevention and treatment of dehydration was made available through the existing health infrastructure. Diarrhocal diseases control would be continued during Eighth Plan as part of the child survival and safe motherhood programme.

Programme for Non-communicable Diseases Control

The increase in life expectancy and the changing life style of the people, have brought in the problem of non-communicable diseases which have added to the already heavy burden of morbidity and mortality due to communicable diseases in the country. Development of models of care and control programmes for non-communicable diseases, therefore, are no longer a luxury but an essentiality.

The strategies for the control of non-communicable diseases have to be based on sound consideration of epidemiology and demography. They must be integrated with the existing health infrastructure to make them cost-effective. Development of appropriate technology and its transfer to the general health services should be an important component of the strategy. Since the life style and high risk behaviour are important variables associated with the rising incidence of most of these diseases, they lend themselves to prevention by health education. Therefore, mobilising community health action through well structured IEC system including mass media will form an important intervention strategy for the control of non-communicable diseases. Development of appropriate learning resource materials for education and training of manpower will be an essential activity. The strategies for the control of specific non-communicable diseases will be as follows:

Cancer Control

Prevalance of cancer in the country is estimated to be 1.5 to 2.0 millions. The Cancer Control Programme, initiated during 1975-76, was converted into a national programme in 1985 with the objective of:

(i) primary prevention of tobacco-related cancer:

(ii) secondary prevention of cancer of uterine cervix; and

(iii) extension and strengthening of treatment (facilities on a national scale.

The last one was the focus of emphasis during the Seventh Plan.

During the Eighth Plan the diagnostic and treatment facilities for cancer would be further strengthened at the medical colleges and other major hospitals. Primary prevention, particularly for tobacco related cancer and uterine cervix cancer, will form the sheet anchor of the Cancer Control programme. It will be carried through IEC activities and early case detection approach, mounted on the primary and secondary health care infrastructure and through mass media.

Iodine Deficiency Disorder

The National Goitre Control Programme which was operated during the Seventh Plan as a "Mission" programme, is a purely Central scheme under the Central health sector. According to the present estimates, about 45 million people suffer from goitre and another 6 to 8 millions from other iodine deficiency disorders. Universal iodization of salt and IEC activities are the main strategies of the programme.

Iodine Deficiency Disorder Control Programme would have continued thrust during the Eighth Plan. The basic approach of the programme being universal iodization of salt, proper co-ordination with major departments concerned with production and distribution of iodised salt namely, the Department of Industry and Railways, will be brought about. Iodized salt will be made available through the public distribution system. To prevent the losses of iodine in the salt due to long-distance transportation under adverse conditions, iodization of salt on small scales in the States far away from the present production centres will be considered and operationalised. Double fortification of the salt with iodine and iron will also be explored to combat the wide-spread problems of anaemia.

Diabetes Control

The National Diabetes Control Programme was launched in 1987 as a Central Sector health programme in the districts of Salem and South Arcot in Tamil Nadu and Jammu and Kashmir on a pilot basis. The main thrust during the Seventh

Plan was to develop an appropriate model for care and control of diabetes mellitus at the district level. The major objectives include:

(i) prevention of diabetes through identification of high risk subjects and early intervention; and

(ii) early diagnosis of disease and institution of management so as to prevent diabetes associated morbidity and mortality.

The programme has been reviewed and would be further extended to cover additional districts in different states during the Eighth Plan. The experience gained in the pilot districts will be used to develop the programme as an integrated model for diabetes, hypertension and heart disease. The learning resource materials, both print and non-print, developed and validated in the pilot districts, will be used for the training of nurses and primary health care workers.

Accidents

For the treatment and rehabilitation of accident victims, accident and trauma services will be started in major cities and also, on pilot scale along some of the high traffic density nasional highways.

Mental Health Services

The Seventh Plan document had suggested initiation of a National Mental Health Programme with emphasis on community based approaches. However, due to fund constraints the programme has not made satisfactory progress.

During the Eighth Plan mental health services will be given priority. The strategies for mental health programme will be community based utilising the existing primary health care and district hospital services. A psychiatric centre in each of the districts/divisions will be established. Also, every medical college will be encouraged to start a separate Department of Psychiatry so that the required manpower, both medical and para-medical, can be trained.

Other Non-communicable Diseases Control Programmes

The programme for control of other non-communicable diseases will also be taken up on pilot basis. Resources constraints will not be allowed to come in the way of developing experience and appropriate technology for implementation of the control programme at a later date.

Medical Research

The Indian Council of Medical Research (ICMR) is the premier institution which is responsible for carrying out bio-medical and operational research in India. Important achievements of the ICMR during previous plans include: demonstration of improved vector control using bio-environmental techniques for control of malaria and filaria; establishment of National Cancer Registry; multi-drug therapy and short course chemo-therapy for leprosy and TB respectively and a national surveillance system for AIDS infection. Various other institutions under the Ministry of Health and Family Welfare and medical colleges have done notable work in the field of medical research.

Research and Development activities by Indian Council of Medical Research and other academic institutions will be pursued during the Eighth Plan through the following strategies:

(i) Establishment of an integrated Bio-medical Research Complex to strengthen research activities and to optimise the utilisation of the available resources and facilities.

(ii) Promotion of excellence by rationalising grants to promising scientists in medical colleges and strengthening of extramural centres for research under eminent scientific leadership.

(iii) Establishment of a network of research units in medical colleges for multi-centric studies.

(iv) Optimal utilisation of resources through coordination and development of proper linkages with sister agencies, commercial utilisation of research findings, constant review of the status of application of research findings by user agencies, continuing interaction with State authorities to determine area specific research needs, and through providing proper guidance and assistance as well as strengthening of research activities under the State Councils of Medical Research.

(v) Development of a Centre for Epidemiological Intelligence.

(vi) Augmentation of research activities in specific priority areas viz., integrated Vector Control Programme for Malaria, Filaria and Japanese Encephalitis, integrated control of non-communicable diseases and development of vaccines for communicable diseases as well as fertility regulation.

(vii) Enhancement of Research and Development on Family Planning and Maternal and Child Health.

(viii) Collaboration with international agencies for transfer of appropriate technology to the Indian scientists.

Indian Systems of Medicine and Homoeopathy

Teaching and training programmes in ISM and H were promoted during the Seventh Plan. Clinical research on drugs of various systems, collection, cultivation and propagation of medicinal plants and standardisation of drugs were encouraged. The Central Councils dealing with these systems of medicine have been strengthened to provide support for training and research in their respective area.

The National Health Policy assigned an important role to ISM and H in the delivery of health services. There are about 5.25 lakhs institutionally trained practitioners of ISM and H. These practitioners are close to the community not only in geographical proximity but also in terms of cultural and social ethos and as such they can play significant role in primary health care delivery. The strategy for utilisation of ISM and H for ealth care delivery during the Eighth Plan would comprise of the following:

(i) There are more than 200 colleges of ISM and H. One of the important tasks during the Eighth Plan would be to provide adequate facilities for training in these colleges so that the graduates emerging from these acquire the desired level of knowledge and skill necessary for patient care. Post-graduate training programmes also require strengthening for the purpose of manpower development for teaching and research in ISM and H.

(ii) To integrate the practitioners of ISM and H in the mainstream of health care delivery system, the graduate curriculum of these systems will be suitably oriented to make them conversant with the national health problems, policies and programes. Refresher courses will also be organised for the inservice practitioners of ISM and H towards the same objective.

(iii) There are more than 5000 pharmaceutical units, engaged in the production of drugs of these systems of medicine. Suitable steps will be taken to enforce the provisions of Drugs and Cosmetics Act to maintain the quality of products of ISM and H produced in the country.

(iv) Research and Development for the production and standardisation of drugs of ISM and H will be supported during the Plan. The existing research institutions will be strengthened for this purpose.

(v) The cultivation, conservation and regeneration of medicinal plants will be supported in State/joint sector farms. There is great potential for internal sale and export of these plants, herbs and formulations.

(vi) Separate departments, directorates and drug control organisations at the Central and State Government level will be established, wherever they are not existing currently.

(vii) Central Councils for Research in ISM and H would continue to receive support during the Plan so that they can discharge their responsibilities efficiently.

Family Welfare Programme

High growth rate of the population continues to be one of the major problems facing the country. Although the 1991 Census recorded a marginal decline in the annual growth rate of population from 2.22 per cent in 1971-81 to 2.11 per eent in 1981-91 this would still mean an addition of 18 million people to the country's population annually.

The fast rate of population growth means that the economy has to grow faster to protect the already low level of per capita availability of food, clothing, housing, employment and social services.

The country is committed to social and economic justice to the millions of people living under conditions of poverty and deprivation. Failure to do so within a reasonable time-frame may generate social tensions and unrest. Besides this, the environmental degradation which is associated with unchecked growth of population carries the inherent risk of natural calamities and disasters.

In this context, population control as sumes an overriding importance in the Eighth Plan.

Review of the Performance

The basic premises of the Family Welfare Programme till now have been:

(i) Acceptance of the family welfare in voluntary.

(ii) The Government's role is to create an environment for the people to adopt small family norm. This is done by spreading awareness, information and education by ensuring easy and convenient availability of family planning aids and services and by giving incentives for adopting family planning.

(iii) The programme, which is a 100 per cent Centrally Sponsored Scheme has integrated family planning and Mother and Child Health (MCH) services and is being implemented through countrywide network of primary health centres and supporting institutions.

In spite of massive efforts in the form of budgetary support and infrastructure development, the performance of family welfare programme has not been commensurate with the inputs. Right from the beginning the achievement of the set goals has been unsatisfactory, resulting in the resetting of targets, as indicated in Table 12.1.

TABLE 12.1

Year	*Specified demographic objective (CBR)**	*Year by which the goal gas to be achieved*	*Actual achicvement*
1962	25	1973	34.6
1966	25	as expeditiously	
1968	23	1978/79	33.3
1969	32	1974/75	34.5
Beginning of Plan	25	1979/81	33.8
1974	30	1979	33.7
Beginning of lan	25	1984	33.8
April 1976	30	1978/79	33.3

I. Population	25	1983/84	33.7
(reduce the gap)			
April 1977	30	1978/79	33.3
II. Population	25	1983/84	33.7
Policy			
January 1978			
Central Coucil of	30	1982/83	33.8
Health			
National Health	31	1985	32.9
Policy	27	1990	29.9
	21	2000	
Seventh Plan	29.1	1990	29.9
Eighth Plan	26.0	1997	

*CBR: Crude Birth Rate.

Seventh Plan Performance

With the long-term objective of achieving the Net Reproduction Rate (NRR) of unity, the Seventh Plan had set the following demographic goals:

	Seventh Plan Target	*Current Status*
Couple Protection Rate (C.P.R.)	42.0%	44.1 (31.3.91)
Crude Birth Rate (BR)	29.1	29.9 (1990)*
Crude Death Rate (DR)	10.4	9.6 (1990)*
Infant Mortality Rate (IMR)	90	80 (1990)*

*Provisional (SRS Data)

While the Seventh Plan targets of achieving CRP of 42 per cent was achieved, this was not matched by a commensurate decline in the birth rate, possibly because of improper selection of the cases.

The performance in terms of various methods of couple protection were not uniform. While the targets for Intra Uterine Device (IUD) were fully achieved and those for oral contraceptives and conventional contraceptive were exceeded, the targets for sterilisation operations fell short by about a quarter. The targets and performance of the Seventh Plan and the year wise break up of performance are given in Tables 12.2 and 12.3.

State-wise analysis of performance of the programme reveals that Punjab, Kerala. Maharastra and Tamil Nadu have performed very well in achieving the targets while Assam, U.P., M.P., Bihar, Rajasthan and some North-Eastern States have performed poorly.

Under the Maternal and Child Health Programme, which is an integral part of family planning programme, targets for reducing Infant Mortality Rate to 90 per thousand live births and for reducing maternal mortality were fixed for the Seventh Plan. The Universal Immunisation Programme (UIP) launched in 1985 with the objective of providing universal coverage of immunisation to pregnant mothers and infants was a major initiative in this direction. Although all the districts in the country have been brought under UIP, the targets for immunisation could not be fully met due to problems of cold chain facilities, inadequate trained manpower, logistic problems, etc. Other programmes aimed at women and children viz,. control of diarrhoeal diseases among the children, prophylaxis against anaemia and Vitamin A supplementation for prevention of nutritional blindness achieved varying degrees of success. Nevertheless these efforts wers able to achieve a substantial reduction in IMR from 97 per thousand live births in 1985 to 80 in 1990.

Constraints

Containment of population growth is not merely a function of couple protection or contraception but is directly correlated with female literacy, age at marriage of the girls, status of women in the community, IMR, quality and outreach of health

TABLE 12.2

Target and Proformance of the Seventh Plan

(in million)

	Target	*Achievemeut*	*Per cent Achievement*	*Remarks*
1. Sterilisation	31.00	23.70	76.50	There is a shortfall of 7.30 million sterilisations.
2. I.U.D.	21.25	21.28	100.14	Targets fully achieved.
3. CC and OP Users*	14.50	15.94	109.93	Achievement exceeds the targets.

*Indicates terminal year targets and achievement.

TABLE 12.3

Yearwise Performance of the Seventh Plan

(Nos. in million)

	1985-86	*1986-87*	*1987-88*	*1988-89*	*1989-90*
Sterilisation	4.9	5.0	4.9	4.7	4.2
	(88)	(84)	(82)	(87)	(76)
IUD	3.3	3.9	4.4	4.8	4.9
	(101)	(105)	(103)	(97)	(93)
BC and OP Users	10.7	11.6	13.4	14.3	15.9
	(103)	(100)	(104)	(94)	(99)

Note: The figures within brackets indicate percentage achievement.

and family planning services and other socio-economic parameters. Table 12.4 illustrates this.

The Family Welfare Programme has essentially remained uni-sector programme of the Ministry of Health and Family Welfare. It has yet to be recognised as a major national concern drawing priority attention and concommittant strong political, social and administrative commitment for the purpose of making it a significant part of our economic development strategy. A national consensus and strong public opinion in its favour, cutting across political, ethnic, religious and geographical boundaries is as yet lacking.

The family welfare programme has also suffered on account of centralised planning and target setting from the top. Regional variations and diversities have not been generally taken into consideration, with the result that similar set of approaches and policies and targets have been applied in States like U.P., M.P. Bihar and Rajasthan where the health infrastructure is weak and related social inputs are lacking and also for the states like Haryana and Andhra Pradesh where factors other than development of infrastructure contributed to poor performance. Monitoring mechanism under the programme has been reduced to a routine target reporting exercise incapable of identifying roadblocks and applying time correctives.

Both pre-service and in-service training of programme personnel is poor because of lack of due emphasis at all levels on training programmes for family welfare. Absence of proper training, education and motivation of the programme personnel including supervisory staff has led to an ineffective, insensitive implementation of the programme.

The programme has remained a Government programme, the community's active involvement and participation being marginal. Due to inadequacy of Information, Education and Communication (IEC) activities the knowledge of the community about the contraceptives, their availability, safety, etc. are at a low level. Adoption of the family norm and use of appro-

TABLE 12.4

Selected Indicators

States	*CBR (1990)*	*IMR (1990)*	*Female literacy rate (1991)*	*Female age at marriage (1981)*	*People below poverty line in years (1987-88) per cent*
Bihar	32.9	75	23.1	16.5	40.8
Kerala	19.0	17	86·9	21.8	17.0
M.P.	36.9	111	28.4	16.5	36.7
Maharashtra	27.5	58	50.5	18.8	29.2
Rajasthan	33.1	83	20.8	16.1	24.4
Tamil Nadu	22.4	67	52.3	20.3	32.8
U.P.	35.7	98	26.0	17.8	35.1

priate measures for birth control are matters of personal choice and decision. The IEC activities have to take this into account. However, till recently, the IEC activities have been directed more to national issues rather than personal issues. Undoubtedly, this incongruity of perception between the people and the providers of services has cost the programme dearly.

Family Planning Programme is being run as a 100 per cent Centrally Sponsored Scheme. The entire outlay is included in the Plan with the result that a major portion (60—70 per cent) of the outlay goes for meeting the expenditure of maintenance nature, leaving very little resources for further expansion, and strengthening of the programme or for any new initiatives. Further, the entire expenditure is borne bp the Centre, although the implementing agency is the States Government.

Lot of incentives and awards have been built into the programme. The incentives and awards have not been unequivocally shown to be very effective in the promotion of small family norms. On the other hand, defects such as over-reporting, low quality acceptors and neglect of non-terminal methods of contraception and MCH activities have often been observed to creep into the programme. The element of disincentives is also missing from in programme.

The efforts for the containment of population growth have to be intensified simultaneously on several fronts. This calls for an integrated approach and concerted efforts through both the government and the non-government organisations, besides social and political commitment to make it a national movement.

Strategy for the Eighth Plan

Containing population growth has been accepted by the Government as one of the six most important objectives of the Eighth Plan, with the aim of reducing the birth rate from 29.9 per thousand in 1990 to 26 per thousand by 1997. The IMR will also be brought down 80 per thousand live births in 1990 to 70 by 1997.

To give a major thrust in this priority area, which constitutes the pivotal point for the success of all developmental efforts, a National Population Policy needs to be enunciated and adopted by the Parliament. Given the political commitment at all levels, it must generate a cascading effect to become a people's movement. Social determinants such as female literacy, age at marriage, employment opportunities for women, and their status in society are as important as achieving a reduction in infant mortality, improving health and nutrition of pre-school child and providing a comprehensive package of maternal health care services. Such in inter-sectoral interaction, supported by political commitment and a popular mass movement, will constitute the approach to strategic interventions during the plan period. A Committee of the National Development Council (NDC) on Population has been constituted in February, 1992 to consider these issues and based on its report, a concrete plan of action will be worked out.

Within the above mentioned broad guide lines, which have been enunciated in the Eighth Plan Directional Paper already accepted by the NDC the following strategies will be adopted for achieving the goals of family welfare during the Eighth Plan:

(i) Convergence of services provided by various social services sectors, *e.g.*, welfare, human resource development, nutrition, etc. Based on a holistic approach to social development and population control, integrated programmes for raising female literacy, female employment, status of women, nutrition and reduction of infant and maternal mortality will be evolved and implemented. The strategy will be:

(a) to pool the existing resources available for individual and fragmented schemes on these activities. and provide additional resources required;

(b) to restructure, redesign and integrate these under a common umbrella; and

(c) to evolve proper mechanisms for planning, implementing and monitoring these programmes at various levels.

(ii) Decentralised planning and implementation will be another strategy, Although there are likely to be commonalities of approach in the general contours of population policy, it is critical that the programme content relates to area-specific planning at the district, the sub-district and the panchayat level based on critical and indepth dissegregated analysis of a constellation of sociobiological indices and demographic determinants. Area specific strategies would mean flexibility of approach and fund utilisation. Targets, if any, will be determined, fixed and monitoried at the district level and the process will be from below upwards.

(iii) As a natural corrolary to decentralised planning and implementation, Panchayati Raj institutions like Gram Panchayat and Zila Parishads, etc., will have to play significant role in planning, implementing and administering the programme. The role of the Centre will be limited to general policy planning and coordination, providing technological inputs where required, safeguarding critical areas and taking innovative leads.

(iv) With greater involvement of the people in the population control and family planning programmes through the Panchayati Raj System as envisaged in the Constitution (Seventy-Second Amendment) Bill 1991, the programme will become one of "people's operation with government cooperation." The health planners and administrators must not only become sensitive and responsive to the felt needs of the people but must also adapt to the instrumentality of local self-government.

(v) The younger couples, who are reproductively most active will be the focus of attention, with necessarily a greater emphasis on spacing methods, although the terminal methods would continue to remain the important means of birth control. Medical Termination of

Pregnancy (MTP) will have to play an important role in the entire scheme of family planning in the Eighth Plan. The coming generation will have to be, therefore, prepared well to accept the small family as a social responsibility. Population education and family life education need to be made a part of general education in which school teachers' role, both as an educator as well as a role.

(vi) The targetted reduction in the birth rate will be the basis of designing, implementing and monitoring the programme against the current method of couple protection rate. While broad guidelines may be prepared by the Centre, suitable parameters would be designed by the individual States for this purpose. Identification and registration of eligible couples, enforcement of civil registration scheme, registration of mothers and children for child survival and safe motherhood activities are areas requiring special monitoring.

(vii) The outreach and quality of family welfare services will be improved. For this, the health services infrastructure will have to be made fully operational and efficient. This would involve:

(a) completion of infrastructural facilities initiated during the earlier plans like buildings for sub-centres, PHCs, CHCs, etc., and installation of necessary equipments;

(b) ensuring placement of adequate number of well-trained workers specially at the grassroot level;

(c) providing mobility to workers, specially the peripheral ones ; and

(d) ensuring adequate drugs and other essential supplies at the Sub-centre and PHC by suitably increasing the funds for the purpose.

(viii) The entire chain of CHC, PHC and Subcentres will be equipped to deliver general health and MCH services in an integrated manner with a strong referral support and linkage at the District level. For this, facilities for services for mothers and children including reservation of beds for them at different levels will be ensured. Setting up of Regional Maternal and Child Health Institutes will be part of the strengthening process of MCH infrastructure.

(ix) Child survival and safe motherhood initiatives will be vigorously pursued. These initiatives will include:

(a) strengthening of Universal Immunisation Programme,

(b) greater emphasis on Diarrhoea Control Programme and effective implementation of ORT programme,

(c) Acute Respiratory Infections Control Programme,

(d) Anaemia Management Programme and not just Anaemia prophylaxis,

(e) Safe Motherhood Programme with high risk pregnancy approach and

(f) intensified effort for training of birth attendants.

(x) Any system is as good as the people who operate it. Therefore, major emphasis will be laid on health manpower planning along with a review of the education and training programmes of all categories of health care providers. Training will not only aim at providing requisite knowledge and skill, but also ensure development of such behavioural attributes that will be conductive to a closer interaction with the community. The methodology, the logistics and the content of training programme will be continuously reviewed. Special programmes would be chalked out for imparting pre-service and inservice training in programme management and IEC activities. To meet the training needs, various training institutions will be strengthened or new ones established, by providing adequate funds, staff, equipments and modility.

(xi) The entire package of incentives and awards will be

restructured to make it more purposeful. Individual cash incentives have not made any impact and hence will be phased out. The payment of compensation to the acceptors for the wages lost due to hospitalisation, etc., will be left to the discretion of the States, thus providing flexibility in approach to suit the local requirements. Community incentives in the form of priority consideration under IRDP programmes, *e.g.*, opening of schools, provision of drinking water facilities, linkage by roads, etc., will be built up in the programme. The possibilities of introducing certain disincentives to the non-adoptors of family planning will also be explored and introduced with due regard to the freedom and the fundamental rights of the people. The performance of the States in this vital sector of human and national concern will be recognised through additional resource allocation as a part of Central Plan assistance to those States which show better performance in terms of pre-determined demographic parameters.

(xii) There is an urgent need to secure involvement and commitment of practitioners of all systems of medicine in the Population Control Programme. The practitioners of Indian System of Medicine and Homoeopathy, whose number is estimated to be more than half a million and who are the closest to the community both in terms of place of practice and the socio-cultural milieu of the community will be involved in the programme by:

(a) providing well structured educational modules of instructions and training in population dynamics and family planning at the undergraduate level;

(b) providing short-term re-orientation cources to the practising doctors;

(c) providing incentives and recognition for exhibiting initiative and leadership in population control activities; and

(d) promoting a sense of comraderie between these practitioners and the grassroot functionaries of the health and family welfare programme with a view to synergising and potentiating their mutual input. A similar approach is also needed to strengthen and secure deeper involvement of practitioners of modern system of medicine. Organisations such as Indian Medical Association (IMA) will be involved in a greater measure in this national task.

(xiii) The role of voluntary organisation in a mass movement such as population control is critical for generation of momentum and accelerating the pace of progress. There is a need to incorporate family planning as a major objective of all voluntary organisations concerned with health and/or education-related activities. Substantially increased ammount of funds will be channelised through these agencies during the Eighth Plan. The establishment of an apex organisation to develop networking between all such voluntary organisations committed to the promotion of national efforts in this important area of human endeavour will be considered.

(xiv) As an extrapolation of the concept of voluntary organisations, in the role and place of organised corporate sector which covers approximately 20 million workers and their families. Effective methods will be evolved to get the organished sector involved in the implementation of family welfare programme.

(xv) Special efforts will be made to involve the community in the Family Planning Programme. The strategy will be to prepare the community to accept the responsibility, the ownership and the control of the programme fully in the long run. Panchayats, youth clubs, village committees, Nehru Yuvak Kendras, women organisations, etc., can play an important role in community motivation, organisation of camps and contraceptive distribution. Grassroot level functionaries, *e.g.*, village dais, Village Health Guides (VHGs), Auxiliary Nurse Mid-wives (ANMs), Anganwani workers, village extension workers, primary school teachers, Gram Panchayat staff etc, will play a facilitatory and supportive role to the community organisations for generating the necessary momentum for population control movement by the people. The village level local functionary will be the hingpin of these new initiatives.

(xvi) The village/neighbourhood tea shops, pan shops, public distribution system shops, pharmacies, cooperatives, etc., will be utilised for community based contraceptive sale and distribution.

(xvii) The social marketing programme, which was originally launched for Nirodh distribution has demonstrated the significance and importance of involvement of the corporate sector to achieve the family planning objectives. This programme will be extended to the social marketing of oral pills as well as for market research and educational activities for which the Corporate Sector possesses special skill and sensitivity.

(xviii) Information, Education and Communication, which are critical inputs will be further strengthened and expanded. The IEC activities of the health and the family welfare sector will be integrated. Greater use of the mass media will be made to disseminate the message of family planning to the remotest corner of the country. The entire system of pricing the media time *vis-a-vis* its social responsibility has to be given a fresh look, different from the commercial angle. Area specific IEC material will be developed and produced. At the viewers' level, efforts will be made to pool resources of various social sectors and to provide community TV/radio sets, besides maintaining them. The backbone of the IEC efforts will, however, remain the inter-personal communication for which the grassroot level female worker will have to be trained and effectively utilised.

(xix) A new thrust in the research and development of methods aimed at regulation of fertility in the male, and of vaccines for fertility regulation, both in the male and female, will be given. Fertility regulation practices such as the use of special herbs by the community particularly in the tribal areas, will also be subjected to research. While intensification of bio-medical research necessary, research in social and behavioural sciences to explore the human dimensions is vital. Health systems research to optimise operational framework, to improve the efficiency and effectiveness of the service provided and to evolve cost-effective interventions in various areas of family planning operation, will be given high priority.

(xx) A continuous monitoring, review and revaluation is an essential component for the successful implementation of the programme. Development and strengthening of health management information system, with district and sub-district data bases of health and demographic parameters and linkages aimed at concurrent evaluation of family planning programme will be developed. This will provide critical inputs at the district and sub-district level and the much needed data for area-specific planning and time-bound implementation.

(xxi) The family planning programme has a multi-sectoral dimension. For the purpose of effective intersectoral coordination and to provide the programme appropriate focus and priority, a proper institutional set-up with the backing of the highest political and administrative authority is an essential requirement. The recommendations of the Committee on Population, constituted by the NDC, will be implemented.

To sum up, the base and the basis of the population control programme during the Eighth Plan will be decentralised, area-specific micro-planning, within the general directional framework of a national policy aimed a generating a people's movement with the total and committed investment of community leaders, irrespective of their denominational affiliations and, linking population control with the programmes of female literacy, women's employment, social security, access to health services and mother and child care.

Outlays

The total outlay for the Central Health Sector is Rs. 1800 crores. The outlays for the Central, States and Union Territories Plans under the Health Sector are shown in Annexures 4 and 5.

The outlays for the Family Welfare Programme are Rs. 6500 crores. Details are given in Annexure 6.

Annexure 1

Progres of Establishment-Minimum Need Programme

Scheme	No. as on 1.4.85	7th Plan Target	7th Plan Achievement	Na. as on 1.4.90	1990-91 Act Ach.	1991-92 Anti. Achievement	Likely No. as 1.4.92	8th Plan Target (1992-97)	1992-93 Target
1	2	3	4	5	6	7	8	9	10
1, Sub-Centres	84263	54612	46937	131200	515	5968	137683	17030	4066
2. P.H.Cs*	9134	12392	10115	19249	1315	1241	21805	4450	759
3. C.H.Cs	813	1523	1261	2047	162	313	2549	1269	259

* Excluding Subsidiary Health Centres, Mini-Health Centres etc.

Source : Working Group Discussions for Annual Plan 1992-93, Planning Commission.

Annexure 2

Construction of Buildings for Sub-centres, PHCs and CHCs

Sl. No.	*Health Institution*	*Number Functioning*	*No. of Bldg. constructed functioning in Govt. Panchayat Bldg.*	*No. of Bldg. under construction*	*No. of Bldg. yet to be constructed*	*Col. 6 as percentage of Col. 3*
1	*2*	*3*	*4*	*5*	*6*	*7*
1.	Sub-centres	131385	52267	7906	71212	54.2
2.	Primary Health Centres	22328	12685	1371	8272	37.0
3.	Community Health Centres	1955	1206	271	478	24.5

Source: Bulletin on Rural Health Satistics in India. December 1991 issued by the Directorate General of Health Services. Ministry of Health and Family Welfare, New Delhi.

Annexure 3

Health Manpower Working in Rural Areas

Sl. No.	*Category*	*Sanctioned Posts*	*Number in position*	*Vacant Post*	*Col. 5 as Percentage of col. 3*
1	*2*	*3*	*4*	*5*	*6*
1.	Specialists in Rural Areas	3523	2481	1042	29.6
2.	Doctors at Primary Health Centres	25671	22078	3593	14.0
3.	Block Extension Education	6068	5513	555	9.2
4.	Health Assistants (Male)	24850	23266	1584	6.4
5.	Health Assistants (Femalc)/LHVs	25726	22999*	2794	10.9
6.	Health Workers (Male)	88182	80701	7481	8.5
7.	Health Workers (Female)/ANMs	130941	119906	11035	8.4
8.	Pharmacists	19225	17702	1523	7.9
9.	Radiographers	667	518	149	22.3
10.	Lab. Technicians	10516	8744	1772	16.9

Source: Bulletin on Rural Health Statistics in India—December 1991 issued by the Directorate General of Health Services, Ministry of Health and Family Welfare, New Delhi.

*Includes 67 posts in position in J and K for which corresponding sanctioned postas are not indicated.

Annexure 4

Eighth Plan Outlay—Health Sector

(*Rs. Crores*)

Sl. No.	*Programme*	*States/UTs*	*Centrally Sponsored Programmes*	*Central Schemes*	*Total*
1	*2*	*3*	*4*	*5*	*6*
1.	Minimum Needs Programme/Rural Health	2250.38	—	1.00	2251.38
2.	Control of Communicable Diseases		1031.00	14.75	
3.	Hospitals and Dispensaries		—	94.00	
4.	Control/Containment of Non-communicable Diseases		—	85.00	
5.	Medical Education and Training	3525.54	—	267.00	5324.54
6.	ICMR		—	124.50	
7.	Indian System of Medicine and Homoeophathy		5.00	83.00	
8.	E.S.I.		—	—	
9.	Other Programmes		20.00	74.75	
	Total	5775.92	1056.00	744.00	7575.92

Annexure 5

Eighth Plan Outlays-Health Sector-Distribution by States/Union Terrisories

(*Rs. Crores*)

Sl. No.	*State/UT*	*Outlay*	*MNP*
	States		
1.	Andhra Pradesh	183.32	53.60
2.	Arunachal Pradesh	28.02	12.50
3.	Assam	159.49	81.00
4.	Bihar	676.87	337.22
5.	Goa	59.00	12.22
6.	Gujarat	242.00	117.87
7.	Haryana	176.11	67.68
8.	Himachal Pradesh	121.00	48.00
9.	Jammu and Kashmir	179.90	75.00
10.	Karnataka	342.00	130.50
11.	Kerala	120.00	22.97
12.	Madhya Pradesh	300.87	150.00
13.	Maharashtra	553.26	281.00
14.	Manipur	21.00	10.15
15.	Meghalaya	33.73	18.00
16.	Mizoram	25.50	15.00
17.	Nagaland	50.00	6.40
18.	Orissa	223.23	78.00
19.	Punjab	254.75	80.00
20.	Rajasthan	390.95	150.00
21.	Sikkim	52.20	13.45
22.	Tamil Nadu	266.00	65.00
23.	Tripura	50.00	20.00
24.	Uttar Pradesh	517.57	260.00

25.	West Bengal	281.00	121.78
	Total : States	5307.77	2227.34
	Union Territories		
1.	Andaman and Nicobar Islands	22.51	9.45
2.	Chandigarh	66.82	0.75
3.	Dadra and Nagar Haveli	2.80	1.04
4.	Daman and Diu	2.40	1.00
5.	Delhi	350.00	—
6.	Lakshadweep	3.62	1.80
7.	Pondicherry	20.00	9.00
	Total : UTs	468.15	23.04
	Grand Total : States and UTs	5775.92	2250.38

Annexure 6

Eighth Plan Outlay—Family Welfare Sector

(*Rs. Crores*)

Sl. No.	*Programme*	*Outlays*
1.	Services and Supplies	3086.00
2.	Training	59.00
3.	Information, Education and Communication	127.00
4.	Research and Evaluation	89.00
5.	Maternirnity and Child Health	1982.00
6.	Organisation	71.00
7.	Village Health Guide Scheme	140.00
8.	Area Projects	400.00
9.	Other Schemes	46.00
10.	Provision for Settlement of arrears payable to States	500.00
	Total	6500.00

APPENDIX III

Women and the Teaching Profession

The most important single educational life-chance a child has, as she clambers up her educational ladder, is probably the equality and vision—or the limitations—of her teachers. No single influence for conservation or change, for creating insurmountable hurdles or new opportunities, will ever be as seminal as that of the teachers in our schools—of both sexes.

Back to June 1945 and the crucial 'scholarship' interview which would unlock me from four years of further boredom at the all-age unreorganized village school. I concentrated hard. 'And what', enquired the grammar-school headmistress 'do you want to be when you grow up?'. My reply was as unhesitating as it was decisive. 'I want to be a teacher.' 'Do you? Why?, The question left me (unusually) speechless. I had no idea, only a long, unexamined certainty assuredly not born of the unhappy example of the cliff-top school. My family had staffed a fair number of hospitals over the years; but not an identifiable padagogue among them. Yet already, at eleven, the adult road to happiness seemed to lead me back to a classroom.

Teaching has in fact traditionally attracted girls of proportionately higher academic ability than the equivalent make entrants to colleges of education. As Table 1 showed, a very high proportion of girls with three 'A' levels (15-17%) and with two 'A' levels (41-7%) entered teacher training in 1967, eleven years ago, instead of going to university like the 68 per cent of boys with 3 'A' levels and 26 per cent of boys with two 'A' levels, who aimed at graduate rather than cretificate qualifications. It is reasonable to hypothesize from the figures that the average woman teacher student was more able than the average male teacher student, and that proportionately more women teachers qualifying were in the top ability band than men students (because more men and fewer women opted for universities and advanced FE). It follows that more women should have been capable of reaching the top of the teaching profession; and they have not. A later section on the staffing of our schools and colleges shows indeed a disturbing decline, in fact, of top women in the education service.

It is perhaps important to stress that the presence of women in the leadership of schools and colleges is not only necessary in order to offer women themselves promotion to challenging personal development and economic equality. It is crucial that both girls and boys actually see women in leadership, management, government, making decisions in their daily lives, if we are to break the cycle of under-achievement. As long as children see men taking the top posts, decisions, and higher pay, and women tacitly accepting this from a constant middle role of an Aristotelian 'golden mean', children will believe what they see and not what we say. They will credit the evidence of their eyes and not our exhortations that women are equal to men, have equal talent, and equal responsibility and rights.

I believe it is important for us to understand the undercurrents beneath present trends if we are to disentangle the different reasons for needing a major restructuring of the teaching profession, with both men and women evenly represented at all stages from pre-school to professors, primaries to polytechnics—and probationers to principals.

I see these as having roots in the past, as do so many of the issues and problems that influence equality or discrimination. A brief historical flashback provides a framework for understanding the present.

There is a growing and extremely well documented literature on the history of the main development of the teaching profession and, latterly, on the specific question of women teachers; and there is little point in summarizing it here at any lenght. It is indeed a matter of some regret that academics in education have not studied in equal depth the problem of the employment and promotion prospects of the non-professional, non-academic women whom we have turned out from our schools so illequipped to achieve the equal pay, the free recruitment, and the relative mobility which teaching has offered so many. Asher Tropp's historical account of the teaching profession (1957) has now been overtaken by an admirably thorough and revealing analysis of women teachers since the turn of the century by Geoffrey Partington (1976), while Hilsum and Start's research (1974) analyses in considerable detail some of the reasons why women and men teachers are (or are not) promoted.

Women's commitment to teaching is a tradition second only to her domestic role, throughout recorded history and in both East and West, and has acquired an aura of 'inborn gifts' and extended maternality that seems ineradicable. It is curiously noticeable that from the earliest days of state education, women have gravitated to and concentrated on younger children, on the infant and junior schools, the elementary and non-advanced sectors within the profession. In Victorian times this was of course for practical as well as attitudinal reasons; women themselves had such a poor basic education that they were not yet competent to teach advanced work—hence the pioneering of Frances Buss, Dorothea Beale, Emily Davies. Understandable though it was that women should settle then for less exacting, less advanced work (which was still an improvement on the largely unpaid drudgery of governess employment), it is sad that women teachers should so quickly have set a pattern, which we now seem unable to break, of more limited career horizons, concentration on the lower rungs of responsibility, and over-docile acceptance of less well-paid teaching posts.

There is nothing new about the unthinking part which women tread to the classroom. We were slow to see alternatives from the start.

> 'In June 1900, a hundred students went down from a famous women's college. 75 of them were going to teach and all the rest were going home to arrange the flowers. Six yeare later, another 100 were going down; but this time only 50 were going to be teachers; two were to be journalists, one a doctor in India, one an expert on foods, one a hospital almoner, one a missionary, one an author—and the rest were going home. By 1913 the teachers had dwindled to 13 per cent. By 1932, only 22 per cent were teachers, and none were going back home to idleness, and 10 were to be barristers and 10 journalists.
>
> (*Biscoe* 1932:7)

At the turn of the century in 1904, women were in the majority in the elementary schools—69.5 per cent of all certificated teachers and a reassuring 56 per cent of all elementary headships. By 1914 the elementary sector had not altered; but already the different pattern in the secondary grammar schools was becoming evident (later to become all too familiar). The total teaching force was fairly evenly divided between the sexes—about 52 per cent to 48 per cent in favour of men; but men accounted for 65.7 per cent of headships, women only 34.3 per cent (HM Government 1919:20). This again was a causal relationship, since women had not been educated to as advanced level of personal education in sufficient numbers themselves to be competent to teach advanced secondary education.

Before the Second World War, 66 per cent of the teaching profession were women (and it is important to remember that they were then all unmarried). By 1951, the teaching force (with the help of the 1947 Emergency Training Scheme which planned places for 9,000 men and 4,000 women being demobilized or otherwise specially recruited) had reached 225,000, split again between two thirds women (140,250) and one third men (DES (1963). One extraordinary symptom however of governmental double-think was that they Ministry planned teacher supply and expansion on twin dimensions of 'women teachers' and 'men teachers' long after two World Wars had illustrated women's interchangeability with men in the labour market when need arose.

The Characteristics and Distribution of Women Teachers

The normative approach, which I questioned in the context of children in schools, is in my view equally inappropriate when discussing teachers. Their influence on children and on their personal opportunities, will be more affected by Dahrendorf's inequalities of 'social differentiations of rank' and 'social stratification of status' than by their sex, alone. Characteristics of status such as full-time: part-time; married: single; graduate: non-graduate, are more divisive than sex alone. Women teachers trained in rural, single-sex colleges before 1955 may have more in common with older men teachers, from the same background, than with younger women leaving a multidisciplinary department of a modern urban polytechnic. Although we tend to discuss teachers by sector and by sex, women teachers are more idiosyncratic in relation to their various status factors. Whether or not they have dependents is more relevant than whether they are married or single. Anyone who doubts this should read Please Ms with its thoughtful, if sad. commentary on the difficulties of unmarried teacher mothers (One Parent Families 1975). It has taken the implications of the Sex Discrimination Act, 1975, to lend power to the arms of those of us who have had to fight for years against the unthinking sacking of unmarried women teachers with children, regardless of their individual personal circumstances. (I have yet to see the putative father, often also in teaching, sacked, even when known).

Similarly, the distinction between full-time and part-time is a more influential factor than sex alone, although we know that most part-timers are in fact women. Age is also highly relevant because the educational environment from which the teachers were produced will have heavily conditioned their attitudes as well as their skills.

The inexorable path to teaching is still hammered out. Fogelman's selection of sixth-form opinion includes some stringent criticisms by students of sex-typed career assumptions by their former schools.

> 'Emphasis was put on the teaching profession for anyone who chose to go to college. As teaching did not interest me, I found that it was rather difficult to find any information regarding other courses.'
>
> 'Little help was given by my school to the pupil who did not want to take up teaching. I found myself "one alone" among 50 to 60 girls all going on to college/university. I know that many had no particular leaning towards teaching, but just drifted into it because of no knowledge of an alternative.'
>
> 'I have found that many of the students at college of education are not there because they want to teach, but because their schools and home persuaded them to go to college, and because they themselves had no other ideas of what to do.'
>
> (*Fogelman* 1972: 10-11)

McNamara (1972) quotes extensively to support the 'compatible with marriage, syndrome, while his own research into a sample of student teachers confirms that a majority of women students make the decision to teach at a relatively early schools age. What we do not know however is how many would have still done so if persuaded by careers teachers that business management, administration, medicine, dentistry, consultancy roles as architects, planners, designers, journalism, are all equally compatible with marriage and children. Given, of course, some of the sex-role restructuring we discussed in earlier chapters.

The Distribution of Women Teachers in Schools

All figures that follow are for England and Wales unless otherwise shown. In the primary sector women dominate overall by mŏre than three to one, but when the teaching force is analysed by type of school, decidely different palterns emerge. Table 1 gives the total distribution of teachers for 1975 which shows

TABLE 1

Distribution of Teachers—Primary Schools 1975

(*a*) *Numbers*

	Men	*Women*	*Total*
Infant	324	37,507	37,381
First	2,062	15,305	17,367
Junior with infant	21,112	60,442	81,554
First and middle	1,086	3,109	4,195
Junior	18,506	33,435	51,941
	43,090	149,798	192,888
Middle deemed primary	2,978	5,262	8,240

(*b*) *Sex balance in each sector*

	men %	*women* %
Infant	0.9	99.1
First	11.9	88.1
Junior	25.9	74.1
First and middle	25.9	74.1
Junior	35.6	64.37
Middle	36.1	63.9

(c) *Overall sex balance*

	men %	*women* %
	22.3	77.7

Source. DES Statistics of Education 1975, Schools, Table 14, (excluding independent schools)

clearly the concentration of men in the junior sector, although we now have about 2,400 male teachers in the infant sector—a welcome breakthrough on the lines discussed earlier. When however the figures are compare with those in Table 2 and 3 following, it will be seen that although men represented only

TABLE 2

Primary School Teachers 1974

	Men	*Women*	*Total*
All teachers	45.667	148,414	194,081
Headships	13,565	10,215	23,780
Deputy headships	7,092	10,788	17,880
Senior master/mistress	22	47	69
Scale 5	48	28	76
Scale 4	774	1,096	1,870

Percentages of relevant group by sex

	men	*women*
All teachers	23.5	76.5
Headships	57.0	43.0
Deputy headships	40.0	60.0
Sentior master/mistress	32.0	68.0
Scale 5	63.0	37.0
Scale 4	41.0	59.0

Source. DES Statistics of Education 1974, Vol. 4, Teachers.

TABLE 3

Decline in Proportion of Women in Senior Posts Schools 1965-74

Teachers	Sex balance—Percentages			
	1965		1974	
	Male %	Female %	Male %	Female %
Primary				
All teachers	26.0	74.0	22.3	77.7
Headships	49.2	50.8	57.0	43.0
Deputy headships	37.4	62.6	40.0	60.0
Secondary				
All teachers	58.8	41.2	56.5	43.5
Headships	76.3	23.7	81.2	18.8
Deputy headships	60.0	40.0	65.0	35.0
Second master/mistress	33.2	66.8	34.0	66.0

Source. DES Statistics of Education 1965-74—Teaching staff.

TABLE 4

Distribution of Teachers—Secondary Schools, 1975

(*a*) *Numbers*

Schools	*Men*	*Women*	*Total*
Modern	20,191	16,665	36,856
Grammar	11,547	8,384	19,931
Technical	580	438	1,018
Comprehensive	80,428	58,190	138,618
Other	3,025	2,504	5,529
	115,771	86,181	201,952
Middle deemed secondary	3,637	4,001	7,638
Direct grant grammar	3,533	2,767	6,300

(*b*) *Sex balance in each sector*

	Men %	*Women* %
Modern	54.8	45.2
Grammar	57.9	42.1
Technical	57.0	43.0
Comprchensive	58.0	42.0
Other	54.7	45.3
Middle deemed secondary	47.6	52.4
Direct grant grammar	56.1	43.9

Overall sex balance

	Men %	*Women* %
	56.9	43.1

Source: DES Statistics of Education 1975, Schools and Teachers.

22 per cent of primary teachers overall in 1974 they carried 57 per cent of headships and 40 per cent of deputy headships the leadership role. (They also represented 63 per cent of scale 5 and 41.0 per cent of scale 4 posts.)

We disturbing to both the prospects of women teachers and the implication for children's attitudes, the proportion of women in leadership roles has actually declined from 1965 to 1974 and provisional statistics since then suggest a continuing trend of decline. The adverse implications of this are obvious.

The decline in women holding headships and senior positions (despite an increase overall in women staff) is, however, much more serious (see Table 3, partly because it is more acute than in the primary sector and partly because it is, as we have seen, even more important for adolescent girls to identify with leadership models. (The second master/mistress question is discussed separately below).

The secondary pattern is both very different and more complex. Table 4 gives the distribution of teachers by type of school. Women are in an overall minority, although the sex balance is generally more even.

How Pupils see Staff

We have already noted the feminization of the pre-school and primary sector—and the importance to girls of having both male and female models with whom they can identify in their formative years. But the polarization of roles between women staff as supportive, subordinate, maternal, and caring, and men as the leaders, heads, active members of staff (football, outdoor pursuits, school journeys), and dealing with boys and older children, is not only constant, but increasing. (In 1975 there were in any event no male nursery teachers and only a small minority of men teachers in infant and first schools). In those schools with a woman head (43 per cent in 1974) pupils will have seen women in authority and in control; but those coming from schools with a headmaster, and probably also men teach- primary science and football (the existing 'male' preserved) they have already begun to conceptualize women as the supporters, not the leaders. It is true that, of the graduate scientists in primary schools in 1974, 653 where men and 1,000 were women—although this is still a disproportionate male bias given the overall proportion of women to men in primary education. But in fact, 311 out of the 653 men were physicists of chemists, while only 235 out of the 1,000 women were either, while on the other hand, 501 women science teachers were biologists but only 118 men. The association of women with natural and men with physical sciences is unlikely to be significantly shakes as long as this pattern persists so early in children's education which partly explains also the masculine-oriented primary science projects we more frequently see. Similarly, of the 1,416 primary French teachers, 1,024 were women (DES *Statistics of education*, Vol. 4, *Teachers*: Table 17), implicity registering with both boys and girls that this is a field in which women excel. While it is comforting to be able to establish that girls may expect to achieve high standards like their teachers, it waters the seeds sown in earlier years and starts the germination of assumptione which are taken on to the contrasting secondary schools.

How Alice or Jane will see men and women teachers when they put on their new secondary school uniform in September will depend on their school—single sex, mixed, grammar, modern, comprehensive. They would of course expect to see a girls' school led and mainly staffed by women (although eleven of the seven hundred or so girls' schools, leaving out independent schools, do have a headmaster!). Whas they may not expect is that the 15 per cent male teachers out of twenty-five thousand in girls' schools should predominantly be heads of departments, and/or teaching maths and science, mirroring more sarply the growing primary pattern. The message is implicity earned again—they are male fields. (Yet the girls' schools do acceed in encouraging more girls to read science than mixed schools. Do women science teachers push girls more? Do ten teachers in girls' schools take those posts in the first place precisely because they want to encourage girls to develop?)

The pattern varies considerably moreover between different types of co-educational schools. In mixed grammar schools, men at number women by nearly two to one. In secondary modern schools the balance is nearly even (fifteen to twelve thousand). But in comprehensive schools the proportion of men is steadily growing, currently nearly 60 per cent to women's 40 per cent overall. Suddenly, girls are seeing a world, as they adjust to the few environment, in which women not only are not the main influence. but they are generally in a minority. At least nearly half of all primary schools still have women heads and deputy leads; but fewer than one fifth of secondary schools have head mistresses and only a third have women deputies. This is not only important because it sets a pattern for girls (and boys), but because it leads to a quite different ethos in mixed schools in particular, which are male dominated, from those where both men and women share the leadership. There is a typical pattern of organization which has important implications in the context of both sex typing and the hidden curriculum. I am quoting in full because Bennett's analysis is absolutely typical of so many schools in all four L.E.A. areas where I have administered education, and in the areas surveyed in 1968 and more recently. Bennett appears to be writing for an audience of teachers educational planners, advisers. He postulates the following as a structure which he sees as not open to question. I believe both teachers and parents will recognize this pattern. Both of the schools quoted below are co-educational.

> 'It may be helpful to look at the formal staff structure of two hypothetical schools. Each school of course has a headmaster. In the first, and English school, there is a deputy headmaster who deputises for the head as necessary and who is in charm of the general day to day running of the school. He is responsible for the discipline of boys in the school and for the supervision of male student-teachers in conjunction with heads of departments. A senior mistress is responsible for the discipline of girls and supervises female student-teachers. She also co-ordinates house matters and has a particular responsiblility for social functions in the school. She has a scheme of general administrative jobs.'
>
> (*Bennett* 1972: 46)

Bennett's book is aimed, one might add, at the in-service trading market.

The phraseology is revealing. The head is male of course. The assumption of complete sex typing of men dealing with boys and women dealing with girls is not questioned—either in the context of discipline or in relation to supervision. Typically the senior mistress is landed with the social side—an extension of the domestic syndrome since it usually mean organizing food, drink, transport, and support services.

> 'In the second school, a Scottish one, the duties of a deputy head the similar . . . he deputises when necessary. . . . There are 5 assistant headmasters in the school and 3 of them act as heads of school. . . . It happens that the head of lower school is a woman and so she has been asked by the headmaster at look after the discipline of the girls in the school. She has also been asked by him to take part in Official Functions, acting as hostess when the school has visitors...'
>
> (*Bennett* 1972: 50, my italics)

Bennett's Scottish contrast is equally interesting. All five assistant headmasters are male. It appears to be accidental (and musual?) for the head of lower school to be a women but as a result she is landed with girls' discipline and appears not to deal with boys—even in lower school? She too, predictably temporarily replaces the head's wife, by hostessing his school functions as his wife does the domestic events—instead of directing affairs.

Colleges of Education

The training institutions which produce the teachers in the first place are of central importance not only in producing the basic teaching force but as potential agents of change, and as inhences in inservice re-education of teachers. It is depressing, therefore, to see the same position mirrored yet again as in the schools sector—an overall predominance of women, their consentration in junior posts, but the steady, not to say rapid, decline in the proportion of women in leadership. During the rapid expansion of teacher training in the 1950s and 1960s, women outnumbered men by two to one overall, despite a higher growth rate for men (Ministry of Education 1964);

The position has been, however, reserved in the training Colleges. In direct proportion to their reorganization from single as to co-educational, from small rural to larger urban,

Student in Training—Colleges and Departments of Education

Year	*M*	*W*	*Total*
1953-54	6,825	19,858	26,683
1956-57	7,127	21,323	28,450
1959-60	10.571	24,013	34,584
1963-64	18,510	39,168	57,678
Percentage growth 1953-63	171,21%	97.24%	116.16%

and them single discipline teacher education to multi-disciplinary higher education, women's representation in all levels, but not ably the higher levels has steadily fallen:

Decline in Proportion of Women Holding Senior Posts in College of Education (Teacher Training)

	Percentage of all posts					
	1965		*1970*		*1973*	
	M %	*F* %	*M* %	*F* %	*M* %	*F* %
all lecturers	52.9	47.1	66.7	33.3	68.3	317
deputy principle	31.8	68.2	51.0	49.0	59.1	409
principal	36.9	63.1	45.9	54.1	57.0	450

Source: DES Statistics of Education 1973.

Two thirds of all principals and deputies were hitherto women now nearly two-thirds are men. For the decade 1953-1963, the women's ratio was even higher: 71 per cent of all lectureships in 1953; 61.5 per cent in 1960; 55 per cent in 1962; 32 per cent in 1973. A reduction from two-thirds to one-third in twenty years can only mean a further decline in top women in teacher training. One alleged reason is that the women, carrying as many do, domestic responsibility, fight shy of the work commitment of reorganization, and of the staff-room conflicts and decision-making required. I question this. I suspect overt and indirect sex discrimination by both men and women on governing bodies who reproduce unfounded doubts and assumptions, ('But can she handle the difficult men in the staff-room? What would you do, Mrs Brown, if your children were ill at the peal of the summer term?') When did someone last ask Mr Brown? Moreover, a substantial number of women in teacher training are in fact single or have grown up children.

The time has surely come for some direct and decisive monitoring of the position of women in the policy making levels of education—or where will the leaders of the future be? These sectors—and all in decline. But the situation in further and higher education is if possible, worse. The position of women in further education for example is the least favourable of all

TABLE 5

Full-time Teachers in Grant-aided Establishments of Further Education, 1974 (England and Wales)

Grade	*Men*	*Women*
Principals	660	33
vice principals	501	39
heads of depts	2,371	225
readers	35	1
principal lecturers	2,513	126
senior lecturers	8,718	714
lecturer II	17,515	2,713
lecturer I	16,426	5,171
assistant lecturer	1,842	1,172

Source: DES *Statistics Education* 1974: Vol. 4 Table 3a.

errors, as Table (5) illustrates. Only a handful of women hold in posts at all and the latest statistics show a decline in women principals from 8.3 per cent in 1961 to 4.0 per cent in 1975, a how familiar pattern.

In universities fewer than 10 per cent of professors are men; only 6 per cent of all readers and senior lecturers; and men account for only 10 per cent of all university staff DES *Statistics of Education* 1974). Women academics like Tessa backstone and Margherita Rendel are more qualified than 1 to two of the masculine ethos of Academe, not to say its hidden criminations. We ought perhaps in justice however to register but although higher education was the first barrier to be attached by the Victorian and Edwardian pioneers (in terms of body; Oxford and Cambridge refused women degrees until well to the twentieth century), our great-grandmothers would be heartened to see that today women academics are the least all represented of any sector of education in relation to made errors.

This is of greater significance educationally than the simple one of personal injustice to women academics. It means the work of an adequate feminine (or feminist) voice in the constant structuring of higher education, and the lack of enough intired women to lift the horizons of women students to seek hanced positions in life and—one hopes—to care about lifting the position of the less fortunate in life who did not get through the net.

My discreet spark on behalf of my university colleagues nevertheless remains a pale flash, compared with my more combustible blaze of frequent indignation at the complacent chauvinism of schools and FE colleges who declare that all in right with their world—which houses not the 8 per cent or of so girls who make she graduation lawns, but the 90 per cent of girls who are steadily feeling their way towards greater understanding of their mothers' frustrations, are determined not to follow them, but lack insightful people in their environment to teach them how to think clearly, and to aim higher. If the most highly educated 1 per cent of women in Academe cannot fight their battle on their own ground, it would augur ill for the rest of us. The compelling voice is still needed back at the ranch.

There is no question but that there must be discriminatory practices in the staffing and promotion policies of the education service, and it is difficult to see how far these will be exposed until both women staff in each sector and the Women's Rights groups of the teachers' unions (of which NATFHE is by far the most thoroughly researched and most belligerent) rouse all their field forces to challenge practices that prevent women from attaining leadership (like regarding leadership in polytechnics as immutably linked with engineering or computer studies and not with training in personnel and welfare studies?). The battle for creches in colleges and polytechnics has seen reversals even in its preliminary skirmishes—while more sports halls and discotheques spring up like mushrooms. A policy of social priority.

Hidden Barriers

It will be clear from earlier illustrations that men and women teachers see their roles differently and that men in leadership tend to see women's role as subordinate, caring, and more peripheral to central and major planning. In the same way in which one can identify a 'hidden curriculum' of structural and attitudinal constraints on girls, a collection of hidden barriers, less obvious but more pervasive than the alleged simplistic causes of women's under-achievement (marriage, family, break in employment) can be detected by a keen and interested eye.

They also see themselves differently according to their sex and domestic status. A. Walters' study of 104 mature women students in Survey suggested that even the women on higher status jobs and on vocational courses described themselves first in terms of their domestic role (*e.g.*, married, mother of three) rather than their past working life or present external role (former teacher, student). This is continuing evidence of women's ambivalence to the loyalty to an economic and productive role (Walters 1975).

Hidden constraints also include the difficulty of married women and of single women with dependents in taking part in training courses, whether evening classes at the Teachers' Centre or longer residential courses. It must be said that unconscious chauvinism on the part of the mainly male Assistant Education Officers and Principal Advisers who share out the diminishing in-service education budget in times of recession in selecting for courses, is not unknown ('She'll only be leaving soon to have a family' or 'she'll miss half of the course if the children are ill'). Since many women teachers are married to men teachers it is worth remarking indeed that the most effetive key to unlock one door for married women is for LEAs and heads to make it clear to their male staff as part of in-service education that they are expected to divide the staying-home-to-look-after-Jeannie absences evenly with their wives. A head teacher can in fact often be spared more easily for a day than a class teacher—but his wife pagged on Scale 2 because she followed his promotion, will be expected to cope with all domestic crises still. More attitude changing is needed here.

Women teachers are often less frequently groomed for seniority and for responsibility by their mainly male heads. Their apparently natural gravitation to pastoral work, tutor groups, and counselling places them on the tramlines for a senior mistress post, not a future headship, for which attendance at administrative meetings, local and regional policy discussions, timetabling experience, and curricular restructuring in reorganizing schools, is a better foundation. But a deeper question may be, why do not more apply for senior posts—as many do not who are qualified? Some suggest that women staff tend to create self barriers unconsciously. Evidence is quoted of the self-perception of women as lacking in confidence; less willing to apply fifty times for promotion, but cutting out after five because of rejection; less sure of capacity to tackle work several jumps ahead rather than one step up; less willing (perhaps rightly?) to relinquish the personal satisfaction of classroom teaching and pupil contact, for the chimaera of administration (c.f. Ollerenshaw and Flude 1974; Assoc. of Assistant Mistresses 1976; Hilsum and Start 1974).

For married women, the blind acceptance that they must

follow husband's career promotion (and not he hers, if it occurred first) is a major hurdle, but one to which the remedy lies as much in their hands as in their husbands'. One small but extremely interesting survey of the problems of women teachers, described the cost to women held back by husbands' career as:

> 'nineteen years in one school on Scale I' and
>
> 'five full-time and one part-time jobe in seventeen years.'

It is curiously interesting how, also, the Cinderella hierarchy of subjects operates indirectly to the detriment of women teachers both in financial terms and in confidence-building and their personal development (or otherwise) for leadership. After twenty years of school recognization, since the mid 1950s, it is daunting to see how, even though the shortage areas of teachers (the demand factor) has shifted constantly, the rank order of Burnham top allowances and of prestigious importance in school terms remains constantly in favour of male-dominated areas. It is rarely related to educational and curricular ideologies clearly defined in advance. Thus a typical school of from 1,000-1,500 pupils will possess four or five head of department posts for maths and sciences, often under an overall head of faculty and mostly at scale 4 or 3, to every one allocated for English, languages, the humanities (not only part of core studies but pursued by more pupils overall). Handicraft and technology rank for higher allowances than housecraft and needlework (does equal mean the same?). Economics will frequently out class history. The logic may be individual; the effect when analysed is that because women dominate the arts subjects and remedial work, they draw lower allowances regardless of size of department or importance of work in the schools' scheme, and women teachers' average salaries tend therefore to be less than men's who have comparable years of service.

To the extent that the conditioning analysed earlier has trained the women of the past that decision-making and conflict are 'unfeminine', it would not be surprising that they eschew the trauma of several years of both, in the task of unceasingly reorganizing schools and colleges. The larger organizations, replacing as they do schools which twently years ago averaged from 400-850 in size, mostly homogeneous in intake; and often single sex, have produced many new dimensions which reouire training and new attitudes. Decision and conflict acquire a new sharpness as opposing ideologies have to be discussed, stitched, welded, or moulded into a coherent whole. (mixed ability or streaming? Integrated studies or history and civics?)

Supervision of 160 mixed staff represents a very different scale and cast of management problems from the oversight of three separate and again, identifiable, groups of fifty in three small schools. Requirements for senior posts in both larger shools and merging colleges and polytechnics include vastly increased reading of local reports, internal documents, the endless how of government national discussion documents or Commission reports.

The gradual integration of teacher training into polytechnics is also steadily reducing opportunities for women staff. Of all trends, the removal of single sex institutions seems to me to be the major adverse factor affecting women staff. Believe in co-education as I do, I cannot but believe that if we continue our present headlong flight to totally unisex provision, we should consider two courses of action concurrently. First, some nationally validated research into the performance and skills of men and women in co-educational establishments with a view to counter remedies against under-achievement and polarization of roles; and second, a deliberate manpower/womanpower planning strategy for teacher redeployment which will ensure more balanced recruitment to the different sectors and levels of education. If we do not develop a national policy of deploying teachers in schools and colleges towards a policy of equality we will soon end up with an all-male leadership, thus turning full circle of Victorian times. Conversely, no true educationalist can accept unquestioningly any variation of 'the best person for the job'. There is meat for a substantial national debate.

The answers are no more simple than the problems. Staff development programmes, aimed clearly at both sexes, should take special account of women's needs for management experience and retraining. Credit should be given for work not traditionally accepted as an equivalent gift (*e.g.*, home-mankind and compensation allowed for the illogicality of career pattern solely caused by sacrifice to husband's promotion. Women returning to teaching who held a scale post before, should be given some incremental benefit and not returned to basic scale, unless there is genuine well founded doubt about present capacity. The child-care problem is well rehearsed—but remains central. Married women who leave for a family should be encouraged to keep up contact, even in-service training while away—with support from the LEA or Training Services Agency for local schemes if need be.

Quota, Sex Roles and the Burnham Test Case

In 1976 the newly introduced provisions of the *Sex discrimination Act* resulted in our challenging the ruling of the Burnham report on teachers' salaries and conditions, that the third-tier post in co-educational schools had to be of opposite sex to the deputy head. We should be clear that rule was not, in fact, replicated in the Burnham FE report for colleges, the Pelham report on teacher training staff, nor in universities. It was limited to the schools sector for reasons which are not clear if the need for students to have access to both sexes at senior level were upheld.

The argument ran roughly thus. Girls in school need a senior woman at the top to 'look after them', a euphemistic phrase, Boys need a man. Therefore if one already had, for example, a male head and deputy, one needed a woman at third ties—and *vice versa*. Authorities were legally obliged (they thought (to advertise for the third tier of the opposite sex to the deputy head. Since most heads and deputies are men, the teachers unions welcomed this as a protection for senior women teachers.

The rationale behind this rule was ambivalent. If the unions on the Burnham Committee really wanted equality, why was it not mandatory to appoint a deputy head of opposite sex to the head—a much more influential move. No way was this conceived. Nor, given an existing male deputy when the head resigned, was it mandatory then to advertise for a women headteacher to preserve the alternation. Equality and balance were apparently only designated as necessary at the support, not leadership, levels. Finally, and most specious of all, if the senior master/mistress were ones appointed of deliberately opposite sex to the deputy head, and the latter left, there was no obligation under the original Burnham rule then to restrict the *deputy and* advertisement to the opposite sex to the extisting senior master/mistress, so carefully appointed to obtain sex balance. Thus, although in theory the rule preserved a mix at the top in the school, it was only at third tier level, and this automatic alternation vanished whenever the deputy head teacher solved.

In 1976 the Equal Opportunities Commission supported Mrs Festle against Surrey County Council in the industrial tribunal, in a challenge of this Burnham rule on the technical ground that the provisions of the Burnham report were only mandatory as so far as they were covered by the *Remuneration of Teachers Act* 1965, i.e., were *financial* provisions. The real case being brought behind this technical argument, was, however, the fundamental principle laid down in the *Sex Discrimination Act* that and jobs must be open to both sexes unless a case can be established for a 'genuine occupational qualification' (Section and Neither the local authorities nor the teachers' unions could, however, make up their minds whether they were arguing for a preserved quota system (which is now unlawful) or for a continue occupational qualification' for which no case has yet then proven.

Mrs. Castle won her case, was appointed senior mistress at her primary school although the deputy head was also a woman, led that particular Burnham rule was removed from the report by the relevant authorities, rightly recognizing the ruling was applicable nationally and not merely to Surrey County Council. The value of the case was that it exposed the whole debate on why both sexes were needed at the top of the school and how this should be achieved. What became immediately clear was the fog of mythology surrounding staffing policies. The preservation of posts for both sexes at the top of the schools can only serve originated in the minds of the Burnham Committee from one of two principles; that is a protected promotion avenue for the minority sex in each case (broadly women in secondary schools and men in primary schools) or—in my view man soundly—that it was necessary for the welfare of both boys and girls to have both sexes at the top of the school.

What we did was to call the bluff of the authorities and unions and make them attempt to define which of the principles they thought they were applying. First, to look at the quoti angle is to raise the whole principle of professionalism. It is clear from the statistics already given that qualified women and men are not available in equal numbers in all subjects. The fast moreover that substantial numbers of women leave teaching for a period and return after a gap of from 3-10 years, places in question whether as many women as men have the kind of experience (as distinct from the ability) defined by most LEAs and governors as necessary for an early headship or senior post. Imposition of a predetermined quota may and almost certainly would mean a breach of the right to appoint the best candition for the job. Even the AAM's report on promotion of women teachers confirmed the widely known lack of women applicant for advertised senior posts. Eleven out of 110 applications for headships, eight out ninety-five for head of house; but while the lack of women applicants for head of maths was predictable, the absence of women prepared to take on head of history or head of English—in which the graduate teacher numbers are almost even in history and higher for women in English—must be a matter for especial concern (AAM 1976: 3).

The opposite sex rule, if justified on quota grounds, would be impossible to justify logically. It could only be validly applied if made compulsory for all three top tier posts—head, deputy and senior master/mistress. Supposing it to be applied arhitrarily in 1979. The accident of the then existing pattern of senior staff in each school as at January 1, 1979 (*i.e.*, mostly men would mean that nine out of ten secondary deputy headships would have to go to women. Since more deputy heads are make the same thing would apply at third tier. Even if experiences candidates were not available? This would, moreover, predetermine an alternating sex balance in perpetuity on the as accidental 1979 model.

The argument then shifts to teachers' roles. How, ask my male headteacher and Chief Education officer colleagues, do then obtain advice on girls' problems? Who can I place in charge of girls' welfare? This strikes at the root of two fallacian. I criticized in earlier chapters, that only women can deal with the curricular and pastoral needs of girls and only men with boys; and second, that either sex will look to the same sex or the same person for every problem simply because the counsellor is a woman or a man. The curriculum should be common to both sexes and there should be no question of detailing women off to supervise 'girls' courses' or *vice versa.* Is it suggested that only a senior member of staff in a 1,500 place comprehensive school, can deal with pastoral problems? Demonstrably it is got so. It is, let me stress, crucial that there is the best mix of women and men at all levels, overall, that we can achieve, to avoid the teaching of small children in an excessively feminized environment, and of older children in what often can only be described as girls attending a boys' school and women teaching in a male environment. To designate this sex-balance at senior level on the basis that men and women will each deal only with their own sex is effectively to reject the whole ideology and principles of co-education. It would, even if not invalid psychologically, socially, and developmentally, be logical only if the terms of reference for both sexes were the same. Twenty years of staffing schools has taught me that senior masters, apart from occsionally caning boys, typically deal with school organization, curricular reconstruction, major administration, CSE examining, and resource allocation, while senior mistresses typically deal with social functions, pregnant school girls, difficult parents, coffee for and entertaining of visitors (in my experience), and school attendance. Equal is not held to mean he same here. Any one of these functions can quite adequately be either dealt with by either sex delegated to an appropriate woman or man on the school staff (PE teacher, head of house, fear group leader, class tutor) who happens to have the characteristics needed for the problem. It is interesting that men are regarded as able to deal with girls when appointed as head of maths or science in girls' schools; and women with boys when teaching English and remedial work in boys' schools, as so many in Matrons in boys' boarding schools are women.

Deeper than the reflex born perhaps of fear of personal misunderstandings in dealing with adolescents of the opposite sex who are past puberty, is the problem of how one reaches balance either without quota, or without definitions of 'genuine occupational qualification' on grounds that the job could not possibly be done by the opposite sex. One quite simple method would be for appointing bodies to give priority to the minority sex provided that the successful candidate is equally qualified and suitable. It has never been wrong to select the person most fitting the idiosyncratic staffing position. It may be that a married woman will bring a maturity, understanding of adolescents, and acquired patience lacking in the younger man with drive. Credit for personal qualities and experience as well as professional background is a perfectly valid additional criterion for selection.

This question affects not only schools and colleges, but the youth service, careers education service, and all of the carring professions where adolescents need counselling as well as the professional service being offered. It is the practical demonstration of the polarity of perceived masculine and feminine qualities and characters that I criticized in the opening chapters. Those responsible for training and in-service education have a direct responsibility to question, to rethink, and to retrain their colleagues in diagnosis and not reflex, in matching personal qualities to pupils' and students' needs, regardless of sex stereotypes.

One important footnote should be recorded. It was a widely held view that the Burnham 'Senior Mistress' rule preserved avenues for promotion for women teachers. This may well be true in the case of comprehensive secondary schools, ninetenths of whose heads and deputy heads are male. But from 1965 to 1973 (when the rule still operated) women actually declined as a proportion of senior mistresses in the primary sector, in secondary schools as a whole, in 'other secondary' schools, and in grammar schools, although they increased in comprehensive and secondary modern schools. It cannot therefore be argued that this intermittently applied quota worked universally in women's favour.

Women or People?

I suggested earlier that we should not generalize about women and men, but about functional status differences—that is, the difference between married and single women, women with and without dependents is more influential than between women and men. A single woman (including divorced, deserted, etc.), with three children may be more hindered from promotion than a married woman with no children or whose family has grown up. A widower with three children may be equally constrained from promotion-prone activities like residential training courses, leadership of teachers' unions, or take-up of extra curricular duties. This diagnostic approach is supported by the preliminary findings of a study of the Higher Education Research Unit being conducted at LSE into supply and demand of teacher supply (Turnbull and Williams 1974) and which includes an examination of sex differentials in teachers' pay. Women earned generally less than men; but single women earned consistently more than married women. Differentials emerged that crossed the sexes—men graduates did better in the secondary sector while male non-graduates did better in primary schools. But while women graduates overtook male non-graduates in secondary schools, they do less well in financial terms in primary schools than men. But women non-graduates were more advantaged in secondary schools—a reverse of the male pattern. The two factors which predictably appeared to be most influential were the tendency for married wamen to have a break in service, and the restriction of geographical area in which they can apply because of the socially-induced assumption that they will follow their husband's promotion pattern and not *vice versa.*

Turnbull and Williams, however, suggest that their analysis establishes that both men and women who come back to teaching after a break of two years or more, suffer no loss of earnings when the return in relation to others with a similar length of service, and question, therefore, whether lower pay is solely due to an interrupted career. More influential may be women's limited field of application and their lesser drive for either greater responsibility or more money because of their satisfaction in home life and their protection of a double income. There is no question but that my married women colleagues have a choice that I do not, of deliberately remaining in non-leadership roles for reasons of personal satisfaction at field level, because their double income is not in fact matched double expenses, and is cushioned by income tax allowances for family. The central costs of mortgage, house maintenance, heating, and car are almost constant to single-income and to double-income families. A double-income married woman teacher has therefore a lesser desire for increased financial security against inflation (or incapacity). Hence the small differences between pay of single women teachers and male colleagues.

A second finding of this research is equally interesting. The position of married women *vis-a-vis* single women deteriorated markedly from 1963 to 1971. The authors postulate that co-educational reorganization has resulted in the replacement of male/female discrimination by a form of married woman/single discrimination.

The Part-timer and Married Returner

The whole structure of the profession has changed in two important respects in the last twenty years, the effect of which we underestimate both in terms of the strucutre of schools and in the attitudinal effect on pupils. First, the proportion of teachers who are either married and have continued without a break, or who have returned to teaching after a break has in creased steadily (the abolition of the marriage bar is post-war). Second, proportionately more of the total labour force has been made up by part-time staff, of whom nine-tenths are women. In 1954 there were only 5,000 part-timers in all schools. From 1964 to 1974, part-timers doubled from about 11,000 women is each of the primary and secondary sectors (but only 429 and 2,782 men respectively) to 21,601 women part-timers in primary schools and 15,881 in the secondary sector (but no equivalent increase in male staff—568 and 3,100). I do not propose to debate the conditions of the teachers themselves but to question the cause and effect of this sex imbalance. My Northern fifth formers were incredulous at the idea that Ted also had the right to opt in and out of economic work and that they might take or the breadwinner role. This attitude of assumed dependence by girls and assumed responsibility to work fulltime of boys, is not likely to change while they see throughout up to twelve years of basic schooling only women combining marriage with part-time work. The sextyping of subject areas of teachers high lighted, is also replicated. Part-timers tend to be found in 'feminine' activities like infant teaching, remedia work, music and drama, and in minority subjects not regarded at important enough to warrant inclusion in the core (*e.g.*, foreign languages in smaller schools, the craft areas which already sextyped). In the eyes of both girls and boys, part-time work becomes then pervasively if unobtrusively identified with a female role, and an 'additional', dispensable, external rule.

The original rationale for encouraging recruitment expansion of both part-time teachers and married women returners, was a no way as conscious attempt to improve opportunities for women. It was a response by government to the crisis of the lastic shortfall of teachers needed to cope with the very high fifthrate of the 1940s as the pupils worked their way through the system. Despite, however, the obvious skills, gifts and puriety that the part-timers and returners have brought, it is a matter for serious concern, not to say strong disapproval, that if the educational, social, and organizational arguments brought to pay in the 1960s to persuade LEAs to retrain and to recruit is rich new labour source, have unaccountably vanished as the session has caused authorities to look for convenient savings. Then some teachers' unions have seriously debated (at least at banch level) policies of (a) part-timers out first, or (b) married women to be declared redundant before men. We simply do not hance permanently on any front. When women were a conmient emergency resource, we heard of their own need for a satisfaction and creativity, and the 'earning for pin money' dadrome began to fade. We were told by inspectors and advers of the special skills that bringing up a family and dealing with interpersonal relationships had given wives and mothers, with which our shools would be enriched (as in my view by are). Now that it is convenient to look for cuts by formulae not if by diagnosis, instead of weedling out the poorer quality sale as well as female) or the more dispensable curricular as (however we define these), government is supporting immitly, a reversion to the previous pattern of a mainly full-time and constant teaching force, by allowing the nature and characteristic of financially recessive cuts and redeployment to unmonitored.

A policy of refusing to employ married returners was forehad and criticized in the DES/Lancaster study on returning to thing.

> Moreover, although women who have left teaching to bring up a family have no prescriptive right to an opportunity to return, to deny them effectively any reasonable chance because of oversupply of those newly trained would be tantaamount to the old marriage bar.'
>
> (*Ollerenshaw and Flude* 1974 : X)

There is no easy answer except that of learning to deploy our staffing resources in an overall plan, nationally and locally, to balance the profession with college leavers and with married returners. The Lancaster Survey estimated that given the massive expansion of students in the 1960s who will he ready to return in the next decade, at intervals, there could be 6,500 trained teachers seeking a return by 1984 and 8,000 by 1989. Falling birthrate or no, our school standards are not so high that, as an educationalist, I can accept that we cannot use the skills locked up there—for which we have paid and in which we have invested—for a further twenty years. Nor do I see how any concept of personal or social justice can use women when we are in crisis, and then dismiss them as without right, with out value, and without relevance when economic pressures and therefore increased male competition makes it expedient to do so.

Dare I suggest that if it were married and part-time men who were so affected, they would have used the organized influences at their disposal (unions; the subject associations to defend the preservation of the threatened discipline—music, languages, remedial work) more efficiently than the women have? Why is it, still, that so many women shy away from organized, effective, economic, political, or controversial battles even in their own interests?

The problem is even more acute in further education, which depends heavily on part-time staff. In the tertiary sector part-timers tend to be equated with lower level, non-advanced work, and are more often vital to the maintenance of courses is smaller or rural colleges or those with little advanced work. The policy of part-timers-out-first is therefore placing at risk the courses on which girls in fact also predominate as students and women as staff. The adult education service is almost entirely staffed by part-timers of whom two-thirds are women. There is a growing cycle of deprivation developing, on cuts simultaneously preventing women from. retraining and of depriving those who have, of the one outlet for creative, not home based satisfaction which is compatible with home and family.

Geoffrey Partington's study documents a thorough but depressing historical survey of discrimination against married women teachers (partington 1976 : 28—36). Depressing, because I have heard all of the quotations repeated in modern form in the last three years, and used to justify staffing cuts. The Sex *Discrimination Act, 1975* outlaws discrimination on grounds of marriage as well as of sex; and defines a new concept of indirect discrimination. Any woman teacher dismissed on grounds of marriage or because she is a part-timer (including, in my view, redundancy as part of any overall policy of priority for male 'breadwinners') should take expert advice from her union and/ or a lawyer, to challenge the practice either under the SDA or, possibly, as a case of unfair dismissal under the other relevant Acts.

It is, in this context, revealing to note that no mixed teachers' union has a majority of women on its executive; some not even a significant minority. And with women still the majority in the profession as a whole, that the Burnham Schools' Committee has only five women out of thirty members of the Management Panel; and four out of twenty-seven on the Teachers' Panel, must be a matter for concern. Do women not stand for election? Or do men (and women) not elect them when they do? And if not, why not? The Equal Rights Panels of the unions ought to be examining in some depth the causes of women's absence from this key leadership role.

Traditions, of course, die hard. Despite the merger of the National Association of Schoolmasters and the new Union of Women Teachers in 1975, the General Secretary (Terry Casey) took no women representatives at all to the House of Commons. Expenditure Committee when (using, however, the union figures expanded as a direct result of the merger) he went to argue stronger representation on the Burnham Committee. The women members 'had not won their spurs yet', said Mr. Casey Perhaps the fact that the reprinted NAS/UWT constitution still enthrines a clause, 'To ensure that schoolboys come under the influence of schoolmasters and girls under the influence of schoolmistresses' (*Education*, February 20, 1976) accounts for the union's Nelsonic eye to its prominent and vocal women. Their place is clearly, for the male leaders, still supervising girls' cookery and not arguing teacher politics in the House. If the deliberate reprinting of this clause embodies conscious union policy, the new approaches I have outlined in the early chapters are even longer overdue than I suggested.

During the discussion of the teachers' role in the primary and secondary school environment, the pupils' perceived image of her or his teachers on the child's future adult roles has emerged as of some importance. This is not to underestimate the effect of *parental attitudes*, which have not been reviewed principally because this is a book about the education system, and cannot embrace all aspects of the complex social educative process in one compass. Since, however, the attitudes of small girls are often very strongly conditioned before they enter school, parental re-education in more positive ways of bringing up their daughters must be an important task for school—especially nursery and primary schools; and for the adult education service. Parent-Teacher Associations are an important voice in pressing for change and in the post-Taylor reforms, should be increasingly influential.

Re-training

The re-training problem is perhaps most acute in the area of numeracy and science. As long ago as 1959 the Crowther Committee recorded its concern about innumerate women teachers—they noted 'the considerable number of training college students, especially in the women's colleges, who have done virtually no mathematics *for three or four years before admission*, and had been unable to secure an O level pass' (Crowther Committee 1959: para 150). Innumerate teachers qualifying then in 1959) still have twenty years teaching ahead of them. Many will even have achieved leadership positions in primary schools. In 1974, 75 per cent of maths teachers in secondary schools were male.

A small research survey of thirtynine schools in the West Midlands in 1976 revealed only five women heads of maths departments out of the thirty-nine (four in girls' schools, significantly). But of the men, four were in girls' schools, four in boys' schools, and twenty-four in mixed school a typical pattern which may well illustrate not only the shortage of women maths teachers but a likely bias against appointing women heads of departments in mixed schools (Hall and Thomas 1977).

In 1977, the Secretary of State for Education and Science has enlisted the aid of the Chancellor of the Exchequer, the Training Services Agency, and the Local Government Training Board to mount and fund a special programme of training and retaining, to produce more teachers of mathematics, physics, craft, design, and technology. Some useful characteristics of the pilot scheme create precedents on which we might build. Special one-year courses for graduates or trained teachers are funded either by secondment by LEAs (for which the TSA, through the LGTB will pay a premium to the LEA of £3,500 for each seconded teacher), or by paying training grants direct to applicants; and tuition fees direct to the training institution. One weakness of the scheme is that *mandatory* grants for this scheme were not available to women (or men) wishing to return to teaching after a break in service. These—as usual—are at the mercy of the discretionary grant system. It is too early yet either to estimate the success of the scheme, or even to analyse the characteristics and distribution of applicants and trainees. Its value, however, is not only the obvious one of productivity of a shortage skill. It is the model that is yet for future programmes. Retaining of teachers of cookery and needlework for example; of the alleged 'surplus' of college-trained teachers because of the declining birth-rate; and the retraining of secondary school teachers for further education and *vice versa*, are obvious next candidates for special programmes. Section 47 of the *Sex Discrimination Act, 1975* allows for programmes of positive discrimination' solely for women or for men where either sex was not previously represented in an employment sector. It would be interesting to explore this to establish following programmes for re-training redundant men teachers for infant teaching and redundant women teachers specifically for handicraft (without the technology if need be) and for the apparent male preserves of 'dealing with the boys', discipline, and decision-making—in other words, for school management and government.

As today's five-year-olds reach the legving age in 1991, the retiary of FE colleges to which the may more, will still have to totaly male leadership and women locked up in the typing room and the catering kitchen, unless the FE sector develops a counteractive positive staff development programme, particularly for its women staff. Natural trends make no impact; positive discrimination is needed. Nelson and Colne College under the leadership of David Moore has created a staff development system one of whose main purpose is to help to counteract the 'illogicality' of a woman's career because of the domestic burden, the precedence that the husbands career tends to take, and so on. This is well written up in a Coombe Lodge Report (1977) and points the way both for more research into women's position in FE and the need for interventionist programmes to 'lever more women to the top' in the interests of the further education sector as a whole. We have thirteen years before today's school entrants reach FE; but next year's girl leavers will still be disadvantaged, in lacking women leaders. Regional Advisory Councils for FE/HE and the DES have a clear duty urgently to investigate the problem of women staff in FE as an act of national policy issue. Perhaps the new area Manpower Services Commission Boards can be used as leverage.

HM Inspectorate have recently, probably for the first time in the inchoate history of the educational pragmatism so characteristic of this country, produced a series of reports on the core curriculum. With equally anxious diffidence however they reassure us that there will be no national plan as such.

> 'the case for a common curriculum, as it is presented here, deserves careful attention and that such a curriculum,

> worked out in the ways suggested, would help to ameliorate the inconsistencies are irrationalities which at present exist, without entailing any kind of centralised control.'
>
> (*HM Inspectorate* 1977:1)

I do not believe, in the light of the present accidental distribution of undergraduate entry and the equally incoherent relationship between the actual distribution of specialist teachers and the attainment of a balanced curriculum, that we will have the tools for the job, without more central sponsorship. Alison, Jane, Fiona, and Liz, sitting in today's reception class, will reach eleven plus in 1986, by which time teacher training will be cut by nearly half. If they are to have a full opportunity to learn the handicrafts, two foreign languages (pace the channel, we really are in Europe now), the physical sciences, enjoy real careers education, and profit from new programmes of transition from school to work, we need double the number of specialists pro rata in some subject areas, that we now have.

This means positive, conscious, and long-term re-training of many existing teachers and some mature returners to newer subject areas with a transfer value. If an undergraduate can become a specialist in three year from the sixth form, a graduate or college-trained tearcher with experience can re-specialize in two years. This would both ease the current level of teacher unemployment and call the bluff of those who allege we cannot offer a common curriculum to all because we do not have the resources. Teachers are better re-trained and re-deployed than on the dole or wasting their skills.

Such programmes would give many women teachers an especially valid second chance to top up their deficient earlier imbalance. It would also, ideally, include a national planning dimension for a proper, permanent, and protected staffing establishment of part-time specialist staff—of both sexes—to give greater flexibility in sparsity areas.

Since this is not a book about teaching as such, but a

synoptic glance across the whole spectrum of women in education, much has been left out, many problems under discussed. The complexity of women's under-achievement and stereotyping of roles in the teaching profession will not be solved in one short chapter highlighting some strands only of a complexly woven mix of historical tradition, politics, prejudice, vested interest, and—on the part of many women still—passivity to accept the status quo. It will be solved by sophisticated enquiry across the related fields to training institutions and their recruitment, post-experience education, good school practice, and investigation of discriminatory practices.

It is arguable whether yet another national commission would be competent to handle such an enquiry but any attempt at a national policy must spring from a nationally validated work respected by the education sector itself and therefore handled by qualified innovators. Perhaps the first task of a recalled Central Advisory Council for Education should be to examine the re-deployment of the teaching profession (and hence the restructuring of the whole historical tangle of Burnham structures) towards a balanced profession geared to educating and encouraging girls and boys (in that order) to equal, higher attainment.

A formidable list of action progrmmes begins to emerge. To conclude at sunset is romantic but valedictory. If we are looking for a way ahead, we need to look for innovation, fresh approaches, and beginnings, even if only dawning. The concluding chapter touches lightly on some of these.

APPENDIX IV

The Way Ahead—A Development Plan

'Certum est quia impossibile eit.'
(It is certain because it is impossible)

Tertullian, 225 AD

Late in the evening, late in November 1975, the telephone rang in the study. The voice of a colleague from Westminster came over a line, succinct, tired, but satisfied. 'It's'through.' 'With education and training still in ?' 'Yes.' The *Sex Discrimination Act, 1975* had finally received the Royal Assent, with, as Huxley would have said, 'all its parts of equal strength and in smooth working order'— or nearly. We had won the first hurdle in legislative terms, in the race to convince government that it is useless to attempt to tackle inequality in employment, in pay and salary, or social discrimination, without simultaneouly attacking their causes and counter-remedies—the formative years of education and training. This chapter is not, however, about discrimination legislation as such. It is too soon to judge, even accurately to assess in the context of education, the merits and demerits of the Act, or of the Equal Opportunities Commission set up under its powers to monitor progress and to act as an agent for constructive change. That is for another, perhpas.

a later book. We are here concerned with translating the messages, problems, and diagnosis of this albeit incomplete account of the education of girls and women into a positive action progammes for change. And to do this is only possible if we use the same kind of unstructured, widespreading, but loosely coordinated network of carying people across the country, as that which helped to haul the many draft Bills and their amendments safely up Sisyphus' hill. The word is partnership; of government, professional staffs, community groups, voluntary organizations, collectives, caring individuals. Each has a different but related part to play in bringing about radical but constructive change. I began by translating Kurt Waldheim's declaration, back to the classroom, the high Street, the home, I end by a similar call—for every reader who is in touch with children, young people, women in need, to accept their own individual responsible (not only that of the governmental and detached 'They') to help to alter the structure, attitudes, and policies of society, that we shall not be debating womens' under-achievement when, in retirement; may generation sees the twenty-first centry safely in.

Inequality and discrimination

> . . . discrimination against women violates the principle of equality of rights and respect for human dignity, it is an obstacle to the participation of women, in equal terms with men, in the political, socal, economic and cultural life of their countries and hampers the growth to the prosperity of society and family, and makes more difficult the full development of the potentialities of women in the service of their countries and humanity.'

It is important to distinguish inequality from discrimination because the measures needed to deal with each are radically different in some tactical respects. To combat inequality we need and overall strategy and policy of positive discrimination in investing our resources, based on diagnosis of the greatest need and the most immediately effective of a choice of intervention and affirmative action programmes. These will be carried out through the tools of the policy makers, committees, leaders of the service, as well as through the community. Discrimination is an individual act by an identified person or body (the authority, the Principal or head teacher, the admissions officer, the interviewing panel) and can be attacked at precise decision making stages along the way. Since the new Act, we now have two kinds of discrimination: *unlawful*—that is, which fits the way the drafter of the Bill drafted it, and apparently '*lawful*'—that is discrimination which is blatantly conscious, overtly indefensible if equality means the same, but which does not happen to fit the wording and terms of a legal document. In educational terms, neither is acceptable. While the law is a useful, indeed a vital tool of human rights, effecive overall change (test cases apart) will come by convincing the leadership of education, that discrimination is wrong, unrespectable, non-u, bad education, uneconomic, and harmful to social stability.

Thus the Principal who wrote to a married woman applicant for a further education course that

> 'We regret that we are unable to offer you a place at the present time. The reason for this is that it is not our policy to offer places to mothers with chlidren under school age. However, we should be very willing to reconsider your application as soon as your youngest child is at school'.

Was practising blatant discrimination, not just even accepting inequality, if only because young fathers are not so denied. This breathtaking arrogance of a college principal is based on several complacent assuptions: that he is a better judge than Mrs X of her family's needs and capacity to cope with her parttime absence; that in the magic day of five-years-old, all children, regardless of circumstances, can suddenly be adequately cared for, but at four and a half cannot; that Mrx X is a better mother at home in any circumstances, regardless of her own financial, mental, psychological, or intellectual needs which will also affect her relationship with her children; that he has the right unilaterally to decide on a desirable policy for society, and so on. Some mothers are better at home, and some children need a homeparent until their teens. Other children and parents are better adjusted and stretched with shared lives from the outset. This is for individual families to decide for themselves-not for the men who control the education service to determine as acts of policy.

Similarly, the under-achievement of girls in the sciences may or may not spring from innately inferior capacity; or from psychological or even sociometric difficulties influencing their competitive learning environment. But the former practice now unlawful, of rationing scarce physics laboratories in favour of boys and teaching girls biology in a converted classroom, on the grounds that the boys needed physics for later vocational training and work and girls did not (a widespread practice in my 1968 survey), was clearly discriminatory.

Women's failure to raise their expectation to advanced FE courses rather than shorter skills-based training may spring from conditioned environmental inequalities. But a conscious policy of denying (rationed) discretionary awards to girls and women to enable more grants to be given to boys and men, because the latter are expected to be breadwinners, would be discrimination; as is the continued denial of equal day release to girls under eighteen and to young women seeking career training, at nineteen or twenty.

The Aggregation of Inequality—Jam Tomorrow

The education expenditure cuts which have been cumulatively intensified since 1973 have now produced the basis of a decade of recession and compound deprivation which will make it doubly difficult to persunde government—central or local—that the time to redress the balance in favour of girls is now. It always seems a problem to be dealt with when resources (later) permit. Jam tomorrow, as usual. One reason is the triviality with which the feminist debate is still treated by many who control resources. This, like most aspects has roots in the past which cling tenaciously to their hidden subsoil, in the present. The OECD survey on educational opportunity in the mid 1960s—when the golden expansionist days meant increased available resources for new developments—merely confirmed make neglect and imperviousness to the emergence of girls as a social risk group.

For Westergaard and Little do us scant justice. They sweep aside girls' inequality as of little importance—yet going on to illustrate themselves how stark it actually was ten years ago.

> 'There are other inequalities of educational opportunity besides those of social class—*inequalities between the sexes for example. But these—so far as the present data go—are of little importance until sixth form level.* But fewer sixth form girls than boys leave with the minimum qualifications for university entry; and fewer even among the qualified, in fact gain admittance to a university. Moreover, the disparity between the sexes widens as one goes down the social scale. The resources—cultural, economic, psychological—necessary for a working class child to overcome the obstacles on the way are very rarely expended on behalf of a girl. At the extreme of the scale, an unskilled manual worker's daughter has a chance on only one in five or six hundred of entering a university—a chance a hundred times lower than if she had been born into a professional family.'
>
> (*Westergaard and Little* 1965: 222, may italics)

This major contribution to the OECD study group predictably concentrates on academic opportunity, selective secondary and higher education. There is no mention of further education, day release, or extended (non-academic) secondary education. They concluded that the overall expansion of educational facilities has been of greater significance than any redistribution of opportunities. But as the published statistics now show, this expansion has benefited men at a consistently higher rate than women.

I believe it is now essential for us to find methods of idetifying particular risk groups among our girls and women by the kind of aggregation of factors of deprivation which lay behind the EPA programme, and the National Children's Bureau's risk groups who were 'Born to Fail' (Wedge and Prosser 1973). For example, rural girls in schools in a mainly working-class or lower middle-class catchment area (*i.e.*, excluding the developed rural commuter villages in which we all tend to live in a well-cushioned ring around the towns), who are in the East Midlands or the North East, and who are in the bottom two quartiles of ability, who are thirty miles from a college and have little public transport, will have five or six indices of potential deprivation. They are five times more at risk than urban girls in a large mixed school in the residential outskirts of a large, well serviced South Eastern town. The choice of sample schools, of pilot areas for investment in new approaches to careers education; for development and grant aid for 'bridging courses' for school leavers and adult returners; for the first range of new in-service training courses, should be guided by *aggregated* factors of deprivation, and not by the accidental willingness of Chief Education officers and heads to experiment—for those areas still in most need are unlikely necessarily (with distinguished, but few, exceptions) to have the liveliest of leaders.

A National Policy

> 'We do not believe that there is any hope of carrying out the measures we have outlined . . . unless they are worked out and adopted as a coherent, properly phased development programme.'
>
> (*Crowther Committee* 1959: para 396)

Teachers' in-service training courses regularly hum with the immediate impact of the major stands of new (or reinforced old) philosophies in the wake of each prestigious report. But rarely are they seen as a diagnostic whole.

Unfortunately no post-war committee has been prepared yet to look diagnostically at either the special situarion of girls as others have discriminatorily planned for them on the one hand; or, ironically, to look at them in precisely the same light as boys, on the other. We now need not a simple national declaration that it is no longer British to descriminate, but a positive, planned policy for which national and local resources will be allocated to achieve certain defined objectives by say, 1985 and 1990 and which will improve the educational opportunities and achievements *of those girls and women most in need.* If, as many hope, the Central Advisory Councils for England and Wales are recalled, moreover, to look at the educational needs of girls and women as the *present* system educates them and to make recommendations for improving their opportunities, there should be no deferment of immediate measures, pending publication of their report. The task is sufficiently great for no interim measures to be regarded as abortive.

There are encouraging signs internationally. It is interesting that it is the Nordic countries that principally are seen to share the UK's concern to include education and training in measures to enforce equality. The Nordic Council of Ministers of Education issued a statement on Sex Roles in Education in 1974, declaring that:

> 'the educational policy is an important tool for endeavours to achieve equality . . . for all levels of the educational system the Nordic countries should take measures to increase the individual's opportunity to *choose* an education, a trade, and an adult role without being bound by expectations originating in sex roles.'

Italy, one the other hand, has passed its Anti-Discrimination Act in response to the EEC's Equal Opportunities Directive, in December 1977, but excluding education and training from its provisions.

> 'Attempts to widen the Act's scope to bring general education and training within its ambit, and to include more detailed and potentially stronger enforcement provisions on the model of the UK Sex Discrimination Act, were firmly rejected.'

Similarly, Ireland now has an Employment Equality Agency, set up under the *Employment Equality Act, 1977*; but has no legal monitoring of education and training. The Dutch Emancipatie Kommissie, however, set up in 1974, keeps an interested eye on education. It was asked, for example, to review the 12-16 comprehensive scheme prepared in 1975-76 by the former government in order to monitor is suitability in the context of equal opportunity. On the European level there are encouraging signs. In addition to the increased attention being paid to equal opportunity in education and training in individual countries, the Commission of the European Communities has now started a phased project to attempt to diagnose the prevalence and cause of inequality of education and training in the secondary years in its nine member states, the first stage of which is the production of a diagnostic report to be considered by government experts and, later, by the Minister of Education in 1978 with a view to action programmes to speed the achievement of real equality. Simultaneously, the Ministers of Education of the twenty countries that make up the Council of Europe have designated equal opportunity in education and training for women as the theme for their 1979 biennial conference. One of the many benefits that will come from these international enquiries into the causes and scale of and remedies for inequality between the sexes, is the increased exchange of information and ideas between experts of the different countries —as well as the implicit endorsement of the growing respectability of the sex inequality debate.

In terms of this country, there would be benefit in replacing our pragmatic and decentralized fatalism which accepts, decade in, decade out, the unevenness of our provision and our achievements as between LEA areas, regions, town, and country, by a national policy that has certain common national stands which are binding on all LEAs. The next section suggests some of the contents and principles that might be included.

The Curriculum and Common Core

The oversensitive reaction of the English teaching profession to suggestions of defining a common core of subject areas which every child should study will, if there is not a relaxation and some concession to the accountability of the educational system to pupils, parents, and to the world of work, soon lead to a counter-reaction seeking some national control over the structure and standards (not the detailed content) of the curriculum. We are the only European country to reject so constantly even the concept that there is a proper minimum which children ought to learn and which teachers ought to teach not primarily so that both are 'happy,' but so that both are socially useful and competent and that children are equipped both for survival and to meet the demands of the world of work competently. We should stop being ashamed of our mill chimneys and power stations, of business and commerce (as if we were still Voltaire's nation of shopkeepers), and of our factories and industrial technology.

This means common core of some kind, and an end to any options system for those under statutory school age which enables them to discontinue subjects vitally necessary for recruitment to skilled employment, further training, and later stages of re-education. This final message could not have been more starkly endorsed than by the 1974 report of the (them National Youth Employment Council, whose title of *Unqualified, Untrained and Unemployed* summarizes its main theme in three words, for the 300,000 school leavers who leave every year with no marketable qualifications or skills, and end on the unskilled labour market or unemployed. The Council recommend especially that employers should open boys' jobs to girls and *vice versa* (now legally mandatory under the employment provisions of the *Sex Discrimination Act. 1975*), and asked the new Manpower Services Commission to research into interchangeability of boys and girls in employment. The Council pressed for investment in training for the less able 'in the interests of the nation as well as of the young people concerned' to match the 'great deal of money in educating those who have academic ability.'

It is a nonsense to say that examinable qualifications do not matter, and that external examinations distort the system to the disadvantage of children. We do not adequately stretch either sex today. Twenty years ago academically able children attempted up to ten subjects out of the twenty-five or so generally taught, in School Certificate; and four or five at eighteen elus. That system had some major faults of inflexibility, and ever-specialization, and the examination syllabuses left much to be desired educationally. Nevertheless the pendulum has swung so far, and today far too few able girls now study for more than five subjects at 'O' level or CSE, or for more than one or two Advanced levels. There is no better investment than *measurable* attainment, not because it is educationally 'better' but because society in the shape of employers, training bodies, villeges, and universities, demand it. Until they cease to do to, educationalists should cease to argue that they are right and the rest of the world is wrong.

For those, nevertheless, for whom the examination system held to be inappropriate (although with a 7-grade CSE which can be moderated on school based assignments, these should always be a minority) there should always be a constant second and third chance. Many colleges of further education do now exercise considerable discretion in waiving recruitment requirements for mature (*i.e.*, not school leaver) entrants who lack formal qualifications, and this has been adopted as a policy principle by the new Business Education Council, preserving a sute for the motivated student with an educationally disadvantaged past.

Equal Means the Same

Perhaps the most fundamental curricular question facing the education service is that underlined by the United National Resolution of 1967 which declared the equal rights in education at all levels, meant the *same* curricula, examinations, staff, and grants. Does equal mean the same, or 'of equivalent value'? One major weakness of the wording of Section 22 of the *Sex Discriminetion Act, 1975* is that it speaks of 'not less favourable treatment'; not of the same treatment. Circular 2/76 of the Department of Education and Science which heralded the new Act to the LEAs, regrettably interpreted this as not necessarily meaning identical classroom provisions for girls and for boys. I challenge, refute, and reject this. It is impossible for me as an educationalist to reconcile the historical thousands of pages of educational philosophy demanding education for personal fulfilment we have printed over the years, or the millions of words we have poured out on the need to treat every individual child in their own right on the one hand, with any deliberate construction of different and separate educational objectives, curriculum, routes, and practical resources for a classified and defined group of pupils whose only common element is a collection of hormones which has determined their sex—sex; not gender. The physiological distinction between girls and boys is a matter of sex. Gender is the collection of attitudes which society stitches together (dress, behaviour, attributed personality traits, expected social roles, etc.) to cloths girls and boys in order to help image identification.

The Green Paper on what has come to be known as the 'Great Debate'—curricular reform in our schools and the vexed question of national standards—was, moreover, considerably more ambiguous on this issue of 'equal' or 'equivalent' than is desirable, given an apparent national policy of full equality in educatian and training. Regrettably, the Consultative Document, Education in Schools, started that:

> 'Equal opportunity does not necessarily mean identical classroom provision for boys and girls but it is essential that, in translating their aims into day-to-day practice, schools should not by their assumptions, decisions or choice of teaching materials, limit the educational opportunities offered to girls,' (*DES* 1977: para 10.9)

I reject this utterly. With respect to both policy maker and drafter, it is a nonsense. If girls are deliberately not offered the *same* subjects, practical resources, and teachers as boys (*e.g.*, biology and not physics, cookery and not metalwork, mixed tennis but not mixed cricket, typing but not economics), then schools are in fact quite deliberately limiting educational opportunities not only to girls, but also conversely to boys. The Green Paper goes on tc recommend that schools must prepare pupils for the transition to adult and working life, and that since 'the traditional division of labour between men and women is rapidly breaking down, the curriculum should reflect this by educating boys and girls according to their needs and not according to sexual stereotypes' (para 10.10). This is surely irreconcilable with different courses for girls and for boys. Breaking down the tradition of men's work and women's work starts way back in the schools which educate for adult roles; not at sixteen plus. The latest output from HM Inspectorate (*Curriculum* 11-16, HMI Working Papers, December 1977) make re-assuring progress. The introductory paper says among other things that:

> 'There is the responsibility for educating the autonomous citizen, a person able to think for *herself* or *himself*, to resist exploitation, to innovate and to be vigilant in the defence of liberty. . . . The role of women and men continues to change and with it inevitably the role of men. Both contribute to the care and upbringing of children. . . . Society tends to expect a finished product from schools whereas it appears to need young people who have acquired certain essential skills . . . whose earlier education will enable them to benefit from further education and Training, *This is as true of the education of girls as of boys*. . . . This country is committed to equal opportunity in education, which must lead to some redistribution of responsibilities within the home as well as in the word of work.'

The wider relevance of mathematics to other curricular areas, and the reciprocal relationship with language is well explained in the Working Papers and is a further justification for insisting that *every pupil* studies mathematics to the highest examinable level up to the compulsory school age. The case for an education in technology which is not work-and employer-centred ('school levers should be equipped to look at technology critically and to be part of a society that seeks to master technology, not to be enslaved by it. It is essential to be well-informed in those matters . . . to strengthen the foundations of democracy') also makes its own case for its wider relevances to our future young women.

Meanwhile, whatever continuing debate about the legal effect of the *Sex Descrimination Act*, educationally there can be no question but that the continued denial of the technical crafts for girls is proportionately 'less favourable treatment' than the denial of cookery and needlework to boys, for all the reasons that are spelled out earlier. Girls lose the transfer value of underpinning their spatial development which the handicrafts offer (and which some psycholagists rightly or wrongly suggest they need because of alleged innate deficiency). They are less qualified to enter technical vocational training or skilled trades in industry. And, more insidiously, they miss the whole impact on pupils' attitudes to transition from school to work, which the outward-looking design and technology programmes (based on earlier exposure to the crafts) offers to boys. In its place, they receive a conditioned drive to the inward-looking domestic and child-rearing role, which further restricts their horizons. Ironically, the denial of cookery and needlework to boys is a positive *advantage* to them, and not a parallel detriment; but further disadvantages girls. It frees boys far career-based school studies, and it removes from them the expectation of the later need for them to share in domestic responsibility, enabling them to concentrate in training and career advancement, often at the expense of their wives' outward lives.

Nor can biology be regarded as of equivalent value to physics and chemistry, its transfer and foundation value for later study and training being considerably more limited. Separate physical education programmes are not always necessary. The denial of the higher social status and standing of male sports and FE activities, to girls removes from them the resultant spin-off benefits of the wider clubability and competitiveness beyond their immediate environment, which is one indirect foundation for men's later tendency to organize themselves in business, industry, and society in exclusively male supportive groups.

For the less able my second curriculum reform would therefore be the replacement of the present domestically oriented skills by different practical work which looks to the external field of *work*, of community involvement in their locality; and of personal relationships and their tools for survival in a complex world; and consumer education, not cooking. I personally would remove the latter from the first to third year altogether, and reinstate it as a compulsory minority elements in an overall 'transition from school to career' course for the fourth and fifth year (for both sexes), equipping them with a wider range of survival kills. Failing this, the alleged though not in fact universal reslanting towards 'home economics' should reflect the economics, more than the home.

It will be evident that much of the principal argument in this work, rejects current social mythalogies. Elizabeth Janeway exposes with delicate but perceptive common sense, much of the social mythology surrounding the 'woman's place is in the home' syndrome, and by a different route, arrives at a common remedy to that which is implicit throughout my own argument: what can prevail against these myths? Not logic alone, and not compulsion, but instead an answer in *reality* to those needs which the myths answer in fantasy; (Janeway 1977: 333).

One answer in reality, which she seeks, lies with the restructuring af our eurriculum on the lines suggested.

Triority of Development Programmes for the Less Able

L.H. Huxley wanted a ladder from the gutter to the university. We do not appear, a hundred years later, to be able to build adequate rungs, even to the intermediate tertiary range, even from the safety of the school's secure pavement, for our less able girls. I have also, in all of the argument so far, completely omitted the very substantial programmes now currently being promoted by the Manpower Services Commission and Training Services Agencies in offering second-chance retraining to mature strants. They are described in detail in MSC and TSA publications and are well worth the study, for two reasons. First, the government has, for reasons which are politically understandable but educationally less obvious, swung all of its resources into a massive MSA/TSA programme of short courses, mostly of a maximum of twenty-six weeks and which are clearly job-related. With escalating unemployment and rapidly changing employment patterns, this is short-sighted. In ten years time, a short term TSA course will be of less value than a BEC or TEC vocational qualification with a substantial transferable core of generic studies and it is questionable how far the swing of mature women's recruitment to TSA's 'TOPS' (Training Opportunities Courses) is in their long term interest. Many, however, will be attracted not only by the hope of early employment in the relevant skills-area but by the substantial training allowances which contrast advantageously with the bleaker outlet for LEA grants and awards. Mature entrants are almost all by definition limited to 'discretionary awards' of which women suffer the greatest vulnerability. The public expenditure cuts have hit the discretionary sector very hard, by the admission of the DES itself. In a recent survey, they concluded that aurhorities made 2,000 *fewer* full value discretionary awards instead of the 5,000 extra needed to keep pace with the 18-19 age group (that is 7,000 fewer than needed). They also found that 45 per cent of LEAs made grants to 16-19s less generous than the LEA national standard, and 80 per cent grants to over nineteenth less generous than those recommended as necessary. The aggregation of inequality bites again—where women live determines their level of grant.

Opportunity and a ladder are merely paper power if the resources needed to climb are denied. The overall national policy for which I am pressing should include a major review of the whole mandatory and discretionary antithesis, and its replacement by a system of resource allocation based on real educational diagnosis aud need, and a conscious priority for a decade, for the less able—for the first time this century.

Research and Review

Recommendations have already emerged implicitly in each chapter, for further research and enquiry. Research into the factors of conditioning which affect girls and boys in different kinds of schools; experimental work i n non-sexist teaching materials; in-service training and re-education programmes—these are for both national bodies and local education authorities. Their co-ordinating policy makers (the Association of Country Councils, the Association of Municipal Authorities, and the Society of Education Officers) will need to devote time in their national debates on policy priorities for their declining resources, to this new, imperative need, if we are not only to achieve this equality, but keep up with our European neighbours economically and developmentally.

There seems to me, however, to be a deeper and wider need, which the recommendations of the Taylor Committee (1977) on the increased involvement of parents and governors in the running of our schools, enhances. We are long overdue for a new Education Act.

The current principle Act of 1944 (for England and Wales) was at that time, one of the finest, most visionary, and far-sighted to reach the statute book. It has been amended by a score of smaller Acts and Statutory Instruments but its principles remain little altered. There is need to sit down and redefine that which should be legislatively binding on all areas as a minimum standard of provision, investment, entitlement, and that which is more appropriately delegated to local education authorities to very according to the needs of their area. Written into a new Act, should be citizens' right—regardless of sex, race, creed, or region of origin—to a certain level of *recurrent* education throughout life, including adult education after retirement; and as a right, not a privilege to be argued for with 120 different LEA Committees or officers whose differing philosophies; prejudices, and resources create differing inequalities of access. This would be a major life-chance for the lost generations' of women whose first chance education has not equipped them for economic adult life outside their homes.

A quintessentiol characteristic of the education service at is best, is that the word impossible does not figure in our vocabulary. With the future lives of children and the country's economic and social future in our hands, there can be no room for failure; only if necessary, prolongation of the fight. Somehow, ways have to be found; an act of faith. Ray Strachey tells an anecdote which, if apocryphal, is nevertheless characteristic, of Emily Davias and Elizabeth Garrett in their early years, discussing at Aldeburgh all the great causes to be fought in order to combat the many social injustices suffered by Victorian women. Emily summed the matter up.

> ' "Well, Elizabeth", she said, "It's quite clear what has to be done. I must devote myself to securing higher education, while you open up the medical profession to women. After these things are done", she added, "we must see about getting the vote." And then she turned to the little girl who was still sitting quietly on her stool and said "you are younger than we, Millie, so you must attend to that" .' (And Millicent Garrett Fawcett, of course, did.)
>
> (*Strachey* 1978:101)

I cannot promise my predecessors that we have succeeded as well as they; nor that we will do so in the next two decades. The progress of the last five years, however, gives us a more secure foundation that ever before—if the men as well as women in leadership in the classroom, in government, and in the home, care to combine in coherent planning for an equal future for all. I cannot do butter than to end with Octavia Hill's parting words:

> 'When I am gone, I hope my friends will not try to carry out any special system, or to follow blindly in the track I have trodden. When the time comes that we slip from our places. and they are called to the front as leaders, what should they inherit from us? Not a system, not an association, not dead formulas . . . what we care most to leave them is not any tangible thing however great, not any memory, however good, but the quick eye to see, the true soul to measure, the large hope to grasp the mighty issues of the new and better days to come—greater ideals, greater hope, and patience to realise both.' (*Edmund* 1913:583)

What she did, we can do. That, readers, means you.

Bibliography

Adwaita Ashrama, A Short Life of Swami Vivekananda.

Aiyar Chandrashekhar N., Treatise on Hindu Law and Usage—John Mayne (1950).

All India Women's Conference, Education of Woman in Modern India (1946).

Altekar, Dr. A.S., The Position of Women in Hindu Civilization.

Anshen, Ruth Nanda (Ed.), Freedom, its Meaning (1942).

——Family, Its Function and Destiny (1949).

Ashraf, K.M., Life and Conditions of the People of Hindustan (1200 A. D.—1500 A. D.) (1935).

Barthwal, Pitambar Dutt, The Nirguna School of Hindi Poetry (1936).

Basu, B. D., History of Education in India under the Rule of the East India Company.

Basu, P., Indo Aryan Polity, 1919.

Belden, Jack, China Shakes the World (1950).

Belvalkar, S. K. and Ranade, R. D., History of Indian Philosophy, Vol. II, (1927).

Besant, Annie, Wake Up, India (1923).

——An Autobiography (1917).

Bhandarkar, R. G., Vaishnavism, Shaivism and Minor Religious Systems (1913).

Blyth, Nereon, Which Way To-morrow? (1938).

Bureau of Education, Postwar Educational Development in India.

Buch, M. A., Rase and Growth of Indian Liberalism.

———Rise and Growth of Indian Nationalism, (1939).

———Rise and Growth of Indian Militant Nationalism (1940).

Buhler. G. (Tr.), The Laws of Manu (1886).

Burway, R. G., The Present Position of Hindu Women and Means for Ameliorating their lot. (1941).

Canton, A. R., The Key of Progress: A Survey of the Status and Conditions of Woman in India.

Chakaladar, H. C., Social Life in Kamasutra of Vatsayana.

Chakravarti, S., The Life of Pandit Ishwar-chandra Vidyasagar (1896).

Chattopadhyaya, Kamala Devi, The Awakening of Indian Women.

Chintamani, C. Y., Indian Social Reform (1901).

———Indian Politics since the Mutiny (1937).

Chiplunkar, G. M., The Scientific Basis of Woman's Education (1930).

Cousins, Margaret E., The Awakening of Asian Womanhood (1922).

Cowan, Minna, The Education of the Woman of India. (1912).

Das, A. C., Rigvedic Culture.

Desai, A. R., Social Background of Indian Nationalism.

Diver, Maud., English Women in India (1909).

Dixon, R. B. The Building of Cultures (1928).

Dubois, Abbe' J. A., Hindu Manners, Customs and Ceremonies (Tr.) (1897).

Dutt, R. C., A History of Civilization of Ancient India, Volumes I. II. (1893).

Ellis, Havelock, Man and Woman (1934).

Engels, Frederic, The Origin of the Family, Private Property and State (1940).

Epstein, I., The Unfinished Revolution in China (1947).

Folsom, J. K., Family and Democratic Society (1945).

Freud, Sigmund, Basic Works of Sigmund Freud (Tr.) (1937).

Fyzee, A. A. A., The Muslim Wife's Right of Dissolving Her Marriage.

Gadgil, D. R., Industrial Evolution in India.

Gajendragadkar, K. B., Legal Rights of Hindu Women (1942).

Gandhi, M. K., Autobiography.

——Women and Social Injustice.

Gedge Evelyn C. and Choksi, M. (Ed.), Women in Modern India (1929).

Ghurye, G. S., Culture and Society (1947).

——Caste and Class in India (1950).

——Indian Costume (1951).

Gidumal, Dayaram, Behramji Malabari (1891).

——The Status of Woman in India (1889).

Gokhale, G. K., Speeches (1920).

Government of India (Home Dept. Selections), No. CCXXIII

Papers relating to Infant Marriage and Enforced Widowhood in India (1886).

Government of India, The Constitution of India (1950).

Kurukshetra—A Symposium on Community Development in India (1952-55).

Gaikwar, Maharaja Sayaji Rao, Speeches and Addresses (1877 to 1927).

Halle, Fannina W. Woman in Soviet Russia (1935).

Hate, (Mrs.) C. A., Hindu Woman and Her Future (1948).

Hauswirth, Freida, Purdah, the Status of Indian Women (1932).

Hazra, R. C., Studies in the Puranic Records on Hindu Rites and Customs (1940).

Hirschfeld, Magnus, Woman, East and West (1935).

Hobhouse, L. T., Liberalism.

——Morals in Evolution.

Holthy, Winifred, Women and Changing Civilization (1936).

Horner, I. B., Women under Primitive Budhism.

——Lay Women and Almswomen (1930).

Indra, M. A., The Status of Women in Ancient India (1940).

International Congress of Women (Tr.) 1899., Women in Professions.

Jayaswal, K. P., Manu and Yajnavalkya (1930).

Jolly, J., Hindu Law and Custom (1928).

——Outlines of a History of the Hindu Law on Partition, Inheritance and Adoption (1885).

Jones, Sir William, The Institutes of Hindu Law, Vol. I (1877).

Kapadia, K. M., Hindu Kinship (1947),

——The Hindu Code Bill (1950).

——Marriage and Family in India (1955).

Karkaria, R. P., Forty Years of Progress and Reform (1896).

Karve, D. K., Looking Back (1936).

Kelkar, N. C., Lokmanya Tilak, Life and Times of Vol. I (1928).

Kellock, James, Mahadev Govind Ranade (1926).

Kirkpatrick, Clifford, Hazi Germany, Its Women and Family (1938).

King, Beatrice, Women in Post-War Russia 1947).

Klein, Viola, The Feminine Character, History of an Ideology (1946).

Kulluk, Bhatta (Com.), Manusmruti (1913).

Kunzru. H. N., Copal Krishna Deodhar (1939).

Lajpat Rai, Lala, England's Debt to India (1917).

——Arya Samaj.

Langdon Davies, J., A Short History of Woman (1938).

Laski, Harold J., The Rise of European Liberalism (1936).

Law. B. C., Women in Buddhist Literature (1927).

Limaye, P. M. (Compt)., The History of the Deccan Education Society (1935).

Ludoviei, Anthony, The Future of Woman (1936).

Macdonell, A. A. & Keith, A. B., Vedic Index, 2 Volumes.

Mahmood, Syed. A History of English Education in India (1895).

Majmudar, R. C. and others, An Advanced History of India (1946).

Majumdar, J. K., (Ed.), Raja Ram Mohan Roy and Progressive Movement in India (1941).

Malinowski, D., Freedom and Civilization (1947).

——Sex and Repression in Savage Society (1949).

——Women and Revolution (1938).

Mannin, Ehtel, Commonsense and Adolessence.

——Commonsense and Morality.

Mayhew, Arthur, The Education of India (1926).

McCabe, Joseph, The Religion of Women (1912).

Mead, Margaret, Male and Female (1950).

Mehta, Smt. Hansa, The Woman Under has Hindiu Law of Marriage and Succession (1943).

Mehta, Ramanlal, A Thesis on the Legal Rights of Women Under the Different Communal Laws in Vogue in India (1933).

Mill, John Stuart, The Subjection of Women.

Mitter, Dwarkanath, Position of Women in Hindu Law (1933).

Mookerji, Radha Kumud, Hindu Civilization (1936).

Mukerjee, D. P., Modern Indian Culture (1942).

Mukerjee, Hirendranath, India Struggles for Freedom (1946).

Mulla, D. F., Principles of Hindu Law (1912).

Muller, Lyer F., Evolution of Marriage (1930).

——Family (1931).

Munshi, K.M., Gujarat and Its Literature (1935).

Murdock, John, Twelve Years of Indian Progress (1898).

Myrdal, Alvn and Klein, Viola, Woman's Two Roles—Home and Work (1956).

Naik. J.P. and Nurullah Syed, History of Education in India (1943).

Naik, V. N., Indian Liberalism, A Study (1945).

Nateson, G. A., Eminent Musalmans.

——Chaitanya to Vivekanand.

——Indian National Congress.

National Council of Women in India, Legal Status of Indian Women (1943).

National Planning Committee Series, Woman's Role in Planned Economy (1947).

Nehru, Pandit Jawaharlal, Towards Freedom. An Autobiography (1942).

Nehru, Shyamkumari (Ed.), Our Cause.

North, Cecil Clare, Social Differentation (1926).

O'Malley, L. S. S. (Ed.), Modern India and the West (1941).

Pal, B. C., Mrs. Annie Besant.

Paranjape, M. R., Education of Women in India.

Pekin, L. B., Co-education.

Pinkham, M. W., Women in the Sacred Scriptures of Hinduism (1941).

Radhakrishnan, S. Hindu View of Life (1928).

Ragozin, Z. A.. Vedic India (1895).

Rajgopal, T.S. Indian Women in the New Age. (1936).

Ramabhai Saraswati (Pandita), The High Cast Hindu (1901).

Ramkrishna Centenary Memorial, The Cultural Heritage of India.

Ranade, M. G., The Rise of the Maratha Power, Vol. I, (1900).

——Religious and Social Reform Speeches (1902).

Ranade, Ramabai (Pub.), Miscellaneous Writings of the Late Honourable Mr. Justice M. G. Ranade (1915).

Rao Raja and Iqbal Singh, Changing India (1939).

Rapson, E. J. (Ed.), Cambridge History of India, (Vol. I, III, IV).

Ray, Renuka, Women in Mines (1945).

Rege, Y. M. Whither Woman? (1938).

Risely, Herbert, People of India.

Roy. M. N., Fragments of a Prisoner's Diary (1941).

Roy, Raja Ram Mohan, The English Works of Raja Ram Mohan Roy (1906).

Rusell, Bertrand, Marriage and Morals.

Saletore, B. A., Social and Political Life in the Vijayanagar Empire (1934).

Sarda, Harbilas, Dayanand Commemoration Volume (1933).

——Life of Dayanand Saraswati (1946).

Sarkar, S. C., Some Aspects of Earliest Social History of India (1928).

Scheinfield, A., Women and Men (1947).

Schmalhausen and Calverton (Ed.), Sex in Civilization (1929).

——Woman's Coming of Age (1931).

——New Generation (1930).

Schmalhausen, S. D., Why We Misbehave?

——New Roads to Progress.

Sen, Kshiti Mohan, Medieval Mysticism of India.

Seward, Sex and the Social Order (1946).

Shamshastry, R., Kautilva's Artha Shastra (1915).

Shastri, L. S., The Constitution of India.

Shelvankar, K. S. The Problem of India.

Siddhanta, N. K., The Heroic Age of India (1929).

Sitarammiyya, P., The History of Indian National Congress (1946).

Strachey, Ray, The Cause (1928).

——Careers and Openings for Women (1937).

Strachey, Ray (Ed.), Our Freedom and Its Results (1936).

Sri Prakash, Annic Besant as Woman and as Ledger (1941).

Sverdloy, G. M. Legal Rights of Soviet Family.

Swami, Dharma Teertha, The Menace of Hindu Imperalism (1946).

Tagore, Rabindranath and Underhill, One Hundred Poems of Kabir.

Tata, Herabai A., Short Sketcn of Indian Women's Franchire Work.

Tawney, R. H., The Acquisitive Society (1921).
Equality (1938).

Theosophic Publishing House, Annie Besant, Builder of New India (1943).

Thomas, P., Women and Marriage in India.

Thompson, Edward, Suttee (1928).

Thompson, E and Garrat, G., Rise and Fulfilment of British Rule in India (1936).

Thompson. H. B., The Mental Traits of Sex (1908).

Trevelyan, George, Macaulay, Nineteenth Century and After (1937).

——English Social History (1944).

UNESCO, Education of Women.

UNESCO and Asian Relations Organization, Woman in South Asia.

Upadhya, Bhagwat Saran, Women in Rigveda (1941).

Vaidya, C. V., Epic India.

——History of the Medieval Hindu India (1921).

Vivekanand, Swami, Our Women (1945).

——Complete Works.

Wadia, A. R., The Ethics of Feminism (1923).

Webb, Beatrice, My Apprenticeship, Vol. I & II.

Woolstodecraft, Mary, The Rights of Women (1929).

Yusuf Ali, A., Medieval India (1932).

Zacharias, H. C. F. Renascent India from Raja Ram Mohan Roy to Mohan Das Gandhi (1933).

Zetkin, Clara, Lenin on the Women Question.

Vernacular Books

Dalpatram, Dalpat Kavya. Vols. I & II (1924). Gujarati.

Dhru, G. G. Jivan Na Vamal (1943), Gujarati.

Gandhi, M., Tyagmurti and Bija Lekhe (1930). Gujarati.

Jaguste, M.R. (Publishers), Base Bavan Vaishnava ni Varta. Gujarati.

Government of Boroda (Pub.), Hindu Nibandha (1937). Gujarati.

——Vadodarani Mahila Pragatine Panthe, (1942). Gujarati.

Majumdar. M. R. (Ed.), Sahityakar Akho. (1949).

Munshi, K. M., Thodan Ras Darshan. (1933). Gujarati.

Nabha Swami, Bhakta Mala. Gujarati.

Narmada Shankar, Narma Kavita, (1914). Gujarati.

Oza. G. H., Madhya Kalin Bharatiya Sanskriti. (1928). Hindi.

Parekh, H. T., Arvachin Gujarat noo Rekha Darshan. Vols. I—III. Gujarati.

——Gujarati Vernacular Vernacular Society no Itihas. Vols. I—III.

Parekh, Sumati, Stri-o-nu Arthic Swatantra (1943). Gujarati.

Pandit, Malati, Rama Bai Ranade. (193). Gujarati.

Pandit, S., Ishwar Chandra Vidyasagar Gujarati.

Patwari, P., Striona-Vikas-ma Nadta Kayada-na Bandhan. (1939). Gujarati.

Shastri, D. K., Vaishnava Dharma-no Sankshipta Itihasa, (193). Gujarati.

Shukla, Ramchandra, Hindi Sahitya-ka Itihaas, Hindi.

Shyam Sunderdas (Ed.), Kabir Garnthavali.

Trivedi, Lalshankar Umiashankar, Vidhva Vivah, (1867), Gujarati.

Trivedi, Navalram, Samaj Sundhara-nu Rekha Darshan, (134). Gujarati.

Unpublished Thesis

Desai, Mrs. G. B., Woman in Modern Gujarati Life.

Desai, Sulochana, Socio-Economic Position of Women in India from 1858-1929.

Hate, Mrs. C. A., Economic Condition of Educated Women in Bombay City.

Merchant, K. T., Changing Ideas on Marriage and Family.

Naik, Chitralekha, Education of Women in the Province of Bombay (1818-1947).

Periodicals

Calcutta Review, 1868.

Indian Review, March and April, 1951.

Indian Social Reformer files of the year 1950.

Journal of Bihar and Orissa Research Society, Vol. XXIV.

Journal of Indian History, Vol. XVII.

Journal of the University of Bombay, September, 1945.

Journal of Anthropological Society of Bombay, Vol. 1.

Man, Vol. 22, No. 25.

Modern Review—Issues of the years, 1919, 1920 and 1921.

Social Reform Annual of the Bombay Presidency Social Reforms Association. From 1938 to 1945.

Stree Bodha Silver Jubilee Volume, 1908.

Urmi Ane Navarachna, Issues of 195[illegible].

Praja Bandhu, Files for the year 1950-51.

Reports of the Institutions

All India Women's Conference, Annual Reports from 1927 to 1949.

Arya Directory (1937).

The Decean Education Society, 1944-48.

Directory of Women's Institutes, Bombay Presidency.

The National Social Conference, Annual Reports from 1887 to 1917.

Census and other Reports

India, 1956. Government of India, Publication Division.